Uniqueness

a

FAITH MEETS FAITH
An Orbis Series in Interreligious Dialogue
Paul F. Knitter, General Editor

In our contemporary world, the many religions and spiritualities stand in need of greater intercommunication and cooperation. More than ever before, they must speak to, learn from, and work with each other, in order to maintain their own identity and vitality and so to contribute to fashioning a better world.

FAITH MEETS FAITH seeks to promote interreligious dialogue by providing an open forum for the exchanges between and among followers of different religious paths. While the series wants to encourage creative and bold responses to the new questions of pluralism confronting religious persons today, it also recognizes the present plurality of perspectives concerning the methods and content of interreligious dialogue.

This series, therefore, does not want to endorse any one school of thought. By making available to both the scholarly community and the general public works that represent a variety of religious and methodological viewpoints, FAITH MEETS FAITH hopes to foster and focus the emerging encounter among the religions of the world.

FAITH MEETS FAITH SERIES

Uniqueness

Problem or Paradox
in Jewish and Christian Traditions

Gabriel Moran

ORBIS BOOKS

Maryknoll, New York 10545

Library of Congress Cataloging-in-Publication Data

Moran, Gabriel.
    Uniqueness : problem or paradox in Jewish and Christian traditions
/ Gabriel Moran.
      p. cm. — (Faith meets faith)
    Includes bibliographical references.
    ISBN 0-88344-830-0 — ISBN 0-88344-829-7 (pbk.)
    1. Christianity—Essence, genius, nature. 2. Judaism—Essence,
genius, nature. 3. Christianity and other religions—Judaism.
4. Judaism—Relations—Christianity. 5. Religious pluralism.
6. Jesus Christ—Person and offices. 7. People of God. I. Title.
II. Series.
BT60.M67   1992
261.2—dc20   92-13009
                                           CIP

Contents

INTRODUCTION   1

1. A VERY UNIQUE WORD   9
Usages of Unique   12
The Two Meanings   18

2. IS THE HOLOCAUST UNIQUE?   25
The Ubiquity of the Term   27
Uniqueness A and B   29
Comparisons to the Holocaust   31
Unique Destruction: Given and Received   34
The Uniqueness of the Response   37
Conclusion   39

3. UNIQUE REVELATION   41
Overview   41
Revelation in Meaning A   46
Revelation in Meaning B   50
Conclusion   55

4. UNIQUE PEOPLE OF THE COVENANT   57
Chosen People   60
Covenant   63
The "Two Covenant" Theories   64
Continuity and Discontinuity   70

5. JESUS   73
A Very Unique Person
Uniqueness of What?   75
Jesus or Christ   77
Uniqueness of Jesus   79
Unique Christ   82
Mediation   89
Conclusion   91

6. THE UNIQUE ANIMAL   **93**
Humans at the Center
The Ecological Problem   94
Hierarchy   98
Anthropocentrism   101
Our Next of Kin   105
The Gift of Food   108

7. HUMAN DEVELOPMENT   **112**
Uniqueness unto Death
Person and Community   113
Unique Presents   117
Unique Developments   121
A Most Unique Experience   126

CONCLUSION   **133**

NOTES   **137**

INDEX   **153**

Introduction

I have been waiting twenty-five years for someone to write this book. But having come to suspect that no one else is going to do it, I reluctantly set out to accomplish the task. The reluctance is based upon the fact that there are other people who are more qualified than I am to address some aspects of this topic. Additionally, I forgo dealing with other aspects that are clearly beyond my competence. Thus, despite the ambitious scope of this book, it is still a relatively modest attempt to address the issue of uniqueness.

This book is the kind of book that I like to read. Readers will have to judge for themselves whether it is the kind of book that suits them. I am giving the reader fair warning as early as possible. I like to read books that state on the first page that there is only one idea in this book. Instead of a logical case argued from premise to conclusion, such books explore one idea from various angles.

This book, *Uniqueness: Problem or Paradox in Jewish and Christian Traditions*, explores the idea of uniqueness. Indeed, I might go further and say that the book is about one *word,* uniqueness. Depending on one's understanding of the relation between ideas and words, there may be more than one idea in the word uniqueness. That is something to be presently explored, but what is affirmed from the beginning is the one word. Truman Capote was once criticized for writing only one word in a day's effort. His defense was: "Yes, but it's the right word."

Attending to a single word for several hundred pages could be exceedingly boring. That depends both on what the word is and what the writer does with it. The advantage in such an exploration is that the initial choice signals to the reader what the book's argument is and is not. Books almost inevitably give the impression that they are built on an accepted premise from which a logical argument is to be constructed. If it is a book on religion, the premise may be the Bible or the Qur'an. If it is a history text, the premise is likely to be established documents. If it is sociology, there may be accepted laws of society. In reaching conclusions, the author is expected to go one reasonable step at a time with the evidence before the reader.

Occasionally, a writer refuses to accept the framework that the format of a book suggests. One lazy way to do that is to tell the reader that the chapters can be read in any order that he or she chooses. In this case, the reader may fear that the author, instead of providing flexibility, has simply not bothered to establish any order or unity. One of the most extreme examples in the twentieth century was Marshall McLuhan, who, late in his life, kept writing books on the uselessness of books.

In a less quixotic vein, many writers strain at the limits of the book form and what we usually assume is the way to argue a case. Throughout the centuries, artists have tried to present the truth in ways that resist the inductive/deductive form of arguing. Artists of the written word use poetry, story, dialogue, and a wide range of other forms to present their cases.

In the twentieth century, some of these playful products of the arts have been taken over by philosophers who are intent on resisting Descartes's *more geometrico*, that is, the establishment of truth by way of scientific and mathematical logic. Martin Heidegger's essays became more and more peculiar, until they finally ended in commentary on poetry. Gabriel Marcel always insisted that his main philosophy was to be found in his plays. Many recent philosophers have written novels or autobiographies. I even suspect that John Dewey's terrible writing style was his way of stopping anyone from thinking that there is a Deweyan system.

One of the more influential works of this century is Martin Buber's *I and Thou*.[1] This book is a series of epigrams that begins with the unproved assertion that there are two primary words: I/Thou and I/It. From there the author comments on everything in the universe. As a philosophical treatise, Buber's book has a strange format.

Somewhat similar is the case of Ludwig Wittgenstein, another influential philosopher of this century. Wittgenstein began his career with a system of numbered propositions that sought to explain the whole world.[2] In his later writings, however, Wittgenstein circled his topics with epigrams. In a search for the firm basis of philosophy, Wittgenstein concluded that at the bottom of human life is *trust,* a particular kind of action. He calls this certainty an *Äusserung*, an utterance. "It is just like directly taking hold of something as I take hold of my towel without having doubts."[3] So much for Descartes and his mathematical method.

I cannot pretend to be Buber or Wittgenstein, although this book is influenced by both of them. As I have indicated, this introduction is to warn the reader that the book declares itself here and then circles its theme with six illustrations that touch upon almost everything. The method is not adopted frivolously. I know of no other way to get at the issue. G. K. Chesterton once noted that in matters of great importance a person is convinced not because an argument proves the case but because the whole universe does.[4]

The heart of the first chapter is a linguistic analysis of uniqueness. I ask how people use the word and what they clearly or confusedly mean by it. Before proceeding to that analysis, I must first comment on the book's subtitle: Problem or Paradox in Jewish and Christian Traditions.

There is little doubt that Jewish and Christian claims to uniqueness constitute a problem for many people. Throughout this book, I repeatedly acknowledge the problem and then place it in the context of a paradox. That paradox is inherent to the idea of uniqueness itself. An understanding of what is paradoxically present in all claims to uniqueness is the key to understanding both Jewish and Christian traditions.

Other things in these traditions may be more important than uniqueness, but one needs a key to unlock what is there at all. A person could study the Bible for many years and miss the peculiarity of its logic. Thousands of years of commentary do not necessarily make clear the logic. Undoubtedly someone could make a case for something else being the key of interpretation. My claim is that "unique" is better than any of its competitors, because this term is both the most comprehensive and the most paradoxical.

I am surprised at how seldom Jewish and Christian writers make any comment about the claim to uniqueness, even while they use the term with extraordinary frequency. For example, Karl Rahner's sixth chapter of the book *Foundations of Christian Faith* is entitled "Jesus Christ." In that one chapter Rahner uses the word uniqueness sixty-one times.[5] But at no time does he comment on any peculiarity about the term or its implications. Nicholas Lash's brilliant study of Christianity, *Easter in Ordinary*, has a small section entitled "uniqueness," but it does not advert to the nature of the claim or anything about the meaning of the word.[6] A book entitled *The Myth of Christian Uniqueness*[7] was countered by a book titled *Christian Uniqueness Reconsidered*.[8] Unfortunately, neither book has any extended comment on what the term uniqueness means. S. Mark Heim, reviewing the two books together, found it "difficult to keep the players on their respective sides"; there was no clear thesis on which the two sides were disagreeing.[9] Books for or against uniqueness have to be clear about the meaning of the word.

The prominent use of the term in Christian theology may seem to make its meaning a Christian rather than a Jewish question. Furthermore, I will have to acknowledge in the course of my argument that the Christian assertion of uniqueness is often an anti-Jewish statement. But I wish to argue that Christianity's legitimate use of uniqueness has to be directly related to the Hebrew Bible and the Jewish people. As soon as Jesus of Nazareth is lifted out of his Jewish context, Christianity will find itself defending an indefensible claim to uniqueness.

Christianity is more prominent in this book than Judaism. Nonetheless, I am not simply using Judaism as part of a Christian argument. The term unique is found less often in Jewish writing, but it is by no means absent there. The logic that leads into the constant Christian use of the term is clearly of Jewish origin and, more importantly, continues in Jewish thinking today. In this book, I direct my criticism more to Christianity than to Judaism; my proposals for change of language apply primarily to Christianity, secondarily to Judaism. Christianity is, in a sense, the bigger problem. Furthermore, I am more confident in suggesting to Christians precise changes of language that, far from destroying the tradition, would invigorate it. I say some similar things of Judaism, although I do so with less assurance that I know the exact words needed for a reform of the tradition.

My main concern is not which religion has more to change or, positively phrased, which religion has the more to gain from an examination of uniqueness. The more important point is that both religions might profit from being examined in relation to the term uniqueness. Each religion might find a new way to relate to the other, and each of them might carry on more effective internal reform in the light of being linked to the other through the logic of uniqueness.

Beyond the polite exchanges of Christian-Jewish dialogue that can easily become introverted, both religions are confronted by a world of many religions and no religion. We have not really arrived at ecumenical (that is, worldwide) religious exchange, but the twenty-first century will almost surely usher it in. Individuals who see themselves as forerunners of such worldwide conversation frequently put Christianity and Judaism into the same basket, especially when attacking narrow-minded groups. Joseph Campbell, who late in life achieved popularity as a religious visionary, made no secret of his disdain for both Christianity and Judaism. For example, he wrote:

> The difficulty faced today by Christian thinkers in this regard follows from their doctrine of the Nazarene as the *unique* historical incarnation of God; and in Judaism, likewise, there is the no less troublesome doctrine of a universal God whose eye is on but one Chosen People of all in his created world. The fruit of such ethnocentric historicism is poor spiritual fare today. . . . These were good enough for our fathers in the tight little worlds of the knowledge of their days, when each little civilization was a thing more or less to itself. But consider that picture of the planet Earth that was taken from the surface of the moon.[10]

The point on which I would agree with Campbell is the close relation between the unique Nazarene and the chosen people. The seeming arrogance of each claim, the apparent ownership of God's attention in the mindset of both claims, became apparent long before photography from the moon. Centuries, if not millennia ago, it should have been obvious—and to some people it was obvious—that there is a problem in understanding these apparently intolerant positions. Did the God of the universe divide the world into a few people he sides with and the rest, whom he disregards or opposes? Joseph Campbell is not alone in assuming that is the only possible meaning of the phrase chosen people. If Judaism has another meaning for the claim, it needs to be brought forth.

Do Christians think, and have they always thought, that God was present in Jesus and nowhere else, that God sides with the Christians while opposing other people? If the Christian response is that they believe God is present everywhere but uniquely in Jesus Christ (as Rahner and other theologians say), then the logic of that claim calls for some explaining. Most people who are not Christian either have no idea of what is being said or think it is all too obvious what is being said and find it intolerable. I think that Joseph Campbell and other critics of Christian uniqueness are attacking an easy enemy. Nonetheless, it is a conception of Christianity not so foreign as to be unrecognizable.

The frequent use of the term unique within Christian or Jewish writing is not thousands of years old; in fact, it is rather recent. Thus, my claim that uniqueness is the key to Christian and Jewish traditions is not based on the importance of the word within each tradition's originating documents. Instead, I am bringing to bear a very modern category to name the logic present within Christianity and Judaism. Uniqueness is a compact way to state a twentieth-century understanding.

I have to admit that this fact about the term uniqueness should make one suspicious about its prominence in religious writing. Is it possible that the term is a modern fad, or worse, a mere obscurantism? As used in religious writing today, the word may in fact obscure more than it clarifies. The initial choice, then, is either to eliminate the term as far as possible or to mine the term in all its paradoxical meaning. I have chosen the latter route, both because the term's ubiquitous presence makes its elimination unlikely and because the rise of the term suggests an important characteristic of twentieth-century understanding.

One of the most pointed attacks on the use of the term "unique" is in Jonathan Z. Smith's book, *Drudgery Divine*. Smith writes that "the 'unique' is an attribute that must be disposed of . . . if progress in thinking through the enterprise of comparison is to be made."[11] After noting that the history of the word *unique* in religious discourse has yet to be written, Smith "hazards the guess" that "the 'unique' is a thoroughly modern notion, one no earlier than . . . nineteenth century German Protestantism."[12] Smith sees a misapplication of unique to "Christ event" and "gospel." I express many of the same concerns in chapter 5, although my aim in discussing the meaning of the word *Christ* will be to clarify the application of unique rather than eliminate the term.

One further point should be noted about the era in which *unique* arose. In Christian writing the term may seem to have arisen as defensive apologetic, that is, as a refusal to draw comparisons with other religions. However, if we look to a broader context, unique is one of the main ways people wrestle with a paradoxical relation of sameness and difference. That is, we live in a post-Darwinian world where each thing is itself only by being related to everything else.

Our confusion is captured by the ironic line that Smith quotes from T. S. Eliot: "All cases are unique, and very similar to others." Our confusion would not be eliminated by getting rid of the word unique. Smith maintains that the term unique "forbids comparison by its very assertion." No doubt there are people who try to do that with the word. Nevertheless, the position I will develop in this book is that the word unique *always* invites comparison. Most important to my purposes, the uniqueness of Christian tradition and the uniqueness of Jewish tradition are best seen with the uniquenesses in relation to each other.

I have emphasized in the above section that Christianity and Judaism are related in history and logic. I am proposing in this book to explore a link between Christian thinking and Jewish thinking. Nonetheless, I wish to call attention to the distinction between the two religions, lest my argument seem to be the standard Christian tactic of absorbing Judaism (the religion of the "Old Testament") into being one source of Christian material, in Arthur Cohen's phrase, "a prehensile tail." Liberal Christian writing often does not succeed any better than conservative writing in avoiding the assumption that there is one line of development that goes from Judaism to Christianity. As my subtitle states, I am interested in two traditions. To the extent that I locate a common key, the two traditions might be seen in closer relation, but the two traditions remain two.

The nineteenth century invented the peculiar phrase "Judeo-Christian," which is usually followed by the word tradition. The popularity of the phrase in the twentieth century points up, I believe, a strong tendency to avoid considering how the Jewish and Christian traditions are actually related. The Holocaust, to be encountered in chapter 2, should have put an end to the phrase "Judeo-Christian tradition," but it continues onward.

With only the barest knowledge of the last two millennia, someone should be able to grasp that there are two distinct traditions, the Jewish and the Christian. Often, the two have been in direct conflict; at other times, they have peacefully resided together. Sometimes optimistic thinkers in each tradition have foreseen a future convergence. Even in this last case, however, where the two have stood together in defense of common values, the two traditions did not become one. From a time somewhere near the end of the first century C.E., church and synagogue have represented different traditions.

The assertion of a Judeo-Christian tradition is likely based on the assumption that western secular enlightenment has moved on beyond both Christianity and Judaism. As Arthur Cohen noted in his important book, *The Myth of Judeo-Christian Tradition,* "the Judeo-Christian connection was formed by the opponents of Judaism and Christianity, by the opponents of a system of unreason which had nearly destroyed Western Europe."[13] The idea of a common tradition did not represent religious progress. "European intellectuals came to regard Judaism and Christianity as essentially similar—similar not with respect to truth, but rather with respect to the untruth which they shared."[14]

The phrase "Judeo-Christian tradition" was not absorbed into the language with a totally negative connotation. When it was assumed that both

Judaism and Christianity had been domesticated and could no longer destroy society, then secular thinkers were willing to grant a positive residue from the two religions. Thus, the phrase "Judeo-Christian tradition" is a recognition of a deposit into the secular bank of individualism, autonomy, and belief in the "dignity of man." Ironically, as chapter 6 will describe, such phrases are now being used in an accusatory way of the "Judeo-Christian tradition's" responsibility for ecological problems. But whether celebrated or denounced, the vague contribution ascribed to this tradition acts as an obstacle to investigating the Christian tradition, the Jewish tradition, and the relationship of the two.

This book is an attempt to clarify this relation between Christianity and Judaism and, by doing so, open a wider area of agreement. More modestly put, my hope is to widen the *possibility* of agreement. How far the agreement could go, no one knows, because there was a gap of more than eighteen hundred years in the conversation. It is unlikely, and probably undesirable, that the two traditions will ever become one. But it is certainly desirable that savage conflict be replaced by whatever genuine understanding is possible.

I am claiming that uniqueness is the key to nothing less than the Christian and Jewish traditions. Am I in fact claiming even more, namely, that it is the key to understanding everything? To the extent that Jewish and Christian religions claim to interpret the universe, I cannot entirely avoid that implication. At least, via the route of Christian and Jewish traditions, uniqueness becomes a universal key. Particularly in chapters 6 and 7, I deal with issues that go beyond the explicit affairs of Christianity and Judaism. Even there, however, my point of reference is Christian and Jewish traditions. With the key that unlocks these two traditions, there is a spillover into numerous contemporary issues.

I could almost reverse the question of whether uniqueness is the key to everything. That would be to ask: Is the idea of uniqueness exclusive to Judaism and Christianity? To answer that question, I have to jump ahead and insist that an exclusivistic understanding of uniqueness violates the logic underlying Christianity and Judaism. That is, for Christians or Jews to claim exclusive possession of uniqueness is nearly a self-contradiction. This point will be clear, I hope, by the end of chapter 1, but it is a point concerning which Christians and Jews throughout the centuries have needed regular reminding.

If the unique can be found in other places, including other religions, then why restrict the scope of this book to Jewish and Christian traditions? My answer is that it is presumptuous enough to include even two traditions. They are the traditions that I am closest to; they are also the traditions that show some evidence of a historic thaw.

I do not apologize, therefore, for restricting my focus to Jewish and Christian relations. Living in the United States makes this particular focus both realistically possible and almost unavoidable. Krister Stendahl has written that the United States of today is the first place since Philo's Alexandria where Christian and Jewish communities are together in such numbers and in relative peace that conversation is a realistic task.[15]

A word must be added, nonetheless, about the third member of the family, Islam. A consideration of Islam could no doubt add to the argument of this book. Occasionally, for the sake of illustration or to indicate how the argument might be continued, I refer to Islam. However, this book does not claim to be about Islamic tradition. At this moment in the United States, the participation of Islam in the conversation is very limited. Within the coming decade, this situation may change radically, although the simple increase in the number of United States Muslims does not guarantee a conversation.

For the present conversation between Christians and Jews, Islam offers an important test. Jewish-Christian dialogue will be fruitful to the extent that it is open, in principle, to Muslims. At the least, the conversation should not be offensive to Muslims; at best, some of the categories might be shaped with explicit awareness of Islam. I wish that a three-way dialogue were more of a reality, but it does not come to exist through declaration by me or anyone else. It will emerge only as the halting gestures and unsure words develop into a trust that has to start, but not end, with individual Christians, Jews, and Muslims.

1

A Very Unique Word

This chapter is a reflection on the puzzle of language generally and, in particular, the peculiar uses of the term *unique.* Nearly all the arguments of this book are linguistic. I argue about the meaning of words, a method that to some people may seem abstract and impractical. However, diverse schools of thought in the twentieth century are linked by a common concern with language. The twentieth century did not discover this "problem." The Socratic dialogues of Plato, for example, can be read as arguments about words. Attention to language has varied from one era to another, but in this century the awareness of language is almost always at the center of philosophical, scientific, political, and cultural struggles with communication.

The simplest way to state the concern of this book is to say that it is about the meaning of words. But there are at least two different meanings for the phrase the meaning of words. One can discuss either the meaning of *words* or the *meaning* of words. I am interested in both issues, so a few words have to be said about each of these emphases.

In the first case, the meaning of *words* is in contrast to the meaning of objects, things, or a supposed "real world." In arguing about the meaning of words, attention is called to language itself, rather than the supposed referent for language. I do not deny that words have reference beyond themselves, but I am trying to force reflection back on what may seem to be mere labels attached to things.

Words are not transparencies through which we describe and discuss the world as it really is. When two parties are heatedly arguing, an outside observer can often see that their disagreement is verbal. I do not mean verbal as opposed to real; that would suggest that the argument should be dismissed as illusory, unimportant, "mere semantics." When an argument gets as far as the meaning of the words themselves, then there is a chance of the argument going somewhere and revealing where we agree and where we disagree. Many women have made the comment about sexist language that once you see it, you can never not see it. Words are the powerful

9

reality to be discussed if fundamental change is to occur.

In the second case, "the meaning of words" has the emphasis on *meaning*. Here the contrast is mainly to the *definition* of words. My interest in this chapter and throughout this book is the meaning rather than the definition of words. After many occasions when I found audiences misunderstanding what I was saying, I realized that people thought I was doing almost exactly the opposite of what I was trying to do. That is, they assumed that I was defining words so I could then go ahead and build my system of concepts. When no system emerged, the audience understandably felt cheated; I had never gotten to the end of my definitions. But, in fact, my interest is almost the reverse of defining. Definitions of words are easily available in any dictionary. However, dictionaries flatten out all the mystery; they set limits (de-fine) on a word by equating it with a few other words.

Living language does not operate that way. Meanings spread out in all directions, embodied mainly in statements. The meaning of a word is constituted by its use, by the particular context in which it is found. Words can indeed be misused; we correct children when they use a word in the wrong place. But the correct uses of a word are extremely varied. A master of language uses words that often surprise us in the context, but once used that way, a richer meaning in the word becomes evident.

Important words (the small, old ones) usually have an emotional range that goes beyond either the speaker's intention or the listener's conscious awareness. Words can shift in meaning over time. Usually, a long period of time is necessary for major change, although a single speaker can sometimes shift subsequent usage. John Kennedy used the word *sophisticated* with a very positive meaning, almost the opposite of the then-current meaning. In this case, one person's use of a word shifted subsequent usage. The shifts are surprising, but they usually have some historical basis. In the case of sophisticated, it might be that the sophists' good side was finally getting some recognition.

My interest, then, is in breaking open definitions, because the quest for meaning is in large part antidefinitional. This strategy is not a preliminary step to building a system of ideas. I refuse to leave the words behind and thereby ascend to a realm of ideas. One can search for understanding by going deeper into the words rather than trying to rise above them. If someone should insist that what I am doing is searching for new definitions, he or she is free to describe the process that way. My own description of the process is that of resistance to premature definition. Only by resisting the temptation to settle quickly upon definitions is it possible to have more meaning allowed into the conversation. That requires not simply adding more synonyms but tracing patterns of usage through time and across space.

From the general issue of the meaning of words, I focus in the rest of this chapter on one example: the meaning of the word unique. Most writers and speakers do not seem to notice how puzzling the word is. As the title of this chapter states the case, unique is a very unique word, one of the most unique words in the language. I hasten to add that it is not a totally unique word; no word can be.

Unique, similar to a number of important words in the language, has meanings that go in opposite directions. The nearly opposite meanings have some common root; otherwise, there would simply be equivocation. Important words, those that go deeply into human nature, have this characteristic. For example, the word *power* suggests to most people activity and external coercion. But the etymology of the word and its less prominent meaning suggest the opposite: passivity and receptiveness within. In classical thought, the lowest rung of creation and the highest being were both described by power (*potens*). In the one case, power was the mere capacity for form, that is, being which is not yet formed as *a* being. In the other case, power was beyond form, that is, be-ing beyond *a* being. Modern thought does not speak of power with the same mystical and metaphysical language, but the paradox of power is still evident in politics or psychology. Feminist writers are certainly aware of the paradox.[1] In all its uses, power refers to being able to realize some possibility. Beyond that, an understanding of true or real power can move in opposite directions.

The question of uniqueness is not unrelated to this mystery of power, especially power as a strange kind of receptiveness or passivity. One of the questions that will surface in nearly every chapter is the power of suffering. Human beings have a greater capacity to suffer than do other creatures. Their power is based on the ability to be receptive to other beings. Sane human beings usually avoid suffering, if they can. Nonetheless, the human response to suffering seems intimately connected to the greatest human power. A flight from all suffering seems to lead to the deterioration of the human, while the willingness to bear suffering when necessary is often found in the most admired human actions. In any case, Christianity and Judaism are very much concerned with this theme.[2]

When a word has two meanings that are almost contradictory, its use often leads to high-pitched battles. Each side cannot believe that the other is dense enough to make the claim it seems to be making. Sometimes the two sides are trying to say the same thing or something close to the same thing. Occasionally both sides are saying almost the opposite of what they seem to be saying. The example of writing on the Holocaust in chapter 2 is rich with cases of such confusion.

A different kind of confusion arises when someone uses the word unique with both meanings vaguely present. Not having reflected on the peculiarity of the term, the author attaches the word to a variety of related nouns. The meaning then shifts radically from one usage to another, but the author is unaware of the difference. Christian writers constantly use the word in reference to Jesus and Christian origins. But, depending on what noun is used (gospel, revelation, church, savior, Christianity), these claims to uniqueness can have very different meanings.

I have no clever twist of phrase that would clear up all this confusion. I continue to marvel at the growing complexity of this problem the further one pursues it. Tied into people's use of unique is a way of looking at everything, a way of being in relation to everything. The question of uniqueness concerns the human place in the world.

Ambiguity is present in many words, and particularly in the word unique, because human life is ambiguous. There is nothing wrong with ambiguity; indeed, human life thrives on it. A poem is an exercise in ambiguity, a precisely controlled ambiguity. The old, small words in the language are worth fighting over because most of life's ambiguities reside there. Words such as love, honor, freedom, happiness, or goodness cannot be replaced by scientifically defined words that no one will misunderstand. The word unique does not have as prominent a place in history as any of these terms. But I think unique does get at the ultimate organization of Jewish and Christian thought worlds, and for this role it is necessarily a paradoxical term that is easily misunderstood.

USAGES OF UNIQUE

In this section, I look at various examples of how people use the word unique. After that, I proceed to draw some conclusions about a comprehensive meaning for the term, or at least the most comprehensive meaning that can be stated at this time.

A first tendency to notice about the word is that some writers get impatient with almost any use of the term. I start with an example from Nels Ferre: "There is accordingly no conceivable way in which anyone who takes human experience at all seriously and who believes in human history in any genuine sense can ever meaningfully conceive or use the concept of the totally unique. The unique in all respects is a fallacious verbalism."[3]

Compare Ferre's statement to one by the Muslim thinker Frithjof Schuon: "There is no such thing in existence as a unique fact, for the simple reason that it is strictly impossible that such a fact should exist."[4] Similarly, historian A. J. Toynbee writes: "This word 'unique' is a negative term signifying what is mentally incomprehensible."[5] These three authors seem to agree that unique is not a description of human experience; it is an obstacle to historical thinking.

In contrast to this complete certainty that no historical event, no fact of experience, is unique, there are numerous writers who say quite casually that *every* event is unique. For example, Martin Buber writes: "God never does the same thing twice . . . that which exists is unique and happens once."[6] Michael Marrus writes: "In one sense, of course, every historical event and every individual is unique, in that each is different from any other."[7] Maurice Wiles refers to "a weak sense of the word unique in which every historical happening is unique. Each event is unrepeatable and has no identical twin."[8] Similar to Wiles's acknowledgment of a "weak sense" of unique, Yehuda Bauer writes that "there is of course no unique event in history, beyond the trite statement that every event is unrepeatable."[9] Perhaps the statement that each historical event is unique is obvious, trite, or a weak sense of unique. But in trying to figure out what is being said about history, all of the above statements, made with great assurance of their evident truth, do not easily fit together.

I think that what is revealed in these quotations is a contrast in impatience. Some people get impatient with the word because its claim is so trivial as to be not worth making. If one says "unique fact" or "unique event," that is not really saying more than "fact" or "event." Unique is practically a redundancy. There are other people who become impatient with the word because its claim is so exalted as to be beyond realization. All events and facts are partial; each thing can be compared to other things. A unique fact or a unique event is an absurdity.

Given such impatience and dissatisfaction with the term, it might seem preferable to set it aside. If one of the two protests were obviously valid, then it would seem wise to stop using the term. But can both protests be accurate? The fact that people reject the term for opposite reasons suggests that there is something mysterious at issue. In any case, the passionate attack on the word does not get rid of it. Many people think that they are saying something important when they use the word, and it is still not clear what they are saying or trying to say.

Consider this contrast. Many writers use unique as the opposite of universal. For example, Lawrence Kohlberg asks "whether the aims of education should be universal as opposed to unique or individual?"[10] Likewise, René Dubos comments that "the man of flesh and blood portrayed by the Spanish philosopher Miguel de Unamuno cares little for universality; he cherishes his uniqueness."[11] Margaret Furse writes that neo-orthodoxy's "interest in the 'uniqueness' and particularity of the Christian revelation led it to minimize any universalizing features in the biblical literature."[12] And finally, Lawrence Blum writes that "the uniqueness view rejects the possibility of action grounded in universal principles as ever being morally appropriate."[13] The assumption in these four quotations is clear: A writer can either portray the *unique* individual or can work with *universal* claims and theories.

The difficulty with this contrast between unique and universal is that many writers say that the way to the universal is the unique; or conversely, the more one gets at the unique, the more closely one approaches the universal. For example, Herbert Marcuse, theorizing on art, writes: "Art's unique truth breaks with both everyday and holiday reality which block a whole dimension of society and nature."[14] Ben Shahn, reflecting on art, writes "that the universal is that unique thing which affirms the unique qualities of all things."[15] In Christian writing, the words unique and universal are a standard pairing in reference to Christ. For example, Michael McGarry writes: "Common among the Christologies of discontinuity which we have outlined is an emphasis on the unique and universal salvific efficacy of Christ."[16] Or Gerald Anderson can refer to the biblical tradition "recognizing the uniqueness and universality of Jesus Christ."[17]

On the one side of this argument it undoubtedly seems logical to say that unique and universal are opposites. That is clearly the case in the logic that dominates much of the modern world. However, the profoundest human experience seems to go counter to this logic; that is, the unique and the universal always go together. An interesting example is Lewis Thomas's essay "The Medusa." The author begins with the statement: "A phenomenon can't be unique and universal at the same time."[18] After examining the strange creature of the essay's title, Thomas is forced to conclude: "They are bizarre, that's it, unique. And at the same time, like a vaguely remembered dream, they remind one of the whole earth at once."[19] Perhaps Thomas would not retract his opening statement that a unique phenomenon cannot be universal, but what is unique in the essay seems to point in the direction of universality.[20]

A further peculiarity of the word unique is known to most of us from grammar lessons when we were young. The adjective unique cannot be given a comparative or superlative form. At least, generations of grammar teachers have insisted that something cannot be more unique or most unique. Logically, it seems, something is either unique or not unique. Every modifier, even the word *very* as used in the title of this chapter, seems to violate the rules of logic.

In 1989, John Kenneth Galbraith was invited by Vice President Quayle to join the Republican Senatorial Inner Circle. Galbraith, in a letter dripping with sarcasm, proposed that his contribution would be to correct the grammar in the Vice President's letters. Among his many corrections, Galbraith suggested: "In your letter you write of 'something truly unique to the Inner Circle.' I will urge you to avoid so modifying the word 'unique'; something is either unique or it is not. There is no need for enhancing adjectives."[21] Galbraith is correct according to grammar books, but Quayle has common usage on his side.

Despite the insistence of grammar books and English teachers, people regularly put qualifiers before the adjective unique. Richard Nixon, in his memoirs, writes: "My experience has been somewhat unique."[22] Nixon is being unduly modest here; friend and foe alike would probably agree that Nixon's experience has been *very* unique.

James Charlesworth, in *Jews and Christians,* writes: "The Enlightenment produced a serious critique of Christianity's dogmas, especially the absolute uniqueness of Jesus, and, in the process, removed many barriers separating Jewish and Christian theologies."[23] An intriguing question here regards Charlesworth's modifier of unique. If the problem as he states it is the absolute uniqueness of Jesus, is there a nonabsolute uniqueness of Jesus that the Enlightenment (and Jews) could accept? Does uniqueness come in two forms: absolute and nonabsolute? If not, why use the modifier absolute? In the Ferre quotation used at the beginning of this section, the author attacks the totally unique as absurd. Does that imply that there *is* a uniqueness that is less than total? What at first glance seems to be a reasonable explanation of these qualifiers is offered by Norman Pittenger: "Taken strictly, there cannot be degrees of uniqueness, but there is a well established, though looser way of speaking of something as more or less unique."[24]

I fear, however, that Pittenger's distinction of loose/strict, like Wiles's strong/weak cited above, can obscure more than clarify the mysterious nature of uniqueness. Is there not something strange when a word whose very meaning seems to be exclusion of degrees of comparison is regularly used with qualifiers such as somewhat, very, more, truly, or totally? If the term unique is regularly used in a "loose" way, where are the occasions for its strict sense? Ferre says that the phrase totally unique is absurd; does it make any sense to use the word at all? Could there still be weak senses if there is no strong sense? Can there be imprecise meaning if all the meaning disappears with the attempt to be precise?

The fact that there are degrees of uniqueness or something that appears to be degrees of uniqueness is a point I wish to pursue. But that peculiarity of the word is a clue to a more important distinction within the meaning of uniqueness. Confusion in the use of the term arises from another source than that of people being imprecise or careless. In the disagreements noted above (for example, whether uniqueness is the correlate or the opposite of universal), a deep rift is evident. There are two meanings in use, but they do not exist along a continuum of loose to strict or weak to strong. Instead, the two meanings are almost contradictories.

Some authors, sensing this contrast in meaning, play upon the ambiguity. Consider these two sentences by Lewis Thomas: "We tend to think of ourselves as the only unique creatures in nature, but it is not so. Uniqueness is so commonplace a property of living things that there really is nothing unique about it."[25] Thomas identifies here the contrasting meanings that cause confusion in many of the above quotations. Uniqueness, according to Thomas's usage, is twofold in meaning: It is a property of living things whereby each of these things is a distinctive creation, and it is a condition asserted of some state of affairs, namely, that it is incomparable. The second meaning is easy to grasp, whether or not the condition for its use is ever justified. But how and why does the first meaning come to be used?

The root meaning of uniqueness is "different from all others." Does such a thing exist in reality? Human beings, as the only users of the word, tend to think that there is at least one justified application of the term: Uniqueness is a quality attributed to human beings because they are different from all the others (the nonhumans). Each human being is its own self, so the word unique often becomes interchangeable with "human individual."

Hannah Arendt, choosing her words carefully, makes uniqueness the specifying name for human life: "In man, otherness, which he shares with everything that is, and distinctness, which he shares with everything alive, become uniqueness, and plurality is the paradoxical plurality of unique beings."[26] In Arendt's terminology, uniqueness includes and also goes beyond otherness (each thing) and distinctness (living beings). The human being is unique, referring to both status and importance. Each and every human being stands out from the crowd, at least the nonhuman crowd. The danger here is that the rest of the world can blur into a generalized otherness, even though living beings are said to be distinct.

The affirmation of human uniqueness need not entail an unbridgeable gulf between human individuals and everything else. Both distinctness and otherness can be understood to be degrees of uniqueness. Young children often have a sense of distinctness (a high degree of uniqueness) of this particular teddy bear, blanket, hamster, or goldfish. The parent sometimes assumes that such things should be changeable within their kind. ("Why don't you let me buy you another blanket to replace this chewed up one?") Such thinking is stoutly resisted by the child. *This* blanket is unique, the child implicitly says; it is different from all others.

Some people never give up their childhood wonder, or else they recapture it in adulthood. Artists have this sense of wonder and appreciation for the particularity of the world. An artist could be described as someone who looks upon each thing as if it were different from all the others. Indeed, the artist may be trying to show us that this flower or this grain of sand *is* different from all the others and should be appreciated for itself. In Lewis Thomas's quotation above, he refers to uniqueness being commonplace, which is not to say that it is commonly perceived. Most of Thomas's essays are attempts to call attention to the startling phenomena of the natural world.

Some of the most penetrating writing on uniqueness comes from authors who combine a knowledge of the life sciences (biology, ecology, anthropology) with a poetic writing style. Loren Eiseley, Lewis Thomas, and Wendell Berry are masters of this form of writing.[27] Whatever may be the topic of the essay, the paradox and mystery in the term uniqueness is never far away. The difference between an awestruck child and a scientific poetic writer is that the latter can help us see each unique thing in its uniqueness. If one merely says "each thing is unique," that is a statement of bland generality. To sustain a meaningful use for the word, one has to pursue *how* each thing is unique. That is why a combination of scientific knowledge and poetic style is so helpful in dealing with uniqueness. It is also why—in the absence of such skill—so many uses of the word sound like either outrageous claims or mere redundancy.

Uniqueness, when seen by a Thomas, Eiseley, or Berry, obviously extends beyond the human individual. These writers do not insist on an unbridgeable gulf between man and beast. They heighten the sense of human uniqueness, even as they apply the idea of uniqueness to (other) animals and to plant life. A closer relation of humans and nonhumans need not mean a diminishing of the human; on the contrary, it can be an exalting of the nonhuman. Closing the gulf between man and beast could mean the blurring of any distinction. But for those people who look, who respond, who care for what they see in the nonhuman world, there arise *more and more* distinctions. Each existent is seen as unique insofar as it has a being or self; each thing becomes itself as it interacts with everything in its environment.

The nineteenth century was a time of great confusion concerning uniqueness as applied to human beings. William Clebsch is historically accurate in the following comment about nineteenth-century Christians, but the disillusioning to which he refers need not have occurred: "They who had entered the century sure of their uniqueness among creatures because of their unique relation to the creator, exited from the century aware of their linkage to all living things by evolutionary laws and genetical patterns."[28]

The assumption of these Christians that human beings are not unique because they are linked to all living things has more to do with seventeenth- and eighteenth-century science than it does with the first chapter of the Book of Genesis. Indeed, if Christians had understood the logic of their own book, they would have perceived in evolutionary theory a support for Christian doctrine, insofar as modern biology provides a basis for the uniqueness of persons. Theodore Dobzhansky writes that "this uniqueness is a fact of life which has a simple biological basis. This basis was discovered more than a century ago by Gregor Mendel."[29]

One of the most interesting essays on this topic, "The Uniqueness of the Individual," is written by Peter Medawar.[30] The essay is mostly about skin grafting and the difficulty of matching the human body, as compared, for example, to doing the same with mice. Human beings are more complex than mice in their ability to conserve, protect, and enlarge their fitness. Human tradition leads to greater variety and versatility than is possible among mice.

Medawar finds the basis of tradition in the constitution of the human body or, as he expresses it, in the unique constitution of each individual. "Philosophers make a distinction between differences of degree and of kind, but the inborn differences between individuals cannot be classified in either way ... one individual differs from all others not because he has unique endowments but because he has a unique *combination* of endowments."[31] This vision of uniqueness leads Medawar to conclude "that every human being is genetically unique; the texture of human diversity is infinitely woven."[32] The term infinitely is admittedly an exaggeration, but Medawar is trying to force the rational mind beyond its fixed boundaries.

Even after the Darwinian revolution, we still tend to think that the world consists of fixed kinds. Within each of these kinds would be individuals that are identical in "essence." Differences among individuals would then refer to some characteristic that one individual has and others do not. Uniqueness in this context would be a superficial concern, a surface difference among things basically the same. As soon as anyone else decides to acquire characteristics I have, my uniqueness is threatened. Two of us trying to be different in the same way end up not being unique.

The evolutionary pattern that Medawar describes moves along a different path toward ever-increasing uniqueness. Among the less complex beings, it is type that dominates; individuals have no apparent individuality. But with living organisms, this arrangement is altered. The individual is an interweaving of many strands, and the differences are not superficial additions to a basic sameness. Each individual is not only *this kind* but *that one.* One cat differs from another not by length of tail or color of eyes but by its total makeup, its distinctive self. The process is clearest in human beings, where a personality stamps each developing organism.

The consideration of human beings in relation to (nonhuman) nature will be taken up in chapter 6. Here I am just trying to suggest that the use of the word unique in reference to human individuals need not be imagined as a narrowing. Some philosophers have said that the possession of one characteristic (for example, reason) distinguishes the human being from its next of kin. In turn, human individuals often look in that same direction to establish their own unique, inimitable identity. That could be looking in the wrong direction.

Maurice Friedman, commenting on a Hasidic statement, writes: "The search for originality, which is so strong in our day, usually takes the form of a different twist or a new wrinkle. What we ought to be concerned about is our faithful response. If we respond faithfully, this will bring out our own uniqueness."[33] The surprising new word here is response, which will be central to the meaning of uniqueness. The paradox revealed in the genetics of the human being, as well as in artistic and religious history, is that uniqueness arises by letting the world flow in. Instead of pushing away what has some similarities and might therefore detract from our uniqueness, the distinctiveness of the human (and that of other living beings) depends on responding to all the others.

THE TWO MEANINGS

If we draw up a chart for the above uses of unique (and several hundred to follow), there is in each use of the term a simple assertion of difference. "This one is completely different from all the others." But *how* this is possible and *whether* this is possible are questions not usually raised. If pressed to explain what they mean by saying that something is unique, people may say "there is nothing like it." If pressed further, they would perhaps back off from the literal truth of their claim. To make a point, they seem to have simply engaged in a little hyperbole. Of anything supposedly unique, one can always find another thing that has some similarities. Two things are similar at least to the extent that both are things.

Why then does the word get used so often? I think it is because people sense something else in the word. Especially in reference to human beings and profound human experiences, uniqueness points to a different kind of difference. The distinctiveness that is sought for in the term does not come from excluding differences. There is a sense that this experience is different because it is so inclusive.

From a beginning point of "different from all others," the *how* of uniqueness runs in two opposite directions. These two strongly contrasting meanings reflect two ways of encountering the world. I shall henceforth refer to Meaning A and Meaning B of uniqueness. I resist giving names other than A and B to these two meanings. Although this algebraic choice lacks aesthetic quality, it will keep open the ambiguity of the term during the exploration of meaning.

MEANING A

There is a way of perceiving the world in which each thing is an isolated monad. The world is a world of individuals that are only externally related to one another. Individuality depends on isolation, on being protected from anything intruding into one's space. Here a thing is unique if it shares no common notes with other things. Thus, in the sequence 3,3,3,9,3, the number 3 is not unique, but the number 9 is. Or more precisely, the number 9 is a unique number within this sequence of numbers. In other respects, 9 is not unique; it is similar to 3 insofar as both are numbers. If we change the sequence to 3,3,3,M,3, then M is unique in this sequence; it is unique in a more complete sense. It is not just different within the kind called number, it is a different kind.

Even with this increase in uniqueness, M is not completely unique. It shares with numbers the note of being a drawn figure. Further variations on a set of elements could be made, but one would never get complete or total uniqueness. The elements in the set would always have the similarity of being elements. It is possible to imagine a thing being one of a kind; it is not possible to imagine a thing being the only one—period. If something is the only one of its kind, we probably do not use the term unique because we would not have a sense of its being different from the others, there being no others of that kind for ready comparison. Uniqueness more often assumes that there are others of the same kind, but an instance of that kind startles us with its distinctiveness, its great difference from others of its kind.

Within Meaning A, nothing is simply and totally unique. One can move by a process of excluding common notes in the direction of splendid isolation. This increasing differentness can be called very unique or more unique. What is meant is that something is *more nearly* unique. A thing could not be totally unique unless it were the only thing, but then the word unique would not come into the conversation, because there would not be any conversants. In human experience, a thing cannot be (totally) unique, because it shares at least the common note of thingness with other things. Total isolation is a limit situation that can never be reached. In the sequence 3,3,3,9,3 − 3,3,3,M,3 − 3,3,3,],3, the fourth element becomes more nearly unique as we go from set one to set three, but it can never reach uniqueness.

MEANING B

There is an alternate way of encountering the world, in which the real is relational. Here a thing *is* at all only because of its nonisolation. As soon as one reflects upon this relational world, it becomes broken into isolated segments. Nevertheless, life and language can struggle to rediscover the relations that precede reflective thought.

In this way of being in the world, to be is to be in communion. The greater the receptiveness to others, the more distinct the self. In the case of a stone, the individual is difficult to determine; stones, from all appearances, exist in isolation from one another. Even at the level of living microbes and insects, the individual barely seems to have a life of its own apart from the species; there is some social life discernible, but not much. However, when we come to a chimp, a dog, or a dolphin, we clearly recognize an individual with its own characteristics. The dogs, chimps, and dolphins become themselves through relating to others, especially of their own kind.

When we cross the line to the human being, then we are clearly involved with the open, the inclusive, the communal being. Not only are they social (living in groups), humans are political, artistic, philosophical, ethical, and religious. To be human is to be open to everything, past as well as present. We clearly recognize that recluses (at least extreme cases such as Howard Hughes) who isolate themselves from human contact are not achieving a more complete human self but are humanly shriveling up. Not that the greatest human self is always the one with the largest number of human contacts. The issue of uniqueness is responsiveness to reality as it is embodied in persons, places, and traditions.

From the subatomic particle to the human being, we can trace a complexity based on levels of increasing inclusivity. From the crystalline formation of minerals to genetic components of human beings, things are uniquely themselves in varying degrees.

In the sequence a,ab,abc,abcd, the fourth member of the set is unique. It is different from all the others because it includes all the others. Or more precisely, the third member is more unique than the previous two, and the fourth member is more unique than the previous three. Each successive member is more unique, that is, *more nearly* unique. The fourth member in this sequence cannot be called simply or totally unique, because the logic of the sequence suggests that now or in the future there could be the members abcde, abcdef. The only thing that could be called (totally) unique would be the being that includes the elements of all beings. Within human experience, this case has not been realized. But since the human being is open to all beings, we have an understandable tendency to declare —without qualification—that the human being is unique. One might say that the human being achieves a uniqueness in principle.

I think there is some value to this declaration of each human being as unique, especially in defense of the rights of the weakest human beings. The rights of each person ought to be dependent on personhood, not on the wealth, health, or talent of the individual. The disadvantage in this use of language is that it hides the differing degrees of uniqueness among human beings. Human beings are born (very) unique with the vocation to become (more nearly) unique. The description of the human being's unique development is taken up in chapter 7.

Those of us born in a later century would seem to have an advantage. We can assimilate the work of great thinkers, artists, and saints from the past. We can learn from the mistakes of the past and use advanced means of communication to encounter reality. But alas! The record of success is not unambiguously on our side. The great thinkers, the admirable saints, the artistic geniuses seem to be scattered in unlikely spots throughout history. This fact even includes the area of science. While it is said that 90 percent of history's scientists are alive today, it is not clear that the story of science is one of unswerving progress. The possibilities for greater uniqueness do advance, but the realization of uniqueness depends on each individual responding to concrete possibilities. One suspects that the story of the modern era is that an increase in the possibilities of uniqueness has been accompanied by an increase in the obstacles to the realization of uniqueness.

The Two Meanings Compared

Meaning B, like Meaning A, implies movement toward a limit that is never reached. We move in the direction of inclusiveness with Meaning B, as opposed to a direction of exclusiveness with Meaning A. But there is a big difference in how one moves in these two directions. A high degree of exclusivity can simply be achieved by intention and choice. If I wish to exclude an individual or a group from a statement, it is usually easy to do so. In contrast, a statement intended to be all-inclusive risks emptiness on one side and insult on the other. Unless others consent to their being named and to their contributing to the process of naming, then my inclusive statement is likely to be inclusive only for me or for a group I represent.

The problem is an acute one for any religious group that wishes to be universal. A religious statement intended to be all-inclusive may not only fail in its intention but be quite insulting to people who prefer to speak for themselves. Christians may be offended in conversations with all-inclusive Hindus, just as Jews may be wary of the embrace of ecumenical Christians.

The problem is not so much imperialism or intolerance, although the world still has plenty of both. The problem is in the nature of language itself. Every choice of language begins by excluding everyone whose language is something other; every word within every language is weighted with this problem.

The language of a group cannot suddenly jump beyond itself to be inclusive of all. For example, in chapter 5 I am skeptical of anything calling itself "inclusive christology." No one speaks christology except (some) Christians.[34] It is possible for Christian writers to say that they wish to exclude no one from their christological statements; it is not possible to have christology include everyone. However kindly intended, the language is imposed by Christians and refers to Christian matters. No one wishes to be defined as a player in someone else's scheme of salvation.

The conclusion to be drawn is not that Christians, Jews, or other religious groups should stop trying to be more inclusive with their speech. I am just expressing the caution that a declaration to be more inclusive is the start and not the end of the process. The principle applies, of course, to my use of the term unique in this book. The point of this chapter is not to come up with a shorthand (exclusive vs. inclusive) that solves all problems. The point is to recognize the *direction* in which one is moving.

The claim for uniqueness can only be sustained by showing where it goes in individual cases. The language of Christian and Jewish traditions has to be carefully and consistently used in a way that opens doors. A few terms (such as revelation, which is discussed in chapter 3) are of indispensable importance. Other terms might also play a central role. I suggest in chapter 4 that some of these foundational terms (faith, covenant, grace, redemption, kingdom of God) should not be used with the adjectives Christian or Jewish.

Terms that have their origin in Jewish or Christian history might still function as invitational terms toward the universal. If they are to function that way, their meanings cannot be preset by Christian or Jewish control; the fullness of meaning awaits dialogue. Some of these terms may not get very far in dialogue, but we will never find out as long as the words Christian or Jewish regularly precede them. Language that truly includes arises out of dialogue between those who wish to be included. Inclusive language, and therefore Meaning B of uniqueness, is not under anyone's direct control.

The starting point for investigating Meaning B of uniqueness, I have suggested, is the character of human life itself. We speak of a human being as unique, by which we mean very unique or nearly unique. Among human beings, there are degrees of uniqueness, but it would be foolhardy to rate individuals according to a single scale of a,ab,abc,abcd, and so forth. It could be that someone is moving along a scale of s,st,stu,stuv. We can barely discern in our own lives what the route is to the unique self each of us can realize. A few cases of great success or great failure catch our attention in the historical record. For the rest of us, who can claim to be judge?

In some people's pattern of speech, Meaning A may almost totally exclude Meaning B. When that is the case, they may get impatient with anyone's using the word unique. They are likely to substitute another word for what seems to be either a grandiose claim or else a trivial claim.

The word unique nonetheless continues to be used with great regularity. I think many people have a sense that the word is appropriate, even if they cannot logically explain why. What may be uppermost in their minds is Meaning A, a difference by the process of exclusion; but below the surface there is a sense of Meaning B. And within a single paragraph, if not a single sentence, both meanings may be operating. Especially when the reference is to human beings, both meanings are likely to be there.

The human being is our fullest realization of Meaning B of uniqueness. Nonetheless, human beings exemplify Meaning A to the extent that their characteristics are spread across space and time. Within this spatial experience, the human individual will protect his or her bodily integrity by excluding other things from the space he or she occupies. Similarly with regard to time, a human being experiences time (at least much of the time) as spread out over a continuum. To use one hour of the day for one purpose is usually exclusionary; the hour cannot be used for other purposes. In Meaning B, time is not experienced as an excluding moment. The present contains the past and the future. This profound meaning of time (to be explored in chapter 7) never resolves its tension with a contrary Meaning A, in which the past, present, and future are separate dimensions.

I hope that it is clear by now that I am not talking about a good meaning and a bad meaning of uniqueness. Nor am I advocating that we get rid of Meaning A. When there are different meanings within the same word, the most that one can argue for is that one meaning be brought to center stage, while another meaning occupy the wings. In its proper time and place, Meaning A can be correct and helpful. But when it completely obscures Meaning B, then the paradox of uniqueness collapses, and with it the peculiar logic of Jewish and Christian traditions. Much of my effort, therefore, is to call attention to Meaning B of uniqueness and point out its centrality in relating particular questions of Jewish and Christian traditions to universal issues of humanity and the cosmos.

I finish with one more example, one in which both Meaning A and Meaning B are evident. The example is not profound, nor is the speaker; rather, it is a typical statement, although in an unusual context. In July of 1980, Ronald Reagan toyed with the idea of choosing Gerald Ford for his vice presidential running mate. The idea apparently only lasted the Wednesday of convention week. Mr. Reagan, however, pronounced that the combination would be a "unique opportunity."[35] What was Mr. Reagan saying or trying to say?

In Meaning A, Reagan was saying something obvious: There has never been a former president running for vice president. But why praise this simple fact as unique? A woman (at that time), a black man, a twenty-five-year-old, or a chimpanzee would also have been unique, that is, unprecedented within the kind called vice presidential nominees. Surely Mr. Reagan was saying something more or something other. He was indicating that a presidency would be stronger if it included the experience of a former president. The country would move forward, not by its usual route of trying to lop off former administrations, but rather by recapitulating the past within the present.

What apparently frightened off Reagan from his unique opportunity was that the press immediately called the idea "co-presidents." That would have had the uniqueness of Meaning A but not Meaning B. I tend to think that in this instance Mr. Reagan was more profound than the press and that he never had the slightest interest in a co-president. However vaguely he conceived it, Reagan was acknowledging the sane truth that the country, similar to individuals, would be better off if it incorporated the past instead of pretending that the past simply disappears behind our backs. By the time Reagan became president, however, he seemed to have forgotten this moment of insight into time that he had had in July.

2

Is the Holocaust Unique?

This chapter belongs either at the beginning or at the end of a study of uniqueness. The safer thing might be to have a discussion of the Holocaust as the conclusion of the story. However, by raising the question of uniqueness at this time in history and placing it in the context of Christian-Jewish relations, I cannot postpone the immediacy and urgency of the Holocaust. On the Jewish side, it is the reality that hovers over every Christian-Jewish conversation, whatever may be the topic under discussion.

From the standpoint of the logic I am trying to ferret out, the Holocaust is a brutal reminder that the movement toward uniqueness is not necessarily an unqualified good. In Jewish, Christian, and other religious traditions, the human animal is God's gift to the earth, its steward, caretaker, high priest, viceregent. However, according to a medieval maxim, the corruption of the best is the worst. The Holocaust is testimony to how far wrong uniqueness can go. In order that the succeeding chapters of this book be realistic, the discussion of the Holocaust has to come first.

I begin by acknowledging the severe limitations under which I approach this discussion. Should someone who is a non Jew presume to write on the Holocaust? The prior question is: Should anyone write about it? For more than a decade after the gruesome details became available to the world, there was near silence. For some people, the silence was a denial of the reality's significance, an attempt to eliminate from memory this embarrassing horror. For other people, the silence was a mark of respect, a stunned astonishment before an incomprehensible memory. Theodore Adorno's statement that "after Auschwitz to write a poem is barbaric," seemed to express the feeling of many Jews. And for some, if poetry was barbaric, prose was obscene.[1]

Beginning in the 1960s, a seeming reversal occurred. What had been a trickle of writing on the Holocaust has become a river, and there is no sign of the waters abating. A recent bibliography refers to two thousand books on the Holocaust and ten thousand publications on Auschwitz alone.[2] For those people who wished to preserve the memory, this astonishing change represents a mixed blessing. Turning the unspeakable into a thriving indus-try can do violence to that memory. At the time of television's first big entrance into the area, Elie Wiesel wrote: "I write to denounce writing. I tell of the impossibility one stumbles upon in trying to tell the tale."[3] Faced with the prospect of such criticism, most artists kept their distance. Noting the absence of novels about the Holocaust, Irving Howe points out that "many of the customary resources and conventions of the novel are una-vailable."[4]

Any non-Jew who speaks on the subject is suspect, understandably so. The Christian, in particular, is almost bound to say something that is offen-sive, no matter what his or her good intention may be. When Cardinal John O'Connor visited Yad Vashem Holocaust Museum in Jerusalem, he said of the Holocaust that it "may be an enormous gift that Judaism has given the world."[5] He discovered, one might suspect, that silence would have been a more appropriate response to a reporter's question on that occasion. Of course, Cardinal O'Connor was trying to say something very positive about Judaism. He succeeded only in causing a fire storm of criticism among many Jewish leaders.

Cardinal O'Connor's problem was not an unusual one. In fact, every Christian who draws upon Christian theological language of the last two thousand years is likely to have his or her words misunderstood. Christians do not usually realize the burden that their theological language carries for Jews. The relating of the Holocaust to the sufferings of the crucified Christ may be heard as a cruel joke. Christian theology needs a far greater revo-lution than has yet occurred before there can be a (Christian) theology of Judaism, let alone a "theology of the Holocaust."[6]

Since I am suggesting that Christians might do better with silence, the obvious question is why I think I can and should write this chapter. My first stipulation is that I am not trying to tell the story of the Holocaust. I do not pretend to substitute here for any voice in the discussion. I am only asking about the logic of uniqueness in relation to the Holocaust. Does a Christian nonexpert on the Holocaust have a right to ask this question? If the logic I refer to has any validity, then a Christian may have not only the right but the duty. The message of Holocaust literature is not only for Jews; in fact, some dimensions are meant especially for Christians. My modest aim is to call attention to this fact in the most effective way I know.

My analysis of the term *unique* in discussion of the Holocaust is meant to do two things: clarify a conflict over whether the Holocaust should be called unique, and explain why what may seem to be an intra-Jewish dis-cussion ought to draw in Christian and secular participants.[7] These two aims are connected. The lack of clarity about the term uniqueness can function as a distraction from important aspects of the Holocaust. The uniqueness of the Holocaust, in addition to being about Jewish suffering, is about the inadequacy of both Christian theological tradition and the presumptions of western secular enlightenment. In the logic I am trying to get at, it is not an exaggeration to say, in Elie Wiesel's words, that "the Holocaust is a unique Jewish tragedy with universal meaning."[8] But what does the word unique mean here?

THE UBIQUITY OF THE TERM

Even if one is not interested in the meaning of uniqueness, one can hardly avoid noticing the prominence of the word in writing on the Holocaust. I seldom read a book on this topic in which the word does not frequently appear. Sometimes it is the first theme; other times it is a main theme throughout the book. Numerous writers try to clarify what they mean by calling the Holocaust unique or calling into question other writers' use of the term. However, the issue does not go away, and it can cause heated emotional exchanges. Both sides seem to think: Why doesn't my opponent understand the clear definition of unique, as I have just stated it?

A definition does not clear up the controversy, because the word is more paradoxical in meaning than is usually acknowledged. A person who says "by unique, I mean . . . ," has not begun to grapple with the complexity of the term. A writer's intention does not control what the word means.

What, it might be asked, makes me think I can do any better? To start with, the luxury of space. I am willing to let the word speak for itself over many pages. When the question of uniqueness comes up in Holocaust literature, the treatment of the term usually ranges from a sentence to a few pages. In contrast, I am attending, throughout this chapter and in the context of this book, to the meaning of the *question*. What results from exploring the question is not a definitive answer to a controversial question. Rather, one gets clearer questions that lead to a more profound impact and a wider audience.

From the material in the first chapter of this book, the reader already knows the answer to the question in this chapter's title: Is the Holocaust unique? The obvious answer is yes. But to make sense of the question as well as the answer, we have to sort out Meaning A and Meaning B of uniqueness. Only then can we get to the important questions: (Within Meaning B), how, why, for whom, and to what degree is the Holocaust unique?

One possible misunderstanding should be addressed immediately. When the question of uniqueness is raised, it often seems to pit a philosophical-theological approach against a historical method. Some historians object to the intrusion of claims to uniqueness because they see that as removing the Holocaust to a suprahistorical plane, outside the historian's job of drawing comparisons and tracing antecedents.[9] (Predictably, within the paradoxical meaning of this term, historians will also say: Uniqueness is what we deal in all the time; every historical event is unique.)[10]

My affirmation of uniqueness is not meant to choose the philosophical-theological side of this argument. Rather, it is to reshape the terms of the debate. Both the historian and the philosopher are challenged by the uniqueness of the Holocaust.

The claim to uniqueness is a challenge to assumptions in modern philosophy and history about the human capacity to draw causal connections, to give rational explanations, and to discover intelligible meaning.[11] Nathan Rotenstreich makes the helpful distinction between explaining and explicating. He offers that his job is not to explain the Holocaust but to explicate what he calls the gestalt of Nazism or the facets of the "unique aspect of the Nazi phenomenon."[12] Similar to the way Rotenstreich is using the word unique here, I am interested in exploring all facets of the Holocaust in such a way that non-Jew as well as Jew can hear.

Jewish writers who make the claim of uniqueness can become very impatient with any questioning of the claim by other Jews and, more so, by non-Jews. Arthur Cohen, using the term *tremendum* for horrors of our century, writes: "Every genocidal *tremendum* is unique to the victims; it is only those who feel upon themselves the breath of guilt and contamination that the insistence falls to argue with the claim of uniqueness. The Cambodian does not tell the Jew that Auschwitz is not unique—it is the calm West that makes such announcements."[13] Cohen in all likelihood is correct that arguing against the claim of uniqueness is often based on guilt and bigotry. Nonetheless, arguing about the *meaning* of the claim can be for the purpose of shaking people out of their complacency or drawing in listeners.

Cohen makes a crucially important point that sufferers do not make claims about who is suffering more. I return to that point at the end of the chapter. For the present, I simply make the point that any writer who uses the term uniqueness has to be patient if the reader resists. Five pages after Cohen has excoriated those who "argue with the claim of uniqueness," he writes: "If the *tremendum* is an event unparalleled, unique in every characteristic dimension of uniqueness . . . the history of the past becomes irrelevant."[14] Cohen acknowledges here that uniqueness is a very peculiar claim, one seemingly impossible to sustain. Thus when Jewish, Christian, or other writers argue about the claim to uniqueness, they may simply be unclear about what such a claim could mean.

When two sides, usually both Jewish, do develop over the applicability of the word unique to the Holocaust, there is usually far more agreement than is manifest. Both sides are passionately concerned with the Holocaust being recognized as immeasurably important and deserving of the world's attention. One side thinks that the word unique is just what is needed to describe the reality; the other side thinks that unique is one of the worst words to use, at best irrelevant and at worst preposterous.

If the peculiarity of the term has not been reflected upon, the latter response is readily understandable. This side sees the claim to uniqueness as lifting the Holocaust outside of human history so that nothing in history is comparable. But if something is, in the literal sense, incomparable, then there is nothing to say. The Holocaust, in being isolated outside of history, suffers just the fate that the claimants to uniqueness were trying to avoid. That is, the world is freed from having to attend to the Holocaust. It becomes unnecessary to examine what led to the Holocaust and what effects still reverberate today. Why, it is asked, cannot the claimants to uniqueness recognize that their strategy is self-defeating?

On the side of the claimant to uniqueness, there is often the same impatience. Can the other side not see that by denying the claim to uniqueness, they undercut the importance of the Holocaust? The Holocaust becomes just one of many calamities in recent history. Who will attend to the special suffering of these people if it gets tossed in with the million who died here and the ten million who died there?

Before applying the word unique to the Holocaust, it is necessary to consider how anything can be called unique. The case to be made about the Holocaust in Meaning B of uniqueness is not that some fact about the Holocaust cannot be compared with other facts, or that an event called the Holocaust possesses some note that cannot be found elsewhere in human history. The Holocaust's most important uniqueness lies in a direction almost exactly the opposite, that is, in the direction of greater inclusiveness.

Many writers on the Holocaust do go in the direction that I describe here, although they may do so with a somewhat apologetic beginning. Historians may say that there is something to this claim of uniqueness, or at least they are not willing to argue against it. Michael Marrus, pointing out what the historian's approach is, writes: "Accepting the uniqueness, this approach *nevertheless* insists upon it being a part of history, explicable as other aspects of Nazism and the Second World War."[15] In this quotation, "nevertheless" indicates that the question has been misunderstood. My approach to uniqueness leads to this premise: *Because* the Holocaust is unique, the work of historians is doubly important in tracing the background of the Holocaust, all facets of its past, as well as its effect in the present.

UNIQUENESS A AND B

In the first chapter, I described how the idea of uniqueness emerges. It begins with the note of "different from all others." Such an assertion is likely to provoke the reaction that the claim cannot be true because there is always something comparable. The search for uniqueness can then go in one of two directions: toward an increase of exclusiveness (Meaning A), or toward an increase of inclusiveness (Meaning B).

In neither direction does one reach an end to the process. No thing excludes comparison with every other thing; similarly, no thing is incomparable by including every note. No thing could be so exclusive as to be totally alone; and no thing could be totally inclusive as long as history continues. However, I have pointed out that in Meaning B the movement across the line from nonhuman to human brings about an openness to everything. The human being is open in principle. People feel justified in using the strange word *unique,* because they have a sense of this process of inclusion within human experience.

MEANING A

Is the Holocaust unique? To the extent that we say that every *event* is unique, the answer is obviously yes. If we conceive of history as a series of discrete points along a time (or space-time) continuum, each point is itself and not another point. Here the best way to name the world would be to assign a number to each point, and a thing could be exactly described by numerical coordinates. The numbering system would never be perfect, but it could approach perfection by breaking everything into events, each with its assigned number.

In this frame of reference, the word unique is largely redundant. For practical purposes, each event could be called unique, although it only approaches that point asymptotically. Since every event can be called unique, there is not much point in calling any event unique.

When faced with this kind of logic, people often rebel. They insist that such and such an event is *really and truly unique.* When they do that, they are not usually pressing to reach that final mathematical location in space and time. Rather, they are demanding recognition that something does not fit the framework. The image that is often brought in is interruption. This term seems to assert a discontinuity in the flow of points.[16]

Although one can say of the Holocaust that it is an interruption, I am doubtful that the claim makes much sense. A physicist cannot accept any interruptions or discontinuities in the flow of space-time points. Of course one can argue, contrary to science, that some events do not have antecedent points leading up to them. Religious people have often made such an argument in favor of miracles. With reference to the Holocaust, however, I think the argument is in the wrong world of discourse. If we are going to find the significance of the Holocaust, we have to start at the other end of uniqueness, with Meaning B.

MEANING B

Historians these days can sometimes sound like scientists and technicians. As students of history employ every means to collect and verify data, history could be construed as the assembling of points in space-time. Most historians, however, subordinate the computer search to the telling of the human story. Historians are not second-class physicists assigning numbers to the continuum. When events are spoken of within history, the dividing lines are arbitrary. The discreteness of events is a humanly chosen device for a particular purpose. The English word *event* has an impersonal meaning that locates it more with the physicist than the historian, no matter how common the phrase "historical event" is. Although I will not try to avoid the word entirely, *event* is of limited relevance in most of the chapters of this book. Unique events usually are in the arena of Meaning A.

History involves telling a human story. If told well, the story includes nonhumans, although human beings remain the central players. Each story can be called unique, that is, inclusive of human beings. Some stories are more unique than others to the extent that they are revelatory of the animal who is unique in principle. Some stories become more unique, as they are participated in by a widening circle of listeners.

Within this world of discourse, there should be little argument with the proposition that the Holocaust is a very unique (that is, very nearly unique) reality. If someone were to argue that another reality could be more unique (more nearly unique), he or she would be on good logical grounds. But an argument over whether one reality or another is the *more* unique is usually unhelpful. The issue here is the uniqueness of the Holocaust. If someone chooses not to discuss the Holocaust at all, that is understandable. But if one does discuss it, then the question is not whether some other reality might be more unique.

Meaning A or Meaning B is indicated by the tense of the verb that is used. In Meaning A, by the time we speak of any (unique) event, it is already a past event; thus we always say of an event that it *was* unique. Time flows on at the rate of sixty seconds a minute. In contrast, the uniqueness of Meaning B takes us more profoundly into the present, which includes the past. The question in the title of this chapter is: *Is* the Holocaust unique? We are discussing a present reality, within which is a past that has not disappeared and the possibilities of a future already with us.

In Meaning A, the Holocaust can be spoken of as a past event. To the question: Was the Holocaust unique? the answer is yes. The Holocaust was a unique event; so was the stock market crash, the invention of microwave ovens, the founding of *People* magazine, and millions—billions—of other events. The unique event sits back there in a string of happenings. If it was an unpleasant event, why not just try to forget it?

When Ronald Reagan went to Bitburg, his explanation was that the events of the Nazi era are behind us.[17] The obvious truth of his statement needs countering with a more important truth: The Holocaust as a unique experience for some people is still becoming more unique for other people. There are people who would like to deny that the past has happened. It is important that the past be tied down in our history books with documented names, dates, and places. Nevertheless, the Holocaust is not an event behind our backs; it is a continuing challenge to both Jew and non-Jew.[18]

COMPARISONS TO THE HOLOCAUST

Before proceeding further with characteristics of the Holocaust's uniqueness, some comments have to be made about the comparability of the Holocaust. I have said that the Holocaust's important uniqueness is not to be found in its isolation from everything, but in the opposite direction: its relation to everything. To the question: Can the Holocaust be compared to anything else? the short answer is: Yes, to everything else. The important question then becomes: What *should* the Holocaust be compared to? When speaking of something important, there are comparisons that trivialize, comparisons that indicate the speaker has little sense of the issue.

We recognize something is important by how we name it. Each human being has a proper name, a recognition of each person's uniqueness. In contrast, as a series of events, roles, or functions, the person is reduced to a collection of numbers: Social Security, Mastercard, telephone, street address. Important historical realities likewise have their own names. Sometimes these names are logically imposed (World War II), sometimes the name is a person or place that comes to symbolize the whole (Watergate). It is both a compliment to its significance and an undermining of that significance when the particular name becomes generic. *The* World War became the first and not the only one of its kind. Watergate was followed by Irangate and other -gate neologisms. Does World War III become more thinkable when world wars have simply become a series? Do the sins of particular politicians become less important when they are strung together with similar acts? To the extent that history is imagined to be a series of points, then each calamity gets only its alloted time on the evening news, and all calamities of a similar kind tend to blur together.

Nearly all Jewish writers are adamant in maintaining that there is only one Holocaust. The upper case in English helps to make the point. There is not a series of things called holocausts, of which the Jewish experience of the 1940s is an example. Compare that to the word *genocide,* a term coined in 1943 in reference to the murder of the Jews.[19] The word is itself abstract and suggests that there have been many cases that deserve the judgment of genocide. Examples could include the European devastation of the American continent, the slaughter of the Armenians by the Turks in 1915, or the recent slaughter of the Cambodian people.[20]

When the word *Holocaust* is applied to these and other calamities, Jews protest. Actually, it was only in the 1960s that Holocaust became the agreed-upon term. But it is a word with biblical origin and meaning; Jewish writers feel that it is a term that belongs to them.[21] It is impossible, however, to stop other people from applying one's own term to their situation. If that practice becomes widespread, then those who are trying to protect the particularity of their experience may try to become more particular. One tendency in Jewish writing is to refer to Auschwitz as the particular name that refers to the whole experience. No one is likely to refer to a whole genre of Auschwitzes. Yet even here, as Lucy Dawidowicz notes, the term Auschwitz is used by some people as "a metaphor for the 'ecumenical nature' of the evil that was committed there."[22]

Another strategy has been to replace the word Holocaust with the Hebrew *Shoah.* No one is likely to turn that word into either metaphor or genre. For those whose first or second language is Hebrew, the use of *Shoah* is powerfully evocative. For the wider public, using *Shoah* in place of Holocaust does not seem to be making great headway, and a solution to the problem of particularity by isolating the term from English speakers may not be wise. Comparisons are discouraged, but in the long run that is not the issue in the affirmation of uniqueness.

In Meaning B of uniqueness, the Holocaust can be compared to other things. The two questions to be raised are *what* and *how*. Some things are simply unworthy of the comparison. If a high school newspaper has its privilege of publication suspended, the editors should not compare their plight to the Jews under Nazism. If every petty dictator is called a Hitler, and innumerable agonies are compared to Auschwitz, most people can appreciate the inappropriateness of the comparison. Jewish speakers can at times participate in the tendency to spread the comparison too far. Dawidowicz gives the example of some Israelis comparing an incident at Ma'alot in 1974 to Auschwitz. The Israeli town of Ma'alot was where Arabs killed twenty Israelis and wounded seventy.[23]

The twentieth century, however, does provide legitimate contenders for comparison with the Holocaust. Hiroshima, Vietnam, Cambodia, Stalinism, the Armenian slaughter, the millions of non-Jews who died under Nazism are cases regularly cited. More recently, AIDS has been compared to the Holocaust.[24] And although the term *Holocaust* is seldom called upon yet, I suspect in the near future our ecological disaster will be a promising candidate for comparison. It seems to me that if done with sufficient sensitivity, such comparisons might lead to a deeper appreciation of both realities. Why then do Jewish writers become so upset when comparisons are made?

I choose the writer Emil Fackenheim as an example. In regard to an essay by a Christian writer, Fackenheim complains: "In this piece, Auschwitz is flattened out into a case of atrocity in general."[25] In another place, he writes: "To link Auschwitz with Hiroshima is not to deepen or widen one's concern with humanity and its future. It is to evade the import of Auschwitz and Hiroshima alike."[26]

If the issue here is the inadequacy of "flatten" (in the first quotation) and "link" (in the second), the objection is understandable. But can one deny all basis of comparison?[27] Auschwitz and Hiroshima are words that point to two terrifying revelations of the twentieth century. How the message in these revelations is heard and what should be the personal response to the two realities can vary. Fackenheim, formerly a Canadian citizen, is related to Hiroshima, but not as closely as a United States citizen. As a Jew who fled Nazi Germany, Fackenheim is closer to Auschwitz than are most United States citizens. As a citizen of the United States, I think one can and should compare Auschwitz and Hiroshima.

There are aspects of great difference between these two; there are aspects of sameness; that is what comparisons are for. The comparison is not necessarily saying that the United States government was as bad as

Hitler's Third Reich. But the United States government has yet to give any semblance of an apology to the world for introducing atomic warfare against a defenseless population. How horrible was this atrocity? We do not yet know, although for Japanese survivors who carry the genetic scars, the horror is real. The rest of the human race has hardly begun to absorb the consequences.

To refer to Hiroshima is to isolate a moment within a complex pattern of history. World War II was a balancing act of terrible choices and horrible slaughters. (Remember Pearl Harbor or Iwo Jima or Okinawa.) The case is made that President Truman saved many lives (particularly of United States soldiers). Some kind of cool calculation of numbers was no doubt part of the planning, and in terms of numbers killed, Hiroshima and Nagasaki represent only a small percentage of that number who died.

Was Hiroshima all that different from Dresden, which had been previously fire bombed? Unfortunately, the answer is no. Hiroshima and Dresden are indeed comparable. A moral line was crossed with the bombing of Dresden, a line that can never be restored. The indiscriminate killing of a civilian population in Dresden made Hiroshima thinkable, just as Hiroshima made future nuclear wars thinkable. Dresden was unique; Hiroshima was more unique. The United States government and its people have never acknowledged the degree of uniqueness. An occasional comparison to the Nazis' unique horror might be part of bringing into consciousness the evils that the United States is fully capable of.[28]

The appropriateness of such comparisons returns us to the underlying difference between Meaning A and Meaning B of uniqueness. In Meaning A, human beings are unique insofar as they occupy space and time that is not occupied by another thing (or series of events). In Meaning B, human beings are unique in their composition, and other beings are unique to varying degrees. Human beings are the most clearly unique, because their nature is not to *have* a nature; their identity is found in an openness to everything in the cosmos. Human beings become capable of greater good in the world as they respond to the gift of being. But with slight distortion, human beings can also be capable of greater and greater evil.

While most of this book concerns the human possibilities for goodness, this chapter underscores the possibility of evil and destructiveness. Great evil demands a heroic response. The remainder of this chapter looks first at the uniqueness of the Holocaust's destructiveness, both as given and received, and second at the uniqueness of the response to the Holocaust.

UNIQUE DESTRUCTION: GIVEN AND RECEIVED

The Holocaust was unique in its whirlpool of destruction, with evil unleashed and suffering endured. At the center of the Holocaust's sufferings are the millions of Jews who died. Spreading out from that center are the survivors of the death camps, the remnant of European Jewry, Jews in the United States, Israel, and elsewhere, every Jew of the past and future. At the center of the destructiveness are Hitler and his cohorts. Spreading out from the center are collaborators, standers-by, ordinary anti-Semites, Christians in Europe and elsewhere, religious and secularist thinkers of every stripe. Before anyone says that this is not my story or my responsibility, he or she should consider the breadth and depth of the phenomenon in question. Within Meaning B of uniqueness, the question is not whether or not I am involved. The question is my degree of involvement and the consequent demand upon me to do something in response.

For each person who dies, death is undoubtedly a unique experience. The Holocaust provided six million such uniquenesses. Numerically, there have been greater slaughters. But for the Jews, six million was a large percentage of the entire people. One out of every three civilians killed during World War II was a Jew. The Nazi aim was to exterminate the people as a whole, every last individual. That is why the issue of intention figures so prominently in discussing the uniqueness of the Holocaust.[29] Whether Hitler had his intention clear from the beginning or evolved to it, whether Hitler's intention was the single force guiding the "final solution," the intention had become clear toward the end of the war: the elimination of a people as a people. The translation of a fanatical ideology into an efficient bureaucracy of killing is what makes the Holocaust so unique from the standpoint of the destruction.[30]

The uniqueness of Meaning B does not depend on there being one note that is absent from other disasters. On the contrary, the uniqueness arises from a combination of all the factors that interweave to produce the final result. Because the interweaving here is so complex, so difficult to explain in anyone's scheme of explanations, the Holocaust challenges both religious and secular views of history.

JEWISH RELIGION

The Jewish view of history suffered a stunning blow. The Holocaust was by no means the first calamity, but it was the most unique suffering, that is, one that took up the past and endured more. In previous devastations, the argument was made that suffering was a punishment for sin or a test of faith. The same argument can be and has been made of the Holocaust. It is clear that many Jews are unpersuaded by this line of argument.[31]

The language of Jewish religion has for thousands of years been a highly personal one of a loving, caring God and his freely chosen people. Biblical imagery often has Israel's God intervening on behalf of his people. Did Jews in the death camps really and literally expect divine intervention? Not perhaps on this day or for that offense, but it is the culmination—the whole people's unique experience—that demands a response from the Jewish thinker.

SECULAR THINKERS

At the other end of the spectrum from the cry of "renew your faith" is the secular answer: The absence of God has finally been revealed. In this view, the remnant must henceforth rely on stronger political and military measures. The trouble with this secular answer is that the uniqueness of the Holocaust is as damaging to themes of western enlightenment as it is to Jewish claims of chosenness.[32]

The liberation of "autonomous man" in the West was supposed to replace religious superstition with unadulterated reason. Progress in the good life was guaranteed. The Holocaust is a challenge to the very idea of modernity in which the modern world accepts no final judgments except its own. And, indeed, Nazi Germany was unique not in being set outside the current of rational and technical development, but in being so thoroughly representative of western "values."

Historians who had assumed that logical answers and human progress would become increasingly clear are challenged by the uniqueness of the Holocaust. In the case of Isaac Deutscher, for example, the Marxism which he substituted for his Jewish religion provides no more help in explanation. Deutscher acknowledges: "To a historian trying to comprehend the Jewish holocaust the greatest obstacle will be the absolute uniqueness of the catastrophe."[33] The word *absolute* here is misleading. There is no guarantee that the Holocaust is the last great evil of the human animal. In this connection, the statement of Raul Hilbert misses the point of uniqueness: "The optimists say that the Nazis are unique—that what they did could not happen again."[34] Unfortunately, the uniqueness of the Nazis means that it could happen again—and could be even worse.

CHRISTIANITY

The other party severely under challenge from the Holocaust is the Christian church. As in previous Jewish-Christian conflicts, there were Christians willing to suggest that the victims deserved what they got. The more common defense was to say that Christianity was not a central player. But in any fair account of history, Christianity cannot entirely remove itself from the story.

One can first distinguish between the historic part that Christian theology played and the actions of Christian church people at the time of the Holocaust. It seems safe to say that there was not a necessary and sufficient link between the anti-Judaism of Christian doctrines and the rise of Nazism. A destruction of the Jews was never envisioned by the New Testament or subsequent official teaching. But it is also safe to say that the anti-Judaism in Christian teaching from first to twentieth centuries was one of the factors that prepared the way for Nazi Germany.[35]

The relevance of Christian doctrines to the Holocaust can be endlessly debated, but on the Christian side, the harshest fact is, as Arthur Cohen puts it, "the slayers were baptized."[36] Individual Christians and the church as an institution were elements in the engine of destruction. To be sure, there were Christian heroes who risked their lives for the sake of Jews. The overall record, nonetheless, is not very good.

THE UNIQUENESS OF THE RESPONSE

Meaning B of uniqueness presupposes a being that is open, receptive, and responsive. That is, uniqueness requires participation by someone who can respond. Something becomes (more nearly) unique as I take part in it, as I allow the reality into my life. The Holocaust is obviously unique; however, it becomes more unique to people depending on their involvement in the reality, their willingness to listen, and their responses.

JEWS

For the Jews who were killed in World War II Europe, the Holocaust was undoubtedly the most unique experience of their lives. Concerning the response of those who died, there is not much that the outsider can say. Hannah Arendt caused a stir in the 1960s with the charge that the Jews did not resist enough, that they went passively to their deaths.[37] Isaiah Trunk's 1970 book on the Jewish political council put the discussion on firmer ground, documenting in detail the resistance or lack of resistance.[38] While this is a topic of continuing interest to Jewish historians, the rest of us can only refrain from speculating and moralizing.

For those who survived the camps, the Holocaust has often remained the most unique experience of their lives. They have a memory to preserve and a story to tell which the whole world should hear. The Holocaust may also be the most unique experience for children of the survivors, for Jews in Europe today, for Jews in Israel, in the United States, and elsewhere.

For every Jew of the present and future, the Holocaust is very unique, but that is not to say that the Holocaust must always be the most unique experience of every Jew. What is incumbent on every Jew is to listen to the story of his or her people; what is embedded for all time in that story is the unique experience of the Holocaust. How unique it proves to be remains to be seen. We already know of the founding of the state of Israel in its wake. We know of various social, political, economic, and military movements that have also followed. Only in a much larger pattern of history will a full meaning of the Holocaust's uniqueness emerge.

The philosophical-theological response is probably only at the beginning stage. Some Jews' conception of God died during the Holocaust, and many Jewish thinkers are wary of rushing in with a new concept. In the 1960s Emil Fackenheim wrote that "the authentic Jew of today is forbidden to hand Hitler another posthumous victory."[39] The statement drew wide support because one can negate negation, even if one is not prepared to elaborate a positive alternative. Fackenheim and other Jewish thinkers have begun the long journey of trying to confront the philosophical-theological implications of the Holocaust. Many Jews have only Franz Rosenzweig's prayer of both hands, the believer and the unbeliever.[40] Or as Elie Wiesel put it: "If I told you that I believed in God, I would be lying; if I told you that I did not believe in God, I would be lying."[41]

CHRISTIANS

In turning to Christianity here, we must first distinguish between the response of Christians at the time and the response called for today. The Holocaust was a unique experience for German Christians, European Christians, and Christians generally. What the response should have been can greatly vary. Just as it is unfair to say that individual Jews caught in the Nazi regime should have shown more resistance, so we would do well to refrain from condemning individual Christians who did not become heroes. One major difference, however, is that, whereas organized movements of resistance in the death camps were all but impossible, organized resistance and condemnation were possible by Christians within Germany and beyond.

There were individuals who exemplify what might have been done on a larger scale. For example, Prior Bernhard Lichtenberg decided on *Kristallnacht* to do something. He daily and publicly prayed for the Jews in his church in Berlin. This practice continued from 1938 to 1941, when he was arrested. Notice that for other Christians at other times, saying a prayer for the sufferings of the Jews could be perfunctory or a substitute for political activity. In Lichtenberg's case, however, he had listened, responded, and risked his life with the best form of resistance at hand. He responded uniquely within a unique experience.[42]

Suppose that high church leaders (including the Pope) had responded with the same uniquely relevant activity? Suppose that the encyclical prepared for Pope Pius XI's approval just before his death in 1939 had been issued? Hitler had shown himself sensitive to church criticism, such as the earlier and milder criticism in *Mit Brennender Sorge* (1937) or the protest of church leaders against euthanasia in 1940-1941. Perhaps Hitler's Third Reich would not have been swayed by powerful words of condemnation from the church. That possibility does not exculpate church leaders.[43] The scandalous failure of a proper response is indicated in a letter of Adolph Bertram, Archbishop of Breslau, to the minister of interior. The archbishop's concern was that the sweep for Jews was including Christians of mixed blood. German Catholics, wrote the archbishop, would feel "deeply hurt . . . if these fellow Christians now would have to meet a fate similar to that of Jews."[44]

What kind of response is called for from Christians of today? It would do no one any good for Christians to wallow in a vague feeling of guilt. Instead, their own unique response is called for. Except for a few Christians, the Holocaust is not the most unique experience of their lives. But for those Christians who do listen, it can become more and more unique. The fact that I am a Christian does not make me personally responsible for the actions of a Mengele or Eichmann. The fact that I am a Christian *does* make me responsible for doing what I can today to alter the patterns of Christian thought and action that prepared the way for Nazism.

In the next three chapters, I describe the changes needed in Christian theology. These changes go to the root of anything called theology. J. B. Metz has repeatedly said: "The problem with a view toward Auschwitz is not merely a revision of the Christian theology of Judaism, but a revision of Christian theology altogether."[45] It is not evident that many Christian theologians have heard this message of Metz's.

There is a crisis of Christian belief that is as severe as the crisis facing Judaism. But instead of stunned silence or the prayer of both hands, Christian theology, for the most part, goes its talkative way. One can find casual and comprehensive claims that the world has been "redeemed" or "saved." The past tense in these verbs has always struck the Jew as incredible; after Auschwitz, it seems to the Jew obscene. Metz has said that he can never again do theology with his back to Auschwitz. Every sentence of Christian theology has to be made with full frontal view of Auschwitz.

CONCLUSION

If Jews wish to have non-Jews hear the message of the Holocaust, then the idea of uniqueness has to be carefully examined and precisely used. Sometimes when the non-Jew does not hear, it leads the Jew to become more insistent that the Holocaust was the worst act in all history. This insistence is not likely to persuade. That the Holocaust is unique is not what needs debating. It is unique to varying degrees, according to one's participation. For those of us alive today, it becomes more unique as we listen. However, we all have a finite time for listening (that is, Meaning A of uniqueness never disappears). Suppose I am struck by someone's story. Should I listen for an hour, an hour a week, every day? Should I give up my job and do nothing else?

What we become involved in and our degree of involvement are partly accidents of history. The pattern of our responsibilities, however, is not entirely arbitrary. Should a white United States Christian study the Holocaust? The answer is: Yes, at some time the issue should be unavoidable. If one is going to be a responsible Christian, then a Christian form of education has to include some serious confrontation with the Holocaust. Should a church school curriculum have one day, one week, one semester on the Holocaust? That decision requires intelligent and informed discussion among educators. Most important is the context. The Holocaust is not one more sad story to be stuck into the curriculum. It is uniquely important to the whole story of Christianity.

Should a black woman in Soweto be reading books on the Holocaust? Actually, that might help her understand her plight, but she will probably have neither the inclination nor the time for such study. The sufferings of blacks in South Africa is another (very) unique experience in the twentieth century. That experience is undoubtedly most unique for the black people of that nation. For people in other parts of the world, South Africa's sufferings can be an experience of varying degrees of uniqueness. A comparison between Nazi Germany and South Africa is not necessarily misplaced. If the comparison is carefully done, it can throw light on both of these unique experiences.

A similar comparison might include the sufferings of people in Tibet, Cambodia, Lebanon, Northern Ireland, or a hundred other places where whole peoples have suffered repression and violence. Partly because of genealogy and partly because of the experiences we have along the way of life, we respond in different ways to these tales of horror. We all have a limited amount of time, anger, sympathy, money, and influence in responding to the world's sufferings, though deep involvement in one case should not entail callousness in the others.

I quoted Arthur Cohen above, saying that people who suffer greatly do not spend their time trying to prove their suffering is greater than someone else's. Unfortunately, those who are outside the immediate circle of suffering can sometimes unwisely engage in such a debate. Within Meaning B of uniqueness, this kind of debate is a distraction from understanding the reality of the suffering and trying to do something about it.

There is no "absolute uniqueness" recorded by an impersonal scale. There are degrees of (near) uniqueness that depend on people entering the experience, usually through listening. Christians who have little interest in listening to the story of the Holocaust may simply be bigoted. It might also be the case that the time for the arrival of this truth is not at hand. Perhaps by another route to Meaning B of uniqueness, such Christians will eventually arrive at being able to hear the (very) unique significance of the Holocaust.

3

Unique Revelation

The discussion of the Holocaust in the previous chapter leads to questions about a larger framework of understanding. Concentration on the Holocaust to the exclusion of other relevant concerns—other aspects of World War II, European history in the early 1900s, modern political and economic history—would eventually undermine Holocaust literature itself. As I pointed out with reference to Meaning B of uniqueness, the Holocaust's uniqueness depends on the degree to which it is related to other awesome revelations of human depravity, suffering, and courage. For Gentile as well as Jew, the Holocaust needs to be placed in the context of the claim that the Jew—or more precisely, Jewish history—is unique. The frequent application of the word *unique* to the Holocaust follows almost inevitably from the Jews' view of their whole historical experience.

Philip Lopate, while skeptical of the use of the word unique in reference to the Holocaust, correctly notes the link to the larger framework: "The hostility toward anything that questions the uniqueness of the Holocaust can now be seen as part of a deeper tendency to view all of Jewish history as unique, to read that history selectively and use it only as it promotes a redemptive script."[1]

The argument over the validity of applying the term unique to the Holocaust is neither trivial wordplay nor an empirical question that historical data can ultimately resolve. What is at stake is the peculiar kind of logic that is at the foundation of Judaism (and Christianity). Confusion about the claim of uniqueness reveals a lack of clarity about many of the foundational concepts of the Jewish and Christian religions.

OVERVIEW

This chapter and the two that follow are closely related. The topics of revelation, covenant, and Jesus unite and divide the two traditions. The uniting and dividing occur within each chapter. In this third chapter, I concentrate on revelation, an idea that is shared by Jews and Christians.

The sharing is not total, however, because the introduction of the Christ profoundly influences the Christian meaning of revelation. In chapter 4, the focus is on covenant. This term is clearly of Jewish origin, and despite the Christian claim to a new covenant, the term is still closely associated with the Jews. Chapter 5 is mainly Christian, insofar as it deals with the founder (or foundation) of the Christian religion. But even here, I particularly attend to the (very) unique person, Jesus of Nazareth, who is a possible bridge between church and Judaism. As I shall later develop, while the Christ figure clearly divides Jew and Christian, the person Jesus can unite.

I said above that Christian and Jew to a large extent agree on the idea of revelation. There are various definitions of the word *revelation* that would cause no conflict, perhaps not even debate, between Christian and Jew. But there is a nagging problem behind this placid surface. Jewish and Christian scholars are in equal trouble when it comes to making sense of this idea to contemporary people — including ordinary Jews and Christians. The absence of debate and conflict may be a sign of wishing to let sleeping dogs lie. The idea of revelation is in fact something of an embarrassment to the liberal end of both Jewish and Christian religions.

Such an attitude is not shared by the conservative wing of both groups. They are not at all embarrassed to assert the existence of a "Jewish revelation" or a "Christian revelation." They have a very clear idea of what this body of material is. God once and for all has said exactly what should be known. The fact that the modern world disagrees is not troubling. Indeed, conservatives among Christians and Jews often seem to relish conflict with the modern world because it proves how much the present scene needs their ministrations. But liberals within these religions need a well-thought-out strategy. The Christian or the Jew who has been educated according to the criteria of modern historiography, critical inquiry, and methods of science cannot cavalierly announce that the modern world is simply wrong.

The result of this liberal perplexity is silence, a willingness to talk about almost anything except this foundational idea of revelation. When I was a graduate student writing a master's thesis on Protestant-Catholic differences on this issue, I was amazed at the seeming absence of discussion of revelation. Over the last thirty years I have discovered much more writing on the topic. Nonetheless, the amount of writing on the meaning of revelation is nowhere near what the importance of the topic would seem to deserve. If anything, the silence has deepened over the last few decades.

In the Roman Catholic church, there was a flurry of interest in the 1960s, mainly inspired by the Second Vatican Council. A document on "divine revelation" was the first item addressed in 1962 but the last issue resolved in 1965. The final version of this document was immeasurably better than the first, the task having been transferred from dogmatic theologians to biblical exegetes. A sense of historical vitality was achieved by this latter group of scholars. The drawback was that this group was not at all inclined to raise the issue of revelation itself. Thus the document on divine revelation is really about the biblical meaning of revelation or the biblical form of revelation.[2]

My comment is not meant to be especially negative about the results of Vatican II. I would not expect a church council to be the original source of speculation on the meaning of revelation. I would hope, however, that the church council might embody an understanding of that meaning. Vatican II, in its existence and form, represented progress over most previous councils; one can hope for much more from Vatican III.[3]

Concerning what was published by Vatican II, the "Constitution on the Church in the Modern World" or the "Declaration on the Jews" may be of greater importance for clarifying revelation than the "Dogmatic Constitution on Divine Revelation." At the least, it can be said that the leadership of the Roman Catholic church struggled with the fundamental concept of revelation. It is not clear that this attitude of open exploration has been encouraged in the intervening years since the council. In particular, attempts to tamper with the term revelation by educators have met with stern opposition.[4]

There has not been a single focus in Protestant Christianity comparable to the Roman Catholic discussion of revelation. Given the whole history of the Protestant intention to recover the "Word of God," the Protestant idea of revelation is closer to the Catholic biblical exegete's than to most philosophical or theological speculation. Thus, in the twentieth century, revelation became almost a code word for Protestant neo-orthodoxy. I was continually taken aback when, on telling Protestant Christians that I was writing on revelation, they usually assumed I was a Barthian. My response that I had no interest in using Barth as my way to speak about revelation would either confuse or end the conversation.

A Protestant exception to that rule was Gordon Kaufman. While noting the excitement generated by Karl Barth's revolution, Kaufman also poked a little fun at its narrowness: "For a period of thirty to forty years it was possible and appropriate to engage in large scale and exciting theological reconstruction which had ultimate roots in 'revelation alone' (the somewhat honorific way of referring to the Protestant Christian tradition)."[5] This Protestant revolution based on "revelation alone" has passed into counterrevolutions and counter-counterrevolutions, but it is not apparent what, if anything, has happened with the term revelation. Except for the extreme right wing, no one wishes to imply that revelation is an honorific title for Protestant Christianity. But how does one face up to the intelligibility of the term? By simply letting in other Christians? Jews? Muslims?

Jewish thinkers, like their Christian counterparts, have not speculated much about the term revelation. However, there have been individual thinkers who have focused on the idea and the word. Martin Buber and Franz Rosenzweig are two of the most prominent examples in this century. For Jews, the real instigator of new reflection on the topic is the Holocaust.

But, as today's generation of Jewish thinkers would admit, they are still trying to absorb the impact of the Holocaust; the rethinking of theoretical foundations has just begun.[6]

Jewish thinkers on the liberal side have not been unaware of a problem here with the claim to revelation. For Jews, the problem's standing is not one of a few decades but of several centuries. What I have referred to as the liberal embarrassment hit Jewish thinkers who were trying to cope with modernity at a time when Christian thinkers did not see much of a problem. As early as the seventeenth and eighteenth centuries, Jewish philosophers sensed that "the very possibility of a unique revelation to a unique Moses at a unique Sinai seems to have vanished with the advent of modernity."[7] By the time of the formation of Reform Judaism's platform in 1885, the idea of revelation was almost totally absorbed into post-Kantian rationalism.[8]

The Christian thinkers of the seventeenth and eighteenth centuries did not experience the same kind of problem. It is true that by the eighteenth century the "Christian revelation" was being given a much more modest position than it had earlier occupied. John Locke, for example, wrote approvingly of revelation as something to be accepted—except when it conflicted with reason.[9] Thus the "Christian revelation" was at best a partner with modern reason, more often reason's ward; but at least its existence seemed secure.

To this day in Christian theology there are casual references to the "Christian revelation." There would be ready admission of disagreements over what exactly is within the category, but almost no acknowledgment that the term is problematic, perhaps unintelligible. Christian theologians seem to assume that if there is some problem here, it belongs to philosophy. Christian philosophers (that is, philosophers who are Christians) seldom want any part of the discussion. As far as they are concerned, revelation is the business of theology. Both philosophers and theologians seem to suppose that one can accept the Christian revelation and get into the game. Or else, lacking the Christian faith that enables one to believe in a Christian revelation, then there is little more to be said on the subject.

An unwillingness to defend "Christian revelation" or "Jewish revelation" may be understandable. But silence on the matter of revelation, or a take-it-on-faith attitude, threatens to encapsulate Jewish and Christian religions within conservative bastions. The irony is that the word revelation is abundantly alive in the contemporary world. The idea and the term are quite common in both secular and religious discourse. One can hardly read the daily newspaper without confronting the term, whether in political disclosures, art reviews, sports pages, or the latest scientific advance. In religious discussions, the term revelation and ideas associated with it (ecstasy, spiritual insight, liminal experience, mysticism, peak moments, and many others) are as common, perhaps more common, than ever.

Christian and Jewish scholars may view all this talk about revelation as either vacuous ("In the latest revelation of scandal from the White House today . . . ") or crazy ("The drug induced a revelation of the oneness of being"). Much of it probably is. I am not suggesting that Christianity or Judaism should capitulate to the latest fad of the New Age. But surely something is going on here which should give pause to a strategy of withdrawing the idea of revelation from public discourse.

Christians once thought that they had a large box filled with truths that were not available elsewhere. The size of the claim was gradually diminished, but the idea of the claim has not been thoroughly reexamined. It needs rethinking, not only in the context of seminary classrooms, but in the largest possible context. Of course, the adequate context is not immediately available. One has to find some immediate allies for the journey and also create some distinctions of language that will not prematurely close off the search. Within the Christian church, the immediate allies for Christian scholars are ordinary Christian people, both the simple, pious believers and the perplexed or alienated members.

If the term revelation is to have any meaning in theology, the meaning must arise from and continue to be connected to the most real and intense experiences of people's lives. Many people find their most intense religious experience in sexual encounter. How does one use the term revelation to acknowledge, support, and clarify this reality? For some Christians, the presence of God may be most deeply felt in reading the New Testament. However, many Christians would find God revealed, as did the great mystic writer von Hügel, in "the particular tone of my brother's voice, the leaping of my dog in the grass, the scent of apricot on the one brick, sun-dried wall, the iridescence of this opal, the sound of the grinding pebbles on yonder seashore."[10]

The challenge that faces both Christian and Jewish thinkers is not to trade the ancient body of past wisdom for a vague and romantic experience of today. The challenge is to think about the claim to revelation so that a richer meaning of the term can eventually emerge or reemerge. The challenge is not entirely new; Christian and Jewish religions have had to face this issue from earliest times. The challenge is of greater urgency today because of a context of religious pluralism and a tendency to evade the issue. For the first time in history, Jews and Christians have to work out the answer, if not in complete cooperation, at least with awareness of each other.

I will state the thesis of this chapter in briefest form, and then I will take up in more detail Meanings A and B of uniqueness as they apply to revelation. Both Christians and Jews have laid claim throughout their histories to a unique revelation. It is unavoidable that they should do so; a nonunique revelation would be unacceptable as the basis of a religious life. However, both religions have entangled the two meanings of uniqueness so that Jews and Christians have been forced into defending a meaning of uniqueness that in modern times has become more and more indefensible.

According to the logic of uniqueness that I have spelled out, the claim to a unique revelation has to go in one of two strongly contrasting directions.

MEANING A

In the first case, revelation is a claim to the exclusive possession of truths. Groups other than one's own are viewed as a threat. After all, any truth they possess is one less that my group can call its own. Not accidentally, the closer the religious group (in history, geography, structure), the more likely is conflict. Christians have found it easier to tolerate Buddhists than Jews or Muslims. The closest neighbor can easily become the ultimate enemy. In this meaning of uniqueness, the Christian revelation belongs to Christians. It can be applied to other groups, as in a Christian theology of Judaism, but no one else shares in it.

MEANING B

In the opposite direction, what structures the religion is people's participation in revelatory experience. There are elements that have an exclusive or possessive character, but they are not what is primary. Other people's experience is not viewed as a threat, although realistically there can be some feeling of competitiveness. One can learn something from other people, even though their particular articulations of truth may seem foreign and sometimes bizarre. For a Christian, two of the main sources of truth would be Judaism and Islam, or more exactly, Jews and Muslims. Revelation would not be a thing to apply to people; it would not be a thing at all, but a complex relation. One discovers the meaning of this revelation in the most important experiences of life and from conversations with other people.

REVELATION IN MEANING A

I will now spell out in more detail the first direction that can be taken in the claim to a unique revelation. In Meaning A of uniqueness, a thing is unique (more nearly unique) to the extent that it excludes common notes with other things. Nothing is simply and completely unique in this sense, because it would be literally incomparable; it would be outside human history and human experience. When we say of a historical event or a human construction that it is unique, we usually mean that it is something very unusual, strikingly different, beyond our expectations.

Art is one of the areas, along with religion, where this use of the word *unique* comes easily to the lips. We are not likely to use the language of art and aesthetics where things are mass produced and lack any distinctiveness of style. We value aesthetic productions that seem to be one of a kind, although it should be noted that being one of a kind does not guarantee that it is good art. Other criteria (and perhaps another meaning of uniqueness) come into play for that judgment.

What the modern world calls a religion is experienced by its devotees as *the way,* the only one of its kind. People would not devote themselves — body and soul, life and death, this world and the world to come — to a mere one among many ways. There is *the* way, so that everything else is seemingly a mistake, or at least less than the way. Even polytheistic or nontheistic religions do not view their teachings as "options" comparable to the choice one makes among brands of soap powder.

Religions, insofar as they affirm one way as the way, give the impression of being highly intolerant. This is the case if one infers that the affirmation of *this* way is the negation of *that* way. Actually, most religions make little if any acknowledgment of competing religious ways. Throughout most of history, the opposite of "our religion" was not "their religion" but the unholy, the profane, a life without devotion.

There is a second, and more important, qualification to the seeming intolerance of a religious group. Most religions have some awareness of their own incompleteness, even if one has to look carefully to find that admission. What is prominent in the Christian religion is Christ–church–sacrament as the way. But what is obscurely admitted is that a merciful God could not damn people who through no fault of their own did not find Christ–church–sacrament. In Jewish tradition, the commandments given to Noah occupy a tiny part of the sacred text, but they are the basis for Gentile entrance into the world to come.

Even granting this twofold qualification of the claim to be *the way,* it still must be admitted that religions have been and continue to be sources of arrogance and conflict. This weakness of religion is closely tied to its strength; it causes intolerance because it so completely involves its devotees. This deficiency of religion cannot easily be corrected. Every religion in the world is still on the threshold of trying to retain its strength while finding a way to live peacefully in a religiously plural world.

Some religions have a worse problem than others. Christianity is more aggressive and proselytizing than is Judaism; Islam is more militant than Buddhism. Hinduism is often said to be the most tolerant religion, and perhaps it is. But by claiming a superiority for their religion precisely because of its tolerance, Hindus can end up intolerant of what other groups think are important differences from Hinduism. Much of liberal Christianity seems to be going in a direction similar to this Hindu tolerance, that is, avoiding conflict with the other by claiming to include the other. That can be quite insulting to whoever the "other" is in any discussion. The problem remains for all religions: No serious devotee of any religious tradition will be heard to say that "one religion is as good as another."

At the base or in the background of each religious group lies a claim that *this way* is *the way.* But how does one know that? Where and how did it come about that this way is available, or more exactly, is demanded? In

Judaism, Christianity, and Islam, revelation is the key term for this fundamental idea. Behind every Christian doctrine and every Jewish practice, with every statement in the sacred writings, is the assumption of a divine revelation.

At some time in his or her life, a member of a religious group is likely to ask: Why should I perform this ritual or hold to this belief? The answer to that question from within the religious tradition is: Because God said so. At some point of origin, God told someone what is so and what is not so, what is to be done and what is not to be done. The metaphor of speech has held a special place in both Christian and Jewish histories, indicating the interpersonal character of revelation.

This claim of a unique revelation seems straightforward in its assertions. There have been moments when God spoke to our fathers. That claim suggests that there were moments when God did not speak, or that there were other fathers to whom God did not speak. Moses at the burning bush or at the top of Sinai, Jesus at his baptism or at the top of Golgotha, were not ordinary moments. For later generations of Jews and Christians, certain events are recalled as revelatory; at that moment the heavens opened and a special, surprising, unsurpassed insight was gained. The moments are remembered largely, although not exclusively, with the help of written texts.

In this meaning of uniqueness, revelation comes to be equated with knowledge, with texts, with interpretations of texts, and with memories handed down orally. Revelation becomes special information about the secrets of the universe. The typical image for describing the act of revealing is *intervention*. That is, the usual course of events was interrupted by the intrusion of "God's Word." Somebody, who could not have known otherwise, becomes privy to God's view of things.

After a sufficient number of interruptions on God's part, the knowledge was available for a fairly complete system. Jewish and Christian commentators of the Middle Ages did not claim that their writings were revelations from God. What they did claim was a certainty for their conclusions to the extent that these conclusions were based on "revealed truth." The first principles of theology in Christianity were said to be divinely revealed truths.

Modern theologians, uneasy with "verbal revelation" or "propositional revelation," have tried to soften the claim. Perhaps God only sent ideas, or perhaps revelation is an "event." But both of these modifications remain part of the same pattern of meaning. God is still imagined as intervening to supply information not available elsewhere, though perhaps the information is more vague than once thought. And the theology that speaks of revelation as event does not mean to say that "revelation is an event." It means only that "revelation was an event." In the present, revelation is a body of information that one group claims to possess.

In this meaning of revelation, every other group becomes a threat to the group's existence. If one's most fundamental belief is that this body of material is without comparison, has no similarity to anything else in history, then any suggestion of similarity or borrowing is perceived as an attack. For some years after the Dead Sea Scrolls were discovered, much of the Christian world held its breath. What would be found to be similar between Jesus and the Teacher of Righteousness? Might the origin of some doctrines and liturgical practices be revealed to have non-Christian sources? Even until 1991, controversies in the world of scholarship kept some of these texts secret, so that Christian and Jewish religions still could not come to terms with the challenge of these documents.

The Dead Sea Scrolls are only one of the most famous incidents in this regard. There are Christians who, from the beginning of Christianity, have fought off all comparisons. In recent centuries, the problem has become more acute. Was the Fatherhood of God a new idea with Jesus? Does the belief in resurrection precede Christianity by millennia? Is the Golden Rule found in almost every religion? In back of all such questions is often a fearful question: Is the uniqueness of the "Christian revelation" eroding?

In trying to defend a unique revelation that is a shrinking body of material, Jewish and Christian scholars introduced a distinction within the term revelation. As it was beginning to become apparent in the seventeenth and eighteenth centuries that some of this exclusively unique material was not so unique, part of the holdings were traded to the category of "natural" or "general" revelation. The distinction was not entirely new; medieval Christian theology had "natural revelation," although not as a separate body of materials.

There were many variations on this separation of revelation into two categories. Protestant Christians usually referred to general and special; Catholics almost never used that language, referring instead to natural and supernatural. What Catholics, Protestants, and Jews agreed upon was the duality: There was, besides a Christian or Jewish revelation, this other revelation. For some Christians and Jews this other revelation became the more important, while the revelation exclusive to their own group seemed only an optional accessory.[11] The liberal forms of Christianity and Judaism in the nineteenth century thus followed Hegel's contention that "revealed religion" is good—but as the last step before (the natural revelation of) pure reason.[12]

This bifurcation of revelation was not a step toward toleration of other religions. If anything, this language is one of the great barriers to a language of religious pluralism. For scholars outside Christianity and Judaism, the split was an attempt to neutralize or reduce the claims of the religious traditions. For Christians and Jews, the separation of the "other revelation" from "our revelation" was an attempt to shore up the exclusivistic meaning of uniqueness.

Revelation thus came to have a twofold meaning: knowledge of God available to all reasonable people, and knowledge of God "based on the reports of reliable witnesses about unique historical events."[13] Within such a framework, other religions become a generalized otherness rather than being particular groups from whom one might learn particularities. Christians did study Judaism (that is, the "Old Testament") as a source of divine revelation. But in Christian theology the Jew has been at best "the natural man." And at worst, the Jew, having had the opportunity to receive the unique truth of Christ, is someone less than the pagan who had only natural or general revelation.

With this separation of revelation into two objects, a choice of direction followed. Either the Christian (Jewish) revelation is an unnecessary addition to what is really important, or else the Christian (Jewish) revelation is the really important part, a set of truths to be aggressively held to and advocated as the path of redemption. Christians and Jews who did not wish to liberalize away their religions seemed to have no choice but to go with the second. The attitude that has been called "fundamentalist" in the twentieth century was a logical consequence.

REVELATION IN MEANING B

I have acknowledged that the claim to possess a unique revelation has been a continuing characteristic of both Jewish and Christian religions. No one can go back to the beginning and change this tendency, nor can the tendency simply be excised in the present. But I would claim that Meaning B of uniqueness has also been there from the start, at least implicitly. I also wish to claim that this strand has always been the more genuine one. However, the first thing needed is to explain the uniqueness of revelation in Meaning B. It can then be seen as inherent to Jewish and Christian traditions, and a stimulus to a conversation between these traditions.

Something is called unique in Meaning B if it moves in the direction of increasing inclusiveness. The word "something" can be misleading here. Although "things" are not without a degree of inclusiveness, this meaning of uniqueness comes into clarity in the world of living beings, people, and communities. A person is more unique — more nearly unique — than a stone. Both the stone and the person have an existence that is relational, open to the influence of other beings. But the human being is the most open being we know of, receptive to the influence of the entire cosmos.

Some nouns are more compatible than others when trying to express Meaning B of uniqueness: unique experience more than unique event, unique community rather than unique doctrine, unique person instead of unique institution. But each of these nouns has its own range of ambiguity. I am not saying that terms such as event, doctrine, or institution should never be used in the context of Meaning B of uniqueness. No single word is decisive. We have to attend to the pattern of usage to find which meaning of uniqueness is at issue. The question of uniqueness A or B is the question of the *direction* in which we are moving.

A unique revelation in Meaning B cannot be equated with unique information or unique doctrine; the direction of these words is usually away from Meaning B. Christianity has undoubtedly formulated doctrines that are not found in the same form in other religions. But the Trinity is not the name of a revelation from God; the doctrine was formulated out of several centuries of church speculation and debate. The church believes that its knowledge of this doctrine is closely related to revelation, but revelation is not the intervention of God to impart such truths.

In his great literary study of the Bible, Northrop Frye several times brings up the term revelation. He writes: "In looking at it (the Bible) as metaphor or metaphor complex, we come up against the word 'revelation,' a word that does imply knowledge of a sort, even though it may not be knowledge of history or nature."[14] Frye does not try to explain here a knowledge that is neither of history nor of nature. In another place, he says that revelation is "a word I use because it is traditional and I can think of no better one."[15] He then immediately denies that it is "the conveying of information from an objective divine source to a subjective human receptor." I agree with Frye's negations and cautions, but is there anything positive that can be said?

Martin Buber, in discussing the foundation of religion, makes much the same denial as Frye, that is, a denial that revelation is "a noetic relation of a thinking subject to a neutral object of thought." Buber then offers by way of contrast: "mutual contact, the genuinely reciprocal meeting in the fullness of life between one active existence and another."[16] Revelation is a word that is not separated from knowledge, but it is a word that challenges our widespread assumptions about knowledge; for example, assumptions that knowledge consists in "taking a look," that knowledge is the amassing of data in a computerlike brain, that knowledge is directed toward getting control of the external world. Revelation in Meaning B of uniqueness means a standing open to all knowledge and to silences beyond knowledge.

Whatever noun one associates with unique in describing revelation, there is always a danger of reductionism. I have said that unique information, unique event, unique knowledge are deficient. Even the description that Buber provides may throw too much weight on individual existence. Revelation always involves what is personal but the relational character of personal existence should place community, not an isolated person, at the forefront of a discussion of revelation. Meaning B of unique revelation is a process that is from and for a community of persons. It is people (or a people) who have a way of life; the personal response inherent to revelation takes place within a people. Thus, if one has to locate a bearer for the word revelation, then community rather than the individual is the more appropriate candidate.

I would also say that *experience* is the best available noun in United States English to follow the words revelational or revelatory. Although experience is sometimes used in a narrower sense, it can be a relational term, an active and passive term, a term that connotes knowing and other than knowing. Revelation can be a knowing experience; it can also be a loving experience, a feeling experience, a suffering experience, and many other kinds of experience.

A term that Franz Rosenzweig used for revelation is helpful as summary: orientation.[17] A community that participates in the experience of revelation has its life oriented. Revelation situates a people in a place and gives it a sense of direction. Place is temporal as well as geographical. The community that experiences revelation as its present place has creation in its past and redemption in its future. For Rosenzweig, creation is expressed in the third person and the indicative mode ("God created the fishes"). In contrast, revelation is expressed in the second person and in the imperative mode ("Do not have strange gods before me").[18]

Paul Ricoeur's analysis of the biblical modes of revelation is different in emphasis, but the result has some similarity with Rosenzweig's. For Ricoeur, first-person prophecy establishes the meaning of revelation. But after that, third-person narrative and second-person hymnic discourse can be seen to have revelatory power. Whether one emphasizes the "I am the Lord thy God" or the "thou shalt not have strange gods before me," revelation is the present encounter which alters the past and provides the possibility of a future. All reality and all modes of discourse become potentially revelatory.[19]

Note that for Rosenzweig, creation, revelation, and redemption are not three events in three time zones. Revelation is inclusive of creation; and when revelation is fully inclusive, it will be called redemption. Martin Buber, agreeing with Rosenzweig, says that one can distinguish creation, revelation, and redemption, but that one should not separate them. Buber criticizes Christianity for separating the three, and there are good grounds for the accusation.[20] But Jewish speech, too, often gives a narrow meaning to creation and speaks of redemption as exclusively in the future. The latter tendency is perhaps a reaction to Christian doctrine that speaks of a redeemed world. Nonetheless, redemption as "pure prospect" can distort Jewish tradition. I return to this question in chapter 5 after examining Christian claims about the Christ.

In the logic of Meaning B of uniqueness, the present is not a moving point. The present is presence and openness. The past is found by going down (not back) to rediscover interpretive helps for today. Modern culture tends to view time as a long series of points, with the past stretching back out of sight. The past can only be saved by herculean efforts to gather bits of printed and mechanical material. The effort is admirable, even if our libraries are overflowing and no one can assimilate more than a small portion of what is being stored.

Christian, Jewish, and Muslim religions have been religions of memory more than of history. The past is present in the form of ritual and recital. Anyone's memory is, of course, highly selective. The memory of some moment in one person's life may become an interpretive symbol for a wide stretch of history; the same is true at a communal level, where one experience can be interpretive for untold numbers of people. It is not a question of how far *back* such experiences are; the memory situates them toward the *center* of the community's life. Each year, each week, each day the story can be retold. "This is what we have seen and heard and touched" (or the Muslim variation, "what we have heard, what we have rehearsed, what we have recited").

The orientational terms for Meaning B of uniqueness thus include community, experience, and present. These terms can be bearers of revelation, irrespective of the number of individuals involved. Could ten thousand people carry an interpretation significant to all humanity? Could a thousand people? Ten? If revelation is an orientation by presence, then there is no contradiction in finding a higher degree of uniqueness among this thousand than that million. But if this thousand or this ten are truly a community, they will not talk about "possessing" revelation.[21] The community will understand that it is oriented outward, beyond its boundaries of this space and this time, called to serve some greater cosmic realization than it can imagine. The revelational question is not solely epistemological. The community asks: If we live like this, does revelation occur?

Within such a meaning of revelation, uniqueness becomes greater as persons participate in the experience. They find themselves called to respond to the unveiling of truth in every experience. The meaning of *divine* arises out of the increasing inclusiveness of personal and communal experience.[22] There is not a being called god who interrupts things to convey special information. If the word *God* is used, it is as the last word before silence, a word that is seldom pronounced. An encounter with the One who goes beyond all names arises out of the encounter with All/Nothing.

When one tries to articulate this experience in prosaic terms, the statements are likely to sound vague and murky. A great temptation is to step above the historical religions and lay hold of a grand, all-encompassing oneness. Jewish and Christian traditions rightly insist that love of all should be held in tension with love of *this* friend and *that* stranger. Revelation is not the moments, the rituals, the texts; but revelation needs concrete embodiment in moments, rituals, and texts.

The Jewish people do not *have* a revelation, but revelation has need of a people, ultimately all people. There is no Jewish (Christian) revelation, but there are Jewish (Christian) symbols, expressions, forms, embodiments of revelation. There is a big difference between saying that the Jewish God is unique and saying that Jews believe in a unique God. It is not at all the same to say that Christians have a unique "Christian revelation" and to say that the Christian church participates in the one unique revelation.

In Meaning B of uniqueness, revelation is not the first building block of an abstract system of ideas. Revelation is an immediate practical experience. "When was the Torah given?" asks the Midrash. "It is given whenever a person receives it."[23] Of the experience of Jewish mystics, Gershom Scholem writes that "instead of the one act of Revelation, there is a constant repetition of the act."[24] The same can be said of Christian mystics, that is, revelation is a daily act, the experience of the presence of God.

The great mystics of both religions do not disparage the sacred text or try to substitute for the tradition a vague feeling of cosmic oneness. The text is the necessary interpretive element, but the revelation is the present experience. Mystics are often assumed to be alienated from their traditions. But as Scholem and others insist, the genuine mystic is simply deeper into the center of the tradition.[25] Those people who think that the task is to preserve "revealed truths" of the past are the ones who are on the periphery of the tradition.

A religious body that approaches revelation this way has nothing to fear from competing traditions. It can take a definite stand out of its own history on the great questions of the day. Without abandoning either the Jewish embodiment of revelation or the Christian embodiment of revelation, Jews and Christians can learn more about revelation by listening to each other. A clearer voice would come through, singly and together, to condemn outrageous policies that are destructive of creation–revelation–redemption. We are not always sure what the next best step is, but it should be possible to say that some steps violate all the ways to the redeeming, reconciling, and reuniting of the world.

As an example of such a stand, consider the United States bishops' pastoral letter on peace.[26] At the beginning of the document, the bishops write: "Peace and war must always be seen in the light of God's intervention in human affairs and our response to that intervention. Both are elements within the ongoing revelation of God's will for creation." They daringly put human response within the meaning of divine revelation, even though much of their language trails behind this intention. The statement would be stronger without the word intervention; likewise, the term ongoing does not really capture a revelation that is always present.

Despite the limitations, the bishops' document represents an admirable attentiveness to an issue of world-shaking importance in the light of one group's particular tradition. The conclusion that the whole tradition converges on a position that condemns the nuclear arms race was a strong challenge to the United States government. The fact that the White House rejected the document out of hand does not mean that it has had no subsequent effect on government policies. The point is not that the Roman Catholic bishops should be telling the United States government how to act. The document is rather an invitation to other groups to take similar stands from their particular traditions.

What the Catholic bishops need for completing their task of speaking to war, technology, ecology, economics, and other contemporary issues is a clearer use of the term revelation. They are not alone in that need. Christians generally, and Jews as well, have to locate the word revelation where it belongs, namely, in the present experience of the human race.

Based on the logic of their own religions, Christians and Jews should not speak of revealed truths from the past, of a Christian revelation or Jewish revelation, of a revelation that has ended. What did end was the development of those foundational documents that will never be replaced. These writings provide the specifically Christian or Jewish interpretation of a never-ending process of revelation. For a Christian or a Jew, the fundamental direction has been set; it will not be reversed. But that orientation in space and time has to be filled out in ways that are still daily surprising.

CONCLUSION

This description of Meaning B of uniqueness in relation to revelation indicates a clear direction in which to move. Christians and Jews have to break the knot that has bound each of them since the beginning of western enlightenment. At that time, the founders of modernity succeeded in shifting the foundational metaphor for human knowing from revelation to enlightenment. However, as often happens in such historical upheavals, the nature of the shift was hidden for a time. The word revelation was retained, but its meaning was now to be established by empirical and mathematical science.

Carl Becker, in his summary of eighteenth-century western thought, writes: "Renunciation of the *traditional revelation* was the very condition of being truly enlightened . . . To be enlightened was to understand this double truth, that it was not in Holy Writ, but in the great book of nature, open for all mankind to read, that the laws of God had been recorded."[27] That is, a traditional revelation (the Holy Writ) was replaced by the new revelation of science (natural revelation). After a century or so of this language, the "laws of God" were no longer the framework of discussion and the term revelation could be quietly put aside.

Both Christian and Jewish thinkers fought a largely unsuccessful rearguard action against the advance of the enlightenment. The defense split into two factions, called conservative and liberal, terms that already reflect the domination of enlightenment. What was called conservatism sometimes accepted and sometimes rejected the new knowledge, but in either case it insisted on the need for the revelation in Holy Writ. The spokesmen for modernity, after some early squabbles, found this position easily tolerable. Whoever wishes to read the Bible in private should be allowed to do so.

What was called liberal Judaism and liberal Christianity engaged modern thinking at the more serious level of structure and method. Traditional revelation had to confront the new revelation. Revelation was said to continue and to develop after the Bible; it was "a continuous river of light and life, flowing through the ages with a constantly increasing fulness of development."[28] The intention of these Jewish and Christian thinkers was admirable; but from today's vantage point it is evident that the idea of revelation was absorbed into the progressivist myth of the enlightenment.

Given what seemed to them the choices, the best that a liberal nineteenth-century Christian thinker could say was that "revelation is not a lightning flash; it is rather like the dawn, brightening into the full day."[29] Today, however, what is under challenge is the image of enlightenment itself. If one does not assume the governing image to be enlightenment, then the choice is not between "lightning" and "brightening dawn." Enlightenment should not be rejected; it is usually preferable to endarkenment. But it is of doubtful adequacy for the comprehension of all relations: human–nonhuman, person–community, life–death.

With the image of enlightenment go the well-worn ruts of conservative versus liberal. A religious appreciation of past wisdom does not belong to a group of reactionaries in flight from today. Nor does the present and future belong to a religious group trying to outdo modern science at its own game. The time is ripe for rethinking our image of time and our myth of progress. That also means the time is ripe for reimagining, reconceptualizing, and restating the relation of Christian and Jewish religions to contemporary life. Paradoxically, it is the *restating* that comes first, with one clear, decisive choice in the use of the word revelation. We need a use of the word that conserves more than conservatism does and at the same time is more liberating than liberalism. Revelation is the present, personal, and more than personal experience of all peoples.

Christian and Jewish thinkers can never begin to explore such a meaning of revelation as long as they keep using phrases that undermine such a meaning. They have to let go of a few phrases that have become customary ways of speaking. Some of these phrases are only a century or two old, but others may go back to the time of the emergence of Christianity or rabbinic Judaism. But we are not faithful to the past by simply repeating all its phrases. One can save the term revelation in Judaism and Christianity only by letting go of it and letting it reemerge in today's experience and conversation.

The fundamental challenge, therefore, is not to restate the "Christian revelation" or "Jewish revelation"; the task is to discuss the only revelation there is, the one in which Jews and Christians participate. Jews and Christians, perceiving themselves as sharing in revelation, would be led to a necessary and detailed conversation about the meaning of revelation. Far from ending there, the conversation would open itself to Muslims and any other groups for whom the term revelation is sufficiently intelligible.

As revelation has no historical endpoint, so also it is not geographically closed to any religious groups. Conversations that include eastern religions would probably need other terms as important as revelation is to Christians, Jews, and Muslims. Such terms would include the word enlightenment with different connotations from those of eighteenth-century Europe. Perhaps the word revelation cannot carry much weight in the East, but I do not think that a firm conclusion can be drawn until we have tried the linguistic change that has been outlined here.

4

Unique People of the Covenant

In the previous chapter, the term *revelation* was shown to move in one of two directions. It is either a narrowing and divisive term or an invitational term without a fixed boundary of space and time. In the latter case, the unique revelation participated in by both Jews and Christians is a way of describing the present experience of the human community.

The category of revelation is a chief example of a simple rule of language: Terms that a religious group believes to be ultimate categories can only properly be used in the singular. If Jews and Christians were to observe this rule, they would be challenged to think more deeply about their relation. Although the initial effect might be to make conversation more difficult, Jews and Christians would eventually be better able to talk to the rest of the religious world.

Following Rosenzweig and Buber, I closely linked revelation to creation and redemption. Creation is the beginning of the process of revelation; redemption is the culmination. All three terms are meant to express the ultimate relation between the divine and the universe. Creation is unique; revelation is more unique; redemption is (or will be) most unique. The logic of both Judaism and Christianity dictates that there is one creation, one revelation, one redemption.

This chapter is mainly on the idea of covenant. No idea is more central to the biblical tradition of Judaism and Christianity. As there is a unique revelation of divine initiative and human response, so there is a unique covenant that links the divine and human in historical experience. The uniqueness of the covenant can be developed under Meaning A, Christians and Jews each claiming to be sole possessors of the covenant with God. Or the uniqueness of Meaning B implies a covenant that finds partial embodiment in Jewish and Christian histories, but is open to further expression beyond Christianity and Judaism.

Because Christians and Jews draw upon the same biblical text, there has always been a conflict over the meaning of the Bible's terms. Jews and Christians confront one another for control of key terms of the language:

creation, faith, revelation, grace, covenant, divine law, messiah, redemption, kingdom. In this era of religious tolerance, there is a tendency to blur the conflict and work out a compromise. Many of these terms are now divided between the competitors. There exists a standard language of Christian revelation and Jewish revelation, Christian faith and Jewish faith, Christian covenant and Jewish covenant.

This strategy of dividing the territory breaks down when it is extended to creation, grace, redemption, or kingdom. The phrase Christian faith makes no more sense than Christian grace, but we have become accustomed to talk of the Christian faith. We also refer to Christian revelation or Christian covenant as if there were such things under the control of the church. The scriptural foundations of Christian and Jewish religions do not allow that there can be two faiths, three revelations, or four redemptions. Because there is one God, there is one revelation of that God, one faith in God, one redemption by God.

The policy of dividing the territory does allow Christians and Jews to live next to each other with a minimum of acrimony. It does little to encourage conversation and mutual understanding. It also fails to persuade the rest of the world that Jews and Christians have relinquished their seeming arrogance. Christianity is the more suspect because Christians have often followed imperialistic language with forceful institutional moves. But regarding claims to know the mind of God and what God decrees for everyone, Jews have essentially the same problem as Christians. To outsiders, Christians and Jews look very much alike in the claims they make.

The complaint is perhaps surprising in light of the fact that Jews and Christians have seemingly abandoned their claims to uniqueness. That is, if one acknowledges a Jewish revelation in addition to a Christian revelation, then Christianity thereby abandons the claim to a unique revelation. The same applies to Judaism. Does this not indicate less arrogance? It might, except that the move toward uniqueness now takes place within the newly minted categories of Christian revelation and Jewish revelation. And whereas a unique revelation can have the openness and receptivity characteristic of Meaning B, a unique Christian (or Jewish) revelation necessarily moves along the narrowing path of Meaning A.

The thesis of this book is that Jews and Christians cannot avoid dealing in uniqueness. It can be the unique possession of what nobody else has, or it can be a unique people participating in a process which is not entirely under their control. This latter meaning of uniqueness is signaled by regularly using the most important religious terms in the singular without qualifying adjectives. The oneness of faith, revelation, grace, covenant, and the rest is complemented by a multiplicity of forms. These forms, Christian or Jewish expressions of revelation, are fallible, incomplete, and changing.

Whatever we say of the revelation of God or faith in God is a feeble attempt to articulate something greater than we can think or say. This deficiency is not an individual failing, the result of laziness or sin. The whole tradition does not possess the truth. The whole tradition may embody the truth and may provide the very best way for its adherents, "But woe to the man so possessed as to think that he possesses God."[1]

Consider, as example, the term faith. The Bible (and Qur'an) make it quite clear that there is only one God and that one's response to God is either faithfulness or infidelity. From a Christian perspective, therefore, the Jews are either infidels or believers. Christians have generally stopped using the term infidel, but they have not completed the process by acknowledging Jews to be of the faith, the only faith there is. Jews have the same linguistic problem in acknowledging Christians to be of the same faith.

The language of "Christian faith" and "Jewish faith" simply freezes conversation at the level of polite exchange and political toleration. Worse, Christian life and Jewish life are reified by these terms. Christian (Jewish) faith is a something, a valuable something to be sure, but a something under the control of Christians (Jews). In contrast, the term faith, without qualification, is a daily challenge to live faithfully. The act of believing is directed toward God *within* the process of revelation. With that meaning of faith, church leaders would have to ask whether the church as a whole is responding in faith. And we would need intra-faith (not interfaith) discussion among everyone trying to live a faithful life.

The two meanings of uniqueness can illuminate the choice of how to use the word faith.

MEANING A

A "Christian faith" or "Jewish faith" seeks to be unique by having under its possession what is not available elsewhere. This control is not difficult to achieve if one reduces faith to *beliefs*. The relation of these two ideas is a complicated one; they ought not to be separated, but they are clearly distinguishable.[2] Faith is the richer, more comprehensive, more foundational term. Beliefs are entailed by faith, are expressive of faith, provide a needed form of faith. The affirmation of beliefs, therefore, is not only allowable but necessary. The Christians have usually had the more elaborate system of beliefs, but Jews clearly have their own beliefs.

The beliefs of a group move within Meaning A of uniqueness. The more that the group elaborates its beliefs, the more it can be said to possess its own unique beliefs. For example, Christianity has a doctrine of incarnation that it claims as uniquely its own. If Hindus claim to have the same doctrine, a few more Christian details will indicate that the doctrine is a (nearly) unique Christian belief. The same is true of its other doctrines, including Trinity. Whatever the competitors, the doctrine can always be further secured as uniquely the church's.

MEANING B

When there is only one faith, then the uniqueness of faith moves in the direction of openness toward all. Such faith is possible everywhere but is not immediately obvious anywhere. One has to listen for a voice that sounds through the confusing conflict of beliefs. A religious group, such as the church, offers criteria to judge between faith and infidelity. The whole body of Christian doctrine is an interlocking set of criteria, but the standard is not easy to apply. One criterion, for example, may be that peaceful harmony with others is a sign of faith. But some short-term conflicts that reveal false and premature harmony might be a necessary step to a truer and deeper union of all.

The journey of faith never ceases to be precarious and fallible, dependent on beliefs. One has to look for organic developments out of whatever particularity one starts from. A sudden leap beyond our particular limitations is almost certain to be illusory. The unique truth of Meaning B is a movement toward receptiveness without an impatient grasping after a final truth. We live the uniqueness of faith by patiently peeling off the layers of defense that block us from hearing the truth.

CHOSEN PEOPLE

The preceding comments on the unity of foundational categories, including faith, lead into the main concern of this chapter, namely that God selected one people and established a covenant with them. Jews may not have many beliefs, but this one rings clear: We are the chosen people. Some twentieth-century Jews have tried to mute this claim. Mordecai Kaplan and the Reconstructionist movement reformulated the belief with terms supposedly less offensive to modern ears.[3] But the claim cannot be quietly buried. Neither traditional Judaism nor modern anti-Semites will let the matter rest there.

The issue I wish to examine is the term *covenant*. However, before getting to that word, it is important to locate it with community or peoplehood. As pointed out in the previous chapter, the bearer of the word revelation is not first the individual but a community. The notion of covenant emerged from the experience of peoplehood, or more strongly, for the Jews, peoplehood is founded on covenant. The Jewish experience of itself as a people is the beginning of the articulation of covenant as a foundational term for all peoples.

Previous chapters have noted that Meaning B of uniqueness emerges with the distinctive characteristics of the human being: community, experience, presence. As the evolutionary process narrows into the straits of human being, a countermovement becomes apparent, namely, an increasing openness to what is other. Embodied in the peculiar word *unique* is this double movement toward particularity and universality at the same time. Humans are in principle open to all times and all space, but any particular group of humans has to be in this time (our present) and this space (our place).

The strand of human history that came to be called Hebrew and Jewish was not the first manifestation of peoplehood or community. However, this people self-consciously experienced itself as a people, and much of the rest of the world has been profoundly influenced by the Jewish demonstration. Even when scattered across the nations of the earth, the sense of Jewishness remained. Even for those Jews who would have preferred to leave the people, the connection endured. Far from disappearing in the twentieth century, the mark of Jewishness has continued. To belong to a people is to share in uniqueness; to be a Jew is to be very unique.

The emergence of a Jewish nation state has posed a problem from the start, namely, how to combine the qualities of unique peoplehood with the political, economic, and military realities of the modern nation state. Martin Buber published a book in 1934 entitled *Israel and the World*. The reference for the term *Israel* has changed in the intervening years, but his reminder of the warning of the prophets is still relevant. "It can persist — and this is the paradox in their warning and the paradox of Jewish history – if it insists *on its vocation of uniqueness*, if it translates into reality the divine words spoken during the making of the covenant."[4]

Buber's phrase "vocation of uniqueness" is almost identical in meaning to "chosen people." To have a vocation is to feel called to something; one does not so much choose a vocation as feel chosen. There is an element of choice insofar as one can refuse to be chosen; nonetheless, the experience is simply one of, This is what I must do. Referring to the sense of vocation, Erik Erikson writes of people who are "called by whom, only theologians claim to know and by what, only bad psychologists."[5]

In this case, the Jews were chosen to be a people. The adjective chosen is almost redundant; for them, the experience of peoplehood was the experience of chosenness. With or without the adjective, the Jewish assertion of its importance as a people is, on the face of it, an arrogant claim. But as with many religious claims, there is a countermovement which is in tension with the direction on the surface. This other stream often shows up in Jewish religion as ironic humor. The phrase "chosen people" is a kind of ironic joke that allows people to cope with their sufferings.

The designation of chosen people is not a claim to have achieved success nor a guarantee of superior benefits. On the contrary, it is the experience of a special burden of responsibility and a painful revelation of the human condition. The Midrash says that God offered the covenant to everyone else before offering it to the Jews; the others thought it was a bad deal, the Jews did not ask. In one variation of the story, the Jews, having arrived at Mount Sinai, "the Holy One, Blessed be He, suspended the mountain over their heads like a barrel and said to them: 'If you accept the Torah well and good; and if not, here will your graves be'."[6]

These two explanations of chosen people are in dialectical tension with regard to human freedom. What the two stories have in common is an ironic twist. The idea of being the chosen people is not movement above humanity but movement toward representation at the center. The uniqueness of chosen people means openness to all in a manifestation of the universal. At their self-critical best, Jews have seen their life as a service to the whole human race. They are a stand-in for the real chosen people, namely, the humans. After all, the really frail but presumptuous beings are the human beings who are chosen for the richest life and the most painful suffering.

The Jewish claim to be the chosen people or a unique people needs to be placed in its proper context rather than denied or hidden. A kind of low-key reasonableness about Jewish importance does not get at the logic of uniqueness nor the place of the Jews. At the beginning of David Hartman's *A Living Covenant*, the author states: "The discussion of Judaism is always internal to Jewish experience and in no way pretends to show how Judaism or the Jewish people are unique or superior to other faith communities. I argue strongly for the significance of Jewish particularity, not for its uniqueness." I have no doubt about Hartman's wish to be tolerant of other religious positions, and an author need not spell out in one book how different religious positions are allowed for. Nevertheless, the above passage does not suggest the basis of tolerance. I would argue that the way to avoid claiming superiority to other "faith communities" is to emphasize the uniqueness of the Jewish people. Far from particularity and uniqueness being opposites, as Hartman's last sentence implies, the Jews' particularity is their uniqueness.[7]

It is interesting to trace Reform Judaism's recent movement to recapture some of the logic of chosenness and uniqueness. As mentioned in the previous chapter, the Reform platform of 1885 went far in the direction of bringing Jewish claims into congruence with nineteenth-century rationalism. Neither the category of revelation nor that of chosen people conformed very well to the canons of post-Kantian European thought or United States empiricism. However, twentieth-century Reform Judaism, as reflected in its prayer book, reasserts some of the particularity of chosenness, peoplehood, and uniqueness. For example, at the beginning of the concluding prayers in *Gates of Prayer*, one finds: "We must praise the Lord of all, the Maker of heaven and earth, who has set us apart from the other families of earth, giving us a destiny unique among the nations."[8]

Some people might complain that this is a rather free translation of an ancient prayer that has no word corresponding to unique. A more literal translation would simply stress difference from the multitudes. However, the phrase "giving us a destiny unique among the nations" does capture the spirit and intent of the prayer. The English word *difference* does not capture the double difference of uniqueness. There are two differences in tension with each other: the difference that comes from the narrowing of choice ("from the other families") and the difference of being of service "among the nations." The call of chosenness is not to isolation but to eventual communion, not to saying that we are right and everyone else is wrong, but to saying that we are trying to live our vocation of uniqueness with the hope that uniqueness will be more truly universal.

God's choice of the Jews has always been clear in Jewish rhetoric. However, what that implies about the other peoples is usually left unsaid. Chosenness for the Jews does not necessarily mean non-chosenness for the Gentiles. Nor does chosenness mean that the chosen arrive first at the gates of heaven. There is a story told at the Seder service which says that when the Red Sea was swallowing the Egyptian soldiers who were in pursuit of the Israelites, the angels in heaven began to sing. "But God said: 'My children lie drowned in the sea and you would sing?' "[9] That is a shocking reversal of language, especially in the context; the Egyptian soldiers are called God's people. The story reminds us that to love A does not mean to hate B, even at moments when A and B are in bitter conflict.

There is also the prayer of the great Hasidic master Bal Shem Tov: "Master of the Universe, know that the children of Israel are suffering too much; they deserve redemption; they need it. But if, for some reason unknown to me, You are not willing, not yet, then redeem all the other nations, but do it soon."[10] Once again, we have a startling reminder of what chosen people means. Chosenness entails a willingness to wait until all the rest are saved. God's chosen people are people.

COVENANT

I come now to the particular term that Jews gave to the world in describing their chosenness: *covenant*. Like other religious terms that become metaphors for relations in the realm where language fails, covenant was a term of ordinary experience. Three millennia ago, there were numerous covenants between individual and individual, state and state, king and subjects, husband and wife. Over a period of several centuries, covenant became one of those ultimate terms for the divine-human relation. What is our relation to God? The Hebrew/Jewish answer was: Something like the agreement between king and subject, lord and serf, or husband and wife. It is already evident here that covenant is a term unified around interpersonal agreement, but with a great many possible variations in the form of the agreement. Jewish history is a working out of the details of the agreement.[11]

Insofar as covenant comes to play this part of expressing the divine-human relation, there could not be two, three, or four covenants. The Jews spoke of *the* covenant with God. Thus, when Christianity emerged out of Judaism, covenant was inevitably at the center of its claim to legitimacy. In the first century C.E., the *idea* of covenant linked Christians and Jews, while the *claim* to covenant divided them.

The situation remains much the same in the late twentieth century. Unless Christians and Jews can come to some agreement on how to use this term, other serious conversation is difficult, if not impossible. The possibilities for finding an opening are limited by the rule I have stated: one God, one faith, one revelation, one covenant. If Jews stand by that rule, can they recognize Christianity as having any validity? If Christians claim their covenant, can they do anything but be anti-Jewish?[12]

Before pursuing attempts to solve this problem, there is an interesting linguistic accident to note. Something of a mistranslation of the word *covenant* occurred when the Bible went from Hebrew to Greek. The Septuagint translators used the somewhat unusual word *diathēkē* for *berît*. The Greek *diathēkē* means disposition of property or last will and testament; this is rather different in connotation from the Hebrew *berît*, meaning an agreement between two parties. Jews are likely to think of this choice of word as the beginning of a distortion that was exacerbated by the Christian application of covenant to Jesus. The connotations of the word *testament* served Christian reflection on the death of Jesus and what he left as "his last will and testament." Christian interest in the original connotations of *berît* would be helpful in correcting a possible imbalance in the word testament.[13]

In one respect, the substitution of testament may have been a happy fault. Christians came to call their sacred writings the New Testament. The title is so well established that almost no one proposes changing the name. It is easier to live with a book called the New Testament than the New Covenant. If the Christian book were called the New Covenant, there would be less flexibility for Christian-Jewish conversation on the meaning of covenant.

There is a logic in Christians using Old Testament when they are the only ones doing the interpreting of the Hebrew Bible. When Christians admit that Jews have a voice in interpreting these Jewish writings, then the body of writing in question is no longer the Old Testament. Out of dialogue with Jews, Christians might someday decide to stop using the term Old Testament. Until then, it may be necessary to use convoluted phrases, such as "the Hebrew Bible, which Christians call the Old Testament."

If the term Old Testament does disappear, would there be a problem in having a book called the New Testament? Perhaps there is a logical paradox in having a new without an old but many names in the English language have new in them without implying anything about the nature or even the existence of an old. Those who founded "new" places (New England, New Ulm, New London) probably thought of them as superior to the old. Whatever the presumptions were in the naming of the New Testament, the name can continue, even if Old Testament someday disappears from Christian usage.

This excursion into new and old in reference to covenant and testament may seem a trivial point, but it is a necessary step for Christian–Jewish conversation. We need some linguistic opening to make fruitful exchange realistically possible. After that, we need endless studies on large and small points in our histories.

THE "TWO COVENANT" THEORIES

Much of the rest of this chapter concerns literature of today that speaks of two covenants. For the reasons I have stated, one has to be skeptical of this way of speaking. There can be only one covenant; it is not divisible into two. However, some of the literature under the rubric of two covenants may be trying to get at the issue of multiplicity. If so, it would be better to talk of two, three, four, and more *forms* of covenant. Then we are in the realm of Meaning B of uniqueness. Instead of being possessed by one group, covenant is a people in relation to God. The movement of people's lives can gather in diverse historical elements and be open to further transformation.

The literature that speaks of two covenants is complex and sometimes confusing. One source of confusion is the use of the same phrase to describe two quite different conversations. The issue on which the two conversations *agree* is that the two covenants are *not* the Old Testament and the New Testament. In one discussion, two covenants refers to Christianity and Judaism in the postbiblical era. In the other discussion, two covenants refers to the pattern within the Old Testament.[14]

TWO POSTBIBLICAL COVENANTS

The Jewish use of the phrase two covenants in recent times is largely identified with Franz Rosenzweig. In his great work, *The Star of Redemption*, Rosenzweig was able to look at Christianity in a nonpolemical way.[15] As he saw it, Christianity need not be the enemy of the mother; the daughter religion might be providentially doing things that Judaism cannot do and should not do. Rosenzweig was reviving a theory that has appeared in several Jewish thinkers, perhaps the most prominent being Judah Halevi. This twelfth-century poet and philosopher wrote that "these people (Christians and Muslims) represent a preparation and preface to the Messiah for whom we wait, who is the first fruit of the tree which they will ultimately recognize as the roots which they now despise."[16] Summarizing the position of Rosenzweig, a contemporary Jewish philosopher writes: "By attempting to move from the uniqueness of Judaism to the generality of the world, it (liberal Judaism) inevitably loses itself in apologetics."[17] Rosenzweig's solution is another uniqueness for Judaism's movement to the world. The need for another unique people is what led Rosenzweig to a positive interpretation of Christianity.

While Rosenzweig's project is intelligible up to this point, the phrase "second covenant" skews the meaning. It is true that the phrase is not prominent in Rosenzweig's writing, but it has become the common description of this theory. The idea of a second covenant added to the first does violence to Jewish logic. Jewish reaction to Rosenzweig's proposal has ranged from mild criticism to strong opposition.

It is interesting to note that Rosenzweig's sympathetic rendering of Christianity did not influence his attitude toward Islam. For the most part, Islam appears in Rosenzweig's work as the negative other, the religion that simply does not grasp the meaning of covenant. If he had been able to take a more impartial look at Islam, perhaps he would have had a three covenant theory.[18]

I have previously cited Rosenzweig's helpfulness with the idea of revelation. His meaning for that term and his context of creation and redemption provide a basis for Jewish-Christian conversation. The idea of two covenants is less helpful, because it is not radical enough.[19] While seeming to acknowledge Christian language, it does not allow sufficient autonomy to Christianity. The "Christian covenant" is too much like a deficient Judaism. That may seem a fair return for centuries of Christian writing which has treated Judaism as a deficient Christianity. What we need, however, is a level basis for mutual understanding.

The problem with a Jewish writer granting a second covenant is that it allows Jews to avoid questioning their relation to a first covenant. The language of Jewish covenant and Christian covenant would reduce the meaning of covenant to something under the control of Jews and Christians. The challenge for both Jews and Christians is to discover daily the meaning of the unique covenant that their lives are shaped by, participate in, and respond to. It is also a covenant that others than Christian or Jew may be faithfully living out.

TWO COVENANTS IN THE OLD TESTAMENT

For the last half century, there has been a wide-ranging conversation — mostly among Christian exegetes — on the "two covenants" in the Bible.[20] Whereas Jewish use of "two covenants" would be novel, Christians from the time of Saint Paul have assumed two covenants. (Since logic dictates that there can be only one, the Christian usage assumed that there *was* an old covenant and there *is* a new covenant.) The Christians divided their Bible into two parts, each having the name testament or covenant. It is, therefore, confusing for Christian writers to refer to the novelty of a two-covenant theory. What would be new for Christians is a one-covenant theory. The novelty in this recent discussion is that the two covenants being discussed are both within the Old Testament.

To the outside observer, there may seem to be something strange in the intensity of Christian interest in this topic compared to Jewish interest. The 1989 edition of the *Encyclopedia of Judaism* does not have an entry for the term covenant.[21] Perhaps the editor of the encyclopedia would say that there is no entry for covenant because that is what the whole encyclopedia is about. Jews are certainly interested in covenant; they might also be suspicious of what motivates Christian interest and where this theory of two covenants in the Old Testament is leading.

Jewish Interpretation

I will first recount the Jewish interpretation of the covenant idea in the Hebrew Bible, before looking at the recent Christian discussion. The Jews' perception of their own biblical history is simpler than the Christian rendering of covenant. For Jews, Sinai provides a single focus: God, covenant, Moses, people. The exodus experience is the moment of emergence for chosenness, uniqueness, peoplehood, and covenant. The promise to Abraham is a foreshadowing of a promise that finds its fulfillment in the Mosaic form of covenant.

Reading history backwards (or downward), the Jews perceive an earlier covenantal experience in Noah. In the story of Noah (Gen. 7), the word covenant is used seven times. Explicitly included within the covenant is the whole earth and all flesh on earth (v. 16). In Noah's blessing of his sons, there is an echo of the blessing over Adam and Eve (Gen. 1:20). The covenant extends to the parents of humanity and thereby to all human beings. By going downward to the past, the Bible implies movement outward to all people.[22]

In the other direction, toward the future, the covenant in Israel was in need of continual renewal. The covenant involved a historical people; the consent of each generation was needed. The rabbis debated the original number of covenants, that is, personal forms of the one covenant. One rabbi said 603,500, the supposed number of adult males at Sinai. No, said another rabbi, the number is 603,500 x 603,500, because the covenant includes the relations between the humans. And the number was added to each day in daily renewals of the covenant.[23]

The covenant was regularly renewed in a liturgical ceremony. The text of the agreement was read, witnesses were invoked, and punishments and rewards were promised. At times of national crisis, special reforms of the covenant occurred. The most striking instance of this renewal, at least before the exile, was under King Josiah, when the Book of Deuteronomy appeared. The whole book is a kind of covenant renewal with an impulse toward democratization. During the Babylonian exile, renewals of covenant life faced new problems. With the return from exile, the call for covenant renewal went out again to all the people, exemplified in the book of Ezra. Renewal of covenant is prominent in Ezekiel, Jeremiah, and Second Isaiah. The latter parts of the Bible, as well as postbiblical Judaism, represent a continuing struggle to live by the covenant, with inevitable failures followed by calls for renewal.

The issue is never resolved once and for all. All of history is needed to play out the possibilities of covenant. "God has never stopped talking to his people, and his people have never stopped talking back. The Bible is part one of the argument, and the Talmud is part two; even more argumentative than its predecessor."[24] Beyond the Talmud, down to the present day, "the covenant is carried forward on a flood of talk: argument and analysis, folkloric expression, interpretation and reinterpretation."[25]

Jewish tradition allows for rebellious individuals who protest from within covenantal existence. God and the humans are not equal, but God has made promises. Jews talk back to God "because of the unconvincing performance of divine providence in history."[26] The Holocaust was not the first time that God was called before a Jewish court of justice. The metaphor of covenant excludes a rationalistic and individualistic understanding of human life. It does not exclude passionate outbursts on the side of the oppressed or the the full use of human freedom to relieve human suffering.

Christian Interpretation

Christian writing on covenant within the Old Testament does not contradict the Jewish view, but it does find a greater tension in two strands of the history. Hence, the phrase "two covenants" arises. A sharp contrast is drawn between a Mosaic (or Sinaitic) covenant[27] and a Davidic covenant.[28] In this Christian reading, Abraham is seen as the forerunner of David. Thus, the contrast becomes the covenant tradition of Abraham-David over against the tradition of Moses.[29]

God first makes a universal promise to Abraham; it is narrowed down in God's dealing with Moses, but it is universalized again with David. Even when the Kingdom of Israel falters and the Israelites are taken into exile, the hope of a new and greater king is kept alive. At the same time that the future is looked to for redemption, more of the past is taken up into God's plan of salvation. For Christians, God's covenant begins with Adam and finds universal realization in the link from Abraham to David to Christ, who is called the Second Adam and the Son of David.

Jews do not necessarily deny the tension between covenantal traditions, as long as a Christian ideology is not imposed on the history. For example, if Christians say that the covenant with Abraham was one of grace, while the covenant with Moses represents law, the worst kind of stereotype is perpetuated in this supposedly revised language. The actual interplay of divine graciousness and human response is a mystery that pertains to each person and each historical era. Rules that structure human activity can be a flight from grace or an embodiment of grace. Jews and Christians have different emphases here; each community has its own spectrum of interpretation in the area of grace and law.

As a people lives out its particularity, it comes closer to manifesting the universal, but this movement is not easily distinguishable from a simple narrowing of life. Thus, in a movement from a Sinaitic to a Davidic form of life, the Jews might see a dangerous narrowing from community to king; in the same movement, the Christians might see an opening toward the universal. Is the movement from Abraham to Moses a narrowing, as the Christians see it, or a focusing of the universal, as the Jews see it? Who is right? Possibly both positions have some truth; a longer play of history may be necessary to follow the rhythm of the movement.

The most common contrast in the description of Sinaitic and Davidic forms of covenant is that the first is *conditional* and the second is *unconditional* or *promissory*.[30] The Sinaitic form was apparently modeled on a covenant form of the time, a Hittite suzerainty treaty. The Lord promises certain goods on the condition of obedience by serfs or workers. In contrast, the Davidic form simply promised an everlasting covenant; it would not be broken by human failure. God would be present and would not abandon the line of David, whatever its faults. By a peculiar inversion due to political failure, this politically oriented form gives rise to a hope for redemption in other than historical terms. The term *messiah*, which starts as a name for a human king, becomes, in the midst of political despair, the name for superhuman intervention. This strain of Jewish thought, which Jews see as a subordinate part of the tradition, is seen by Christians as the key to unlocking the whole Old Testament.[31]

Christians are especially attracted to those texts that refer to an inter-iorizing of the covenant. A movement of interiorization can suggest a transcending of mundane historical struggles. In that way, interiorizing and universalizing can go together. However, pursued without attention to ordinary life, the interiorizing can be an escape to a private illusion of self-sufficiency.

The only place in the Old Testament that actually refers to a "new covenant" written in the human heart is Jeremiah 31:31, but the sentiment is common enough in the latter part of the biblical text. If there is one covenant with endless forms of renewal, then there is a new covenant every day in the hearts of each of the faithful. Such language is intelligible to the Jew, but these moments of individual conversion need integration within the whole covenantal history. Jews see Christians as seizing the Davidic promise without accepting the Mosaic discipline; the result is a premature and apocalyptic form of messianism that presses for an end to history.

A central struggle of biblical history is to join the Davidic unconditional and the Sinaitic promissory forms of covenant. A great moment of insight comes with Amos and then with Deuteronomy, Second Isaiah, and the later prophets. God's unconditional promises do not exclude the need for human response; the promise of not being abandoned should not be cause for complacency. One might say that if you are a sinner, the presence of God would be worse than God's absence (Dt. 28:14-22). Psalm 89 brings together the two strands in the line: "I will punish the rebellion with the rod . . . But my gracious favor I will not remove from him" (vv. 33-34). Thus, what are called two covenants are not two objects but two ways of seeing human activity in response to divine initiative. If this integration of the two strands occurs, Jewish and Christian interpretations would not be so far apart as they first seemed.

Conclusion

Both Christian and Jewish readings of the covenant in the Bible can be seen as movements of the inclusivity suggested by Meaning B of uniqueness. The Christian way of reading the Old Testament ends up with the prophets and from there to the Christ figure. The Jewish reading leads to a deepening of God's presence in ordinary life. Each religion has its concern with universality in the lives of a unique people. Which understanding of the covenant is the more unique? I think that the question is unanswerable, and, fortunately, it need not be answered. Each religion can affirm the uniqueness it knows while listening to the other for the correction of possible biases.

CONTINUITY AND DISCONTINUITY

A unique covenant, one in which peoples participate, provides a context in which to relate Christian and Jewish traditions. A common way to address this issue is by the question: Is Christianity continuous or discontinuous with Judaism? Liberal Christianity's answer tends to be that Christianity is, or ought to be, continuous with Judaism. The assumption is that with continuity Christians are more sympathetic to Jewish concerns and there is a firmer basis for dialogue on common themes. From the Jewish side, this assumption is very questionable. If forced to choose between continuity and discontinuity, Jews are likely to find a discontinuous Christianity easier to live with.

The reason for this Jewish preference is clear if continuous and discontinuous are imagined as a line of development. When Christianity and Judaism are placed on one line, Christianity is further up the line. Liberal Christians try to avoid any claim to superiority, but can Christianity really find another place than one which claims to fulfill, supercede, or replace Judaism? The liberal Christian problem is not the negating of Judaism, but something that is harder for Jews to fight, namely, Judaism imagined as an early stage of Christian fullness. Even as Jews are praised—especially the Jew in the Old Testament—Jewish life is subsumed and thereby subverted in Christian statements. As more than one Jewish leader has put it: Continuity plus "Christ event" equals displacement. There really is no alternative within the image of a line of development.

The Jew is likely to see discontinuity as a less objectionable alternative, that is, to view Christianity as having its own line of development which takes its origin largely from Paul. Jews can then view Christianity as a kind of estranged relative who is out doing things (perhaps some very good things) in another part of the world. Jewish history can continue unhampered along *its* line of development with little reference to Christianity.

The choice of discontinuity over continuity within a line of development explains what is a puzzle for some Christian scholars today. Jews do not get very excited over Christian reinterpretation of the epistles of Saint Paul. The new scholarship has amassed considerable evidence that Paul was not attacking the Jews.[32] Should not Jews be relieved or even happy that Paul's enemies were "Judaizers" within the Christian community rather than the Jews? The Jewish answer is: No, not really. Such a change would bring the estranged relative back into the one household. Paul did not intend to disparage the Jewish way; he simply wished to admit Gentiles into the household of faith. Nonetheless, whatever Paul envisioned, the subsequent history was of a new development overrunning the householders who were there first.[33]

That Christianity is in some sense continuous with Judaism can hardly be doubted. But the phrase "in some sense" needs exploring, because in another sense there is obvious discontinuity. What often governs the question is the image of a line. With that image, one is limited to choosing between a single, unbroken line (or if broken, in need of repair) and a line that is interrupted to form two discontinuous lines. The liberal Christian assumption that there should be continuity can subvert Jewish autonomy, and it also does not fit the picture of what has happened in Christian history. The Jewish picture of a Christianity founded by Paul is offensive to Christians and it, too, does not recognize all the facts of history.

A line made up of a series of points is the standard image for Meaning A of uniqueness. A thing becomes (more nearly) unique as it is narrowed down to one line, to few points, and finally to one point. In this context, the *word* covenant can be seen as almost exclusively Jewish, and the Jewish temptation is to think that the covenant is a Jewish covenant. Prophets from biblical times to the present continually warn against this tendency. It is closer to the truth to say that the Jews belong to the covenant than to say the covenant belongs to the Jews.

When Christianity assumes Meaning A of uniqueness, it has to lodge its claim to the covenant in an anti-Jewish way. Liberal Christians try to reduce the number of points of conflict with the Jews. Not only does this reduction not solve the problem of conflicting interpretation, but the movement may be in the wrong direction. If a Christian says "I am in agreement with Jews on numerous points; we just differ on the 'Christ event'," then there is no ground on which to hold a conversation. The uniqueness of the Christian position would simply separate it from Judaism. Jews sometimes find it easier to talk with evangelical Christians who retain a whole body of material.[34] The Jews can then argue with the Christians over the meaning and value of Christian teachings. In any case, however, as long as Christians and Jews move within Meaning A of uniqueness, the arguments are not likely to go very far.

More fruitful discussion and debate require Meaning B of uniqueness. The context and image is not a line with points but community with people. The debate is not between Old Testament and New Testament, but between the Jewish community of the present and the Christian community of the present. Each community includes its past that is preserved in written documents and a tradition of interpretation and ritual. If a unique people engages another unique people, they are almost certain to learn something about their own as well as the other's uniqueness.

Much of Christianity takes its origin from Jewish religion; the continuity is still evident today, both in fundamental ideas and incidental details. Jewish religion, being the earlier of the two, cannot have a similar continuity with Christianity. However, some of postbiblical Judaism necessarily evolved in reaction to Christianity. The arrow of influence goes predominantly from Jewish to Christian, but the starting principle for Jewish-Christian conversation is some overlap of statements and some reciprocal influence. If the Jews and Christians were to engage in honest exchange about their interacting histories, Jewish religion would become more unique, and so would the Christian religion.

The question of continuity between "Christian covenant" and "Jewish covenant" cannot be asked, because neither exists. What can be asked is the relation of Christian and Jewish peoples within the idea of covenant. Jews and Christians share many ideas, beliefs, and practices. Both religions have similar outlooks on the goodness of creation, the sanctity of human life, the reality of sin, the need for grace and redemption. Regarding all these important realities, Jews and Christians *share in* them. That is, the powerful realities of faith, revelation, and covenant are participated in, not divided between, Christian and Jewish traditions.

Within the unique covenant, Christian life is in part continuous, in part discontinuous, with biblical Judaism. Of course, something similar can be said of the relation between modern Judaism and ancient Judaism. The community of the present lives in evolving tension with the community of the past. Since rabbinic Judaism developed out of earlier forms of Judaism, Christianity can be seen as a sibling more than a daughter of today's Judaism.[35]

Competent historians, whether Christian or Jewish, should be able to tell us which Jewish elements were changed by the early followers of Jesus. Beyond that, Christians have to consider which elements were undesirably changed within the history of the church. As Protestant and Catholic Christians have had to discover, two groups may have even more differences than they first thought. But the arguments should be about the real differences rather than accidents of one era, quirks of personality, and misstated positions. Foremost among the particular elements to be examined is the person who belongs to both Christian and Jewish histories: Jesus of Nazareth.

5

Jesus

A Very Unique Person

The title of this chapter refers to Jesus of Nazareth; the content of this chapter concerns the person Jesus and the complex set of ideas and claims that gathered around him. From the very beginning, there has been difficulty in distinguishing between this person and a surrounding system of ideas. Almost two millennia after his death, the questions remain puzzling. But we are perhaps at a good point in history for getting a few things clear about Jesus who is called the Christ.

I enter the arena of this discussion with reservations similar to those that I expressed in discussing the Holocaust. There are Christians for whom any tampering with their set of beliefs is blasphemous. Of course, that is not true of most Christians, who recognize the need to ask probing questions about Jesus and church doctrine concerning him. The bigger problem is with Christian theologians who use a language and a set of assumptions that are extremely difficult to get at. This chapter is not an exercise in Christian theology; it is an attempt to clarify language that influences other choices of language in Christian thinking, starting with the term *theology* itself.

I begin, therefore, by distancing the content of this chapter from a main thread of Christian theology with which it might get confused. From what I have said about the meaning of uniqueness, it might seem that I am about to advocate an "inclusive christology" as opposed to an "exclusive christology." Actually, I am doubtful that the relatively recent invention of the term *christology* has been useful to understanding among Christians or to conversation with others, especially Jews. I do ask in this chapter about the actual and possible inclusiveness of the term *Christ*, but the context and intention of my question are not theology, let alone christology. As I will indicate later in the chapter, christology cannot be more inclusive than Christianity is.

73

I ask a couple of simple questions of meaning in this chapter, but simple questions are not always simple to get at. I am especially interested in the terms *Jesus* and *Christ*, how both terms relate to the question of uniqueness, and how both function in Jewish-Christian relations. As was the case with the Holocaust, I am not presuming to substitute my voice for those voices more expert than mine. Complicated data from history, exegesis, and archeology abound in this area. My modest contribution is to suggest a few distinctions that would lead to clearer and more fruitful discussions. If Christians wish to engage in "christological debates," that is their prerogative; if they wish to have serious coversations with Jews, the starting point has to be different terrain.

From the first to the twentieth century, it was not apparent that Christians and Jews could converse at all. The Jew was asked to accept Christ as Lord and Savior. With few exceptions, the answer was no, and that was the end of the conversation. From each side, the position of the other was a simple negation. From the Jewish perspective, Christianity was the negation of the Jew's right to exist. From the Christian perspective, the Jews were mysteriously perverse in refusing to accept their own savior. The incapacity of Christian thinkers to root their beliefs in Jewish soil blocked their perception of the positive meaning of the Jewish no. As Arthur Cohen notes: "The mystery of Jewish unbelief which confounds Christendom is from the side of Israel the mystery of trust."[1]

In the twentieth century, there has been no quick reversal or total solution. The memory and the formulas linger on, even with some sincere attempts to rethink the question. Whatever progress there seemed to be early in this century proved woefully inadequate in the face of the Holocaust. Indeed, some of the biblical and theological scholarship of Europe became swept up into indirect defense of the Nazi regime.

Despite the Holocaust, or possibly pressured by the fact of the Holocaust, the hesitant steps have continued, and some progress is evident on both sides. There has been more writing on Jesus by Jews during the last forty years than in all previous history. Israeli schoolchildren now find a positive portrait of Jesus in their textbooks. On the Christian side, students of the New Testament have been immeasurably enriched by Jewish scholarship on the first century C.E. Christians are now able to situate the rabbi Jesus in a political and religious context.[2]

Both Christians and Jews need to consider the language that each uses. For Christians, there are some careful linguistic incisions needed before there can be full mutual exchange. These incisions of language are particularly connected with Jesus who is called the Christ. From the Jewish side, some standard formulas that state the eternal division of Judaism and Christianity need examining. For example, Pinchas Lapide, who is not at all unsympathetic to Christianity, writes: "With you the king stands in the middle and with us it is the kingdom. With you the redeemer, with us the redemption."[3] Even if one grants some truth to this statement, is the issue clear, and is the situation unchangeable? Are we dealing with contradictories or with differing emphases?

UNIQUENESS OF WHAT?

As in Holocaust literature, the writing referred to in this chapter is filled with the word unique. One can hardly read a book on the New Testament, theology, or Christian life, without regularly encountering a claim to uniqueness. In reference to the Holocaust, we saw that the claim is more complex than one might first assume; however, the reference for the term unique remained quite clear. Uniqueness referred to experiences of Jewish people in a horror summed up by the word *Holocaust*.

A major part of the difficulty in this chapter is not whether uniqueness applies but what the term is being applied to. I will spend much of my effort in this chapter distinguishing its application to Jesus and to Christ. Before doing that, however, I must take note of other sweeping usages where the meaning may be difficult to establish. For example, John Hick, despite some fine contributions in this area, is not very helpful in statements such as the following: "Until fairly recently it was a virtually universal Christian assumption, an implicit dogma with almost credal status, that Christ/the Christian gospel/Christianity is 'absolute,' 'unique,' 'final,' 'normative,' 'ultimate,' decisively superior to all other saviors, gospels, religions."[4]

Perhaps what Hick says is true, but the three nouns (Christ, gospel, Christianity) combined with the five adjectives (absolute, unique, final, normative, ultimate) could constitute a dozen or more implicit dogmas. That is, *unique* may overlap in meaning with its four neighbors, but the words are not interchangeable, and they represent different claims. And I think even the most unsophisticated Christians make some distinction among Christ/gospel/Christianity when it comes to the most exalted claims. Some Christians may say that Christ is unique and also say that Christianity is unique, but I dare say that few of them would think that the two statements are interchangeable in meaning.

Arnold Toynbee, leading the attack on Christianity's uniqueness earlier in this century, writes: "We ought also, I should say, try to purge our Christianity of the traditional Christian belief that Christianity is unique ... We have to do this if we are to purge Christianity of the exclusive mindedness and intolerance that follow from a belief in Christianity's uniqueness."[5] I would not deny that Christianity can be intolerant and that intolerance can follow upon a misunderstanding of uniqueness. But telling Christians to give up their "traditional belief that Christianity is unique" fails to specify what it is that Christians should "purge."

When other writers come to the defense of "Christian uniqueness," they usually do not carefully delineate the meaning and the uses of the term unique. John Cobb, responding to the question of Christianity's uniqueness, writes: "Christianity, like all traditions, is unique. Its role in history has been unique for good and ill. Its response to our pluralistic situation is unique. Its potential for becoming more inclusive is unique. Let us celebrate Christian uniqueness."[6] Unfortunately, the body of the essay does not contain any analysis of the meaning of uniqueness that would clarify and support these claims.

According to the meanings of uniqueness sketched out previously, it is difficult to make much sense of the statement: Christianity is unique. In Meaning A of uniqueness, a thing becomes more nearly unique as it excludes common notes with other things. The historically complex set of ideas and practices called Christianity can hardly be fitted into this meaning. It has been apparent from quite early in Christianity that there are similarities elsewhere; in addition, Christianity is a great absorber of Greek, Roman, Byzantine, and other cultures. So perhaps "Christianity is unique" does not mean that it excludes all other religions, but, on the contrary, that it includes the others. That sounds more like Meaning B of uniqueness.

Meaning B of uniqueness, it will be recalled, refers to an increasing inclusiveness. The most obvious example is the human being who includes other levels of being and whose nature is to be open and receptive to the whole world. Perhaps the attribution of uniqueness to Christianity refers to a similar capacity to include its competitors. Christians may be claiming that Christianity can absorb the truth(s) of every other religion. Such a uniqueness seems more fitted to Hinduism than to Christianity's more aggressive stance, which includes drawing a firm distinction between what Christianity is and what it is not.

Critics who complain about the "traditional claim to Christianity's uniqueness" may have mislocated the claim. Far more common is the claim that the gospel is unique. To many people the difference may seem slight, but in the context of scholarly debate, there is a marked difference. Jonathan Z. Smith writes that "the proposition of the uniqueness of the gospel genre seems to be a variation on the Protestant model of a pristine originary moment followed by corruption."[7] What that means is that the assertion of a unique (early) gospel is made in direct opposition to a nonunique (later) Christianity.[8]

With this contrast, the claim for a unique gospel becomes more intelligible. Christian writers who assert the uniqueness of the gospel are affirming two things: the utter novelty of the gospel in comparison to any other document of its time, and that the return to a pure gospel is the principle of church reform. Meaning A of uniqueness is clearly at issue. Christians have complete control over the word *gospel* and most of its meaning. The gospel is a message of vitality, surprise, and originality. There are very few similar documents in world history.

Non-Christians as well as Christians would grant a considerable degree of uniqueness to the gospel. When Christians assert an absolute uniqueness, they may be undermining rather than defending the gospel.[9] A truly incomparable gospel would be an isolated gospel. The isolation of the gospel from historical and literary criticism saves the gospel from maltreatment, but at the expense of making it irrelevant to the ordinary concerns of ordinary people.

What can be claimed with little debate is that the gospel is a very unique document. As for the claim that Christianity is unique, I would suggest that both the defenders and the attackers have the wrong noun being modified by the adjective unique. The argument over a Christian claim to uniqueness belongs elsewhere, beginning with the person who is the foundation of Christianity.

JESUS OR CHRIST

Where the word unique can clearly be applied is to the person, Jesus of Nazareth. Before developing the meaning and significance of this assertion, I have to make a distinction that is indispensable to asking the right questions in this chapter. "Jesus" is indisputably the name of a first-century Jew about whom the gospel speaks. "Christ" is a title representing a claim about that person. The title was already a complicated story when applied to Jesus in the New Testament. It has since then been layered with further meanings in subsequent centuries. Starting in the synoptic gospels, the claim of Christ was placed after the name Jesus, so that people came to think of Jesus as the first name and Christ as the surname.

This way of speaking among Christians causes more confusion than is usually noticed. As for conversation with Jews, an insensitivity on the point is one of the biggest obstacles to a conversation beginning at all. Most Jews are able to carry on a conversation about Jesus, if they are interested in doing so. Most Jews cannot discuss Christ, either because it is unclear what the topic of the conversation is or because the topic is a belief that they do not share. I find it astounding that so many Christians are oblivious of this fact.

The problem here is not only an insensitivity to Jews but confusion among Christians themselves regarding what or whom they are talking about. I would not propose that Christians excise the phrase Jesus Christ from their prayers and doctrines. But in asking many questions and in having conversations that will take us somewhere, the casual interchanging of Jesus, Christ, and Jesus Christ is a severe obstacle.

Christians have a legitimate concern with the claim to uniqueness; it pertains to the logic that underlies their religion. But who or what is unique? And how is he or they or it unique? I would suggest that the statement "Jesus Christ is unique" is unintelligible; it is neither a true nor false statement. If one is going to ask the question of uniqueness, that phrase first has to be broken down.

The thesis of this chapter is that Jesus is unique and Christ is unique, but they are unique in almost opposite ways. I qualify the contrast as *almost* opposite because the term Christ itself has to be broken down into contrasting claims. That fact makes a comparison between the uniqueness of Jesus and the uniqueness of Christ a complicated one.

I should note here that a sharp and consistent distinction between the meanings of Jesus and Christ is not a new and externally imposed rule of usage. The distinction is fairly simple and obvious; it stems from the beginning of Christian history. The distinction takes nothing away from Christian belief. It is not a denial of anything that has been attributed to Jesus in the development of the Christian church. What the distinction does do is clarify many statements for Christians and non-Christians alike.

What is unfortunate is that many Christian scholars associate the distinction between Jesus and Christ with a particular debate that raged in the late nineteenth century and has continued to surface in the twentieth century.[10] The debate used a contrast between the "Jesus of history" and the "Christ of faith." Not accidentally, this debate used the distinction I am referring to (that is, "Jesus" and "Christ"), but it also involved various polemical positions about history, faith, and the Bible. In the twentieth century, as the debate subsided (the Jesus of history now said to be a Jesus of faith), many people might now assume that a sharp distinction between Jesus and Christ is passé. But my point is a simpler truth that precedes and succeeds the categories born in the nineteenth century. Jesus is the man's name; Christ is a title, attached to which is a set of ideas. That someone can and should recognize the difference between the meanings of *Jesus* and *Christ* is as valid in the late twentieth century as in the eighteenth, eighth, or second centuries. The distinction is the basis of a common speech among Christians and between Christians and non-Christians.

Most talk about the uniqueness of Jesus Christ is simply a stopper in the conversation. Christians are making a claim that is not clear; non-Christians are usually uninterested. Sometimes, however, the claim leads to strange and confusing conflicts because the claim can be interpreted in opposite ways. One of the most interesting battles in Christian history concerned iconoclasm in the Eastern church.

The story is brilliantly recounted in Jaroslav Pelikan's history of the Eastern church. The worst conflicts come about, writes Pelikan, when two sides share the same fundamental assumption.[11] In the icon controversy of the eighth century, both sides ardently believed "that Jesus Christ was uniquely the image of God." From this premise, "it was possible either to conclude that therefore he must not be portrayed in a pictorial representation or that therefore he could be portrayed this way."[12] If I can paraphrase and sharpen Pelikan's contrast, one side logically concluded that "if Jesus Christ is uniquely the image of God," then *nothing* else could represent God. The other side logically concluded from the same premise that *everything* could represent God. In a sense, both were right; they were using different meanings of uniqueness and different referents for the relation of "Jesus Christ" and icons.

Pelikan notes that the iconoclasts were not opposed to images; far from it. They believed that "a proper image of God could only be as noble as the human mind."[13] They thought that the community acting in response to the command "Do this in remembrance of me" was a worthy image of God but that a wooden statue was not. They sensed that uniqueness is a quality of persons. Like the later Protestant reformers of Western Christianity, the iconoclasts had hold of a large truth, although they may have missed a smaller but still important truth of their adversaries. Wooden statues may be a poor representation of an infinite God, but in the divine-human relation that Christianity says it believes in, not even wooden statues are excluded.

Christians of the twentieth century may be no clearer than those of the eighth century when they assert the uniqueness of Jesus Christ. The assertion can still issue in almost opposite conclusions. The phrase can lead to the most narrow-minded intolerance toward everyone who will not accept Jesus Christ. Or in the hands of Archbishop Nathan Söderblom, an ecumenist early in this century, the uniqueness of Jesus Christ compels the affirmation that "God reveals himself in history, outside the church as well as in it."[14] A confusion on this point is tragic, because it means that Christians spend their energies on accusations of heresy instead of getting on with their vocation of helping to transform the world.

UNIQUENESS OF JESUS

If we temporarily prescind from the use of the term Christ, and ask about the uniqueness of Jesus, the issue is fairly clear or can be made clear. We are talking about a person whose existence is denied by almost no one. I have pointed out that Meaning B of uniqueness applies to every person. Modern evolutionary theory supports ancient wisdom that the human being is a microcosm, a recapitulating of its fellow inhabitants on earth. Other animals have some share in the meaning of uniqueness. But with the human individual, the openness to being, the receptivity to all levels of life, is most clearly apparent.

In asking the question is Jesus unique, the answer is easy, perhaps too easy. For writers who are aware that *unique* is an adjective to describe every human being, the question is answered with a somewhat impatient yes. A writer discussing Christian-Buddhist relations answers the question about the uniqueness of Jesus by saying: "That Jesus is unique is obvious even to Buddhists, just as Christians would hardly question the uniqueness of Gautama. Is not each of us unique?"[15]

The affirmation of Jesus' uniqueness deserves more consideration than "Of course, isn't everyone?" The uniqueness of each human individual, far from being a simple fact of perception, is an idea that slowly emerged in history. One could surmise from the practice of some governments that the idea has not yet emerged everywhere, even though the worst governments today profess respect for the right to life, the right to liberty, the worth and dignity of each person.

Not all historical eras, nations, and individuals have been equal contributors to the recognition of personal uniqueness. On any scale of measurement, the Jewish nation has been a contributor disproportionate to its size. Among those Jews, Jesus of Nazareth is certainly one of the most important individuals in the emergence of the idea of unique personhood. To affirm the contribution of Jesus of Nazareth is not to disparage the contribution of other great historical figures, such as Rabbis Akiba or Hillel, near contemporaries of Jesus.

Jesus did not go around saying, "I am unique." According to the best records we have, he did say some startling things about himself. Mostly, however, he talked about the important issues of his people, his place, and his time. He talked about the universe and its relation to his Father in heaven. He manifested an extraordinary tension of contrasts typical of the great leaders of his people.[16] Those who were inspired by him struggled to find words to describe the experience. So intense and extensive has been the reflection, involving the invention of new philosophical categories, that the simple gospel story is constantly in danger of being overwhelmed. But the portrait of this very unique person, the one who helped to give birth to the very idea of person, has continued to inspire people throughout the centuries.

Christians have the right and the duty to emphasize the uniqueness of Jesus. They need not make the claim that Jesus is more unique than anyone else, although they can hardly avoid claiming that he is among the more unique. The insistence that Jesus is the most unique person who ever lived is unnecessary and perhaps unintelligible.

If Christians would attend to the actual lived uniqueness of Jesus' life, they would be able to develop a richer version of the Christian life. Here I am brought to one of the major theses of this chapter, a statement that may be surprising but which follows from the above. Christians ought to affirm the uniqueness of Jesus *more strongly* than they have. Jesus is more unique than most Christians recognize.[17]

To affirm Jesus' uniqueness is to recognize the need to appreciate the Jewish people, the land, and the time that formed the context of Jesus' life. Most Christians cannot sufficiently appreciate Jesus' uniqueness because they do not know Jewish history well enough. Ironically, some Christian writers seem to think that affirming the uniqueness of Jesus is a denial of his Jewishness and even his humanity. For example, James Charlesworth writes: "Many Christians, including some who are erudite and sophisticated, tend to assume that Jesus must have been unique and have had little relation with his contemporaries. To begin with, this improper perspective—or unexamined supposition—ensures that any conclusion will be deficient, and certainly docetic (a denial of Jesus' humanity)."[18]

This passage is typical of the author's concern throughout the book, in which he criticizes other scholars and warns "how dangerous and indeed misleading are the caricatures that tend to *emphasize* Jesus' *uniqueness* in early Judaism."[19] The concern is based upon a false idea of what the uniqueness of a person means. Personal uniqueness depends on being deeply rooted in a people, a place, and a time. When the unique Jew of first century Palestine has been *underemphasized*, other kinds of claims have taken his proper place.

Norman Cousins once made the perceptive comment: "Jews and Christians have at least one thing in common; both have been unwilling to live with the idea that Jesus was a Jew." Christians have been ignorant of Jesus' person and teaching because they have never fully acknowledged that he was a Jew. Jews have been deliberately ignorant of Jesus in reaction to the abstracting of Jesus out of his Jewish history. Both religions have been the poorer, with Christianity suffering the decidedly greater loss. Judaism has all its important teachers except Jesus; Christians have none of their important Jewish teachers except Jesus.

This situation, however, has been changing. Both Jews and Christians may be on the verge of recognizing that Jesus of Nazareth was a very unique person, a first-century Jew whose powerful image could still be a bridge of understanding between Christians and Jews.[20] It will not be easy overcoming nearly two millennia of deliberate refusal to accept the Jewishness of Jesus. But if Christians really believe in the God that Jesus reveals, they will be attentive to Jewish as well as Christian scholarship that reveals the unique person of Jesus.

What is clear today is that Jesus arose out of the long tradition of ancient Israel. As with great innovators before him, the presence of his person was the meeting place of past and future, the renewal of the covenant between God and his people. He gathered up disparate strands of Jewish thought and practice; he was, for example, both exorcist and charismatic healer. Messianic expectation was one, though only one, strand of Jewish thought. The interweaving of such strands is what very unique people do. "The great synthesizer who alters the outlook of a generation . . . is apt to be the most envied, feared, and hated man among his contemporaries . . . Such a man is a kind of lens or gathering point through which past thought gathers, is reorganized, and radiates outward again into new forms."[21]

Christians should have no argument with Jewish writers who insist that all of the best points of Jesus' teaching are already found in the Hebrew Bible. Presumably, it was Jesus' chief reading material. Where there is a place to argue is with the contention, most clearly articulated by Joseph Klausner, that Jesus preached an impressive ethical ideal, but that its very impressiveness as ideal makes it impractical as a way of life.[22] More recent studies in the twentieth century locate Jesus' teaching in the very practical give-and-take of Jewish disputation. For example, Pinchas Lapide's book on the Sermon on the Mount analyzes Jesus' teaching sentence by sentence, to show that it is not a call to an impossible ideal. The Sermon on the Mount is, rather, a down-to-earth instruction on how to act in a hostile world, how to begin changing enemies into friends, and how to observe the law with greater attentiveness.[23]

The apparent contradictions of the law ("You have heard . . . but I say") arise from misreadings or misinterpretations of the text. The sense of the text is not "I am contradicting" but "I am pushing your commitment still further." There remain some disputes about whether any of Jesus' teachings—for example, some points concerning Sabbath observance—contradicted the tradition.[24] Even if one thinks that there are such points, the main story is clear: Jesus was uniquely rooted in the Palestinian Judaism of his time. The Jewish writer Geza Vermes summarizes the matter in these words: "Jesus the teacher and leader, venerated by his intimates and less committed admirers alike as prophet, lord and son of God."[25]

Jesus was a Jew who was in dispute with Judaism. That was not unusual for a Jew of those times, nor for a Jew today. The gospels, written at a time when church and synagogue were splitting, portray Jesus as doing argumentative battle with the Pharisees. Recent scholarship places Jesus close to the pharisaic school. He argued with the Pharisees because his teaching was so similar to theirs. He was perhaps at the "liberal" end of the spectrum of pharisaic opinion, arguing for the spirit of the law rather than the outward performance of every letter of the law. Such an interpretation, however, could be a case of importing modern formulas. A very different reading of the gospels is possible. John Howard Yoder, for example, arguing from the text of Luke's Gospel, sees Jesus as demanding a stricter observance of the Sabbath and Jubilee prescriptions. If one reads the gospel through the lens of justice for the poor, then Jesus might emerge not as a nineteenth-century humanist but as a radical religious reformer who condemns the rich for their escapes from forgiving debts and from returning land to the poor.[26]

Christians tend to think of Jesus as the founder of Christianity. Haddon Willmer suggests that Jesus is in dispute with Christianity as much as with Judaism. Willmer asks: "Was there anything distinctive about the fact that Jesus was a disputer, or about the manner and intention of his disputing? What, for instance, is the significance of a parabolic method of teaching for the interrelation of Christianity and other faiths?"[27] Willmer's question, so potentially fruitful, has yet to be explored. Parables have been thought of as moral tales for the individual or as stories that shift one's consciousness. But what would it be like to be in parabolic relation with other religions? The answer to that question requires that we have first situated Jesus in Jewish tradition, disputing with his own people so as to bring forth a profound truth from that tradition.

UNIQUE CHRIST

The uniqueness of Christ, I said above, is almost the opposite of that of Jesus. Such a contention is in no sense an attack upon the meaning of

Christ. If one takes account of several distinctions in the use of the word Christ, then the uniqueness can be intelligible, inspiring, and ecumenically helpful. Ultimately, the words *Jesus* and *Christ* do have to be held in close tension with each other for the development of Christian doctrine. That is why Christians coined the phrase Jesus Christ, although if they had followed one of the Pauline uses, Christ Jesus, it might have been easier to remember that *Christ* is a title, an idea, an ideal, a hope, rather than a surname. Before the words are related, it is important to sharply distinguish them. I have examined the fairly simple statement that Jesus is unique. What sense is there to the claim that Christ is unique?

An answer to this question requires a set of distinctions within the term itself. There is, first, a distinction between the word Christ and the ideas associated with the word. Second, there is a needed distinction between Christ and the Jewish word Messiah, which it originally translated. Third, there is a meaning of Christ that comes from the past and a meaning that Christians impute to the future. Fourth, there is a distinction between the meaning of Christ that the church intends beyond its boundaries and the actual meaning of Christ in the non-Christian world.

WORD AND IDEA

The first distinction between word and idea is fairly obvious, although in many discussions it is not adverted to at all. Sometimes a distinction of this kind is not particularly relevant. In the case of religious doctrines — and Christ as a chief example — the distinction is indispensable.

The *word* Christ is very unique according to Meaning A of uniqueness. The Christians coined the term at the very beginning and have exercised almost exclusive possession. Somewhere on earth there may be someone saying, "I am Christ," but none of the major religious traditions has offered serious competition for possession of the term. While the word Christ is unique to Christianity, the idea that Christianity expresses, or tries to express, through that word may not be so unique. First, however, let us attend to the word.

Each group, including a religious group, develops its own technical language for its own members. Sometimes the intent is to create a secret society, to use a language that says outsiders are unwelcome. Sometimes a technical language is simply unavoidable for discussing the phenomena of archeology, biology, physics, and so forth. Outsiders are welcome on the condition that they learn the discipline. In either case, the language spoken within the group is uniquely its own. The fundamental assertions of the language are simply definitions.

The statements of Christian doctrine and Christian theology are not propositions that in isolated packages can be proved true or false. One has to know the fundamental terms of the language in order to judge. In Christian language, there is no doubt that *Christ* is a fundamental term, and it takes its meaning from other terms that have helped to define it.

George Lindbeck, in his study of religious language, says that the phrase "Christ is Lord" is important to Christians, but is not a (true) proposition.[28] The statement becomes true as it is used in activities of adoration, obedience, service, and so forth. "Christ is Lord" or "Christ is the unique way of salvation" are formulas that define what Christianity is. One could not eliminate Christ or place Christ on equal footing with other saviors, while still having Christianity exist. *Outside* the context of Christian doctrine, the question whether Christ is Lord (or whether Christ is the unique way of salvation) is neither true nor false. The statement's meaning is indeterminate.[29]

This example may seem to suggest that each religious group is totally encapsulated within its own statements and an interreligious conversation is impossible. Such conversation is indeed difficult and cannot proceed by comparing a statement in one religion with a statement in another. There are patterns of meaning, however, that transcend particular groups. In the case of Judaism and Christianity, the origin of the latter is a guarantee of considerable overlap of meaning. Most of the time when Christians say "Christ," the context which defines the term means that no debate with Jews is possible. But with some terms that are regularly associated with Christ (for example, redemption, salvation, revelation, mediator, kingdom), Jews and Christians have the possibility of a lively and fruitful debate.

If we are speaking of the *word* Christ, then the Christian belief in the uniqueness of Christ is unassailable. Neither Jews nor any other non-Christians have been arguing for possession of the term. Presumably, however, Christian writers have more in mind when they relate uniqueness to Christ. They are referring to a meaning that does overlap with a Jewish term.

CHRIST AND MESSIAH

The second distinction is between the meanings of Christ and Messiah. For most of the world, this distinction is a minor squabble; for Jews and Christians it is indispensable before there can be a serious conversation. Christ is the anglicized version of the Greek *Christos* that in the New Testament translates the Hebrew *Mashiach* (the anointed one). As in all translations, there is some difference of connotation, because language does not consist of words so much as patterns of speech.

In some cases, two words that were not far apart at the time of translation later diverge. Christ is a supreme example of such a history. In the first century C.E., it could have been plausibly argued that Messiah and Christ represented the same meaning. By the fourth or fifth centuries, after the long christological debates, the two words had separated in meaning. In the twentieth century, after the evolution of Christian piety and doctrine, as well as persecution of Jews in the name of Christ, the assumption that Christ and Messiah are equivalent in meaning is staggering. Messiah remains a Jewish word having, if not a central role in Jewish history, indisputable Jewish roots and connotations. Christ is a Christian term that has acquired layer upon layer of connotation. It overlaps with the meaning of Messiah, but also with complicated metaphysical and ethical beliefs.[30]

In the synoptic gospels, the word Christ very closely approximates the meaning of Messiah. But in Paul, "the name Christ receives its content not through a previously fixed conception of messiahship but rather from the person and work of Jesus Christ." In the contemporary scholarship on Paul, he is understood to be speaking to the Gentiles, not to the Jews or against the Jews. The word Christ is already beginning its own history. Paul uses the word as a proper name and the description of God's activities. This double usage had profound influence on such Christian writers as Clement, Ignatius, Polycarp, and their successors.[31]

It would make no sense to complain that Paul should have spoken differently. But Paul has been badly understood in much of Christian history, so Jews to this day are wary of his influence. N. A. Dahl may be correct in saying that "Paul's proclamation of Christ has a unique character. The revelation of the Son of God signifies for him an abrupt break with the past."[32] The word Christ and some of the meaning attached to the word may be a break with the past of the Gentile world. The meaning in that setting could not be in smooth continuity with the Jewish Messiah. However, it would be incorrect to infer that Paul was thereby attacking or rejecting Judaism.[33]

In summary, the Christian word Christ cannot be equated with the Jewish Messiah, but neither can it be entirely separated from that history. If Paul is taken in isolation, then the uniqueness which Dahl referred to will be of Meaning A. But if Paul and the four gospels are kept in healthy tension, then a distinction without a separation of the meanings of Christ and Messiah is possible. Paul is not the enemy of the Jews, even though his "gospel" evolved into a non-Jewish strand of Christianity.[34]

For many Christians, "Christ" is another name for God; they have probably been taught that Christ fulfilled the Jewish hopes for a Messiah. Such a belief merely functions as a lead into the "divinity of Christ" or the "redemption of the world by the Second Person of the Trinity." I am not judging whether the evolution of these formulas was good or bad; I am certainly not proposing that the evolution of Christianity be undone. My sole point is that when Christians say Christ and Jews say Messiah, they are not saying the same or even approximately the same thing.

Such a distinction does not dissolve Christian and Jewish differences over the titles attributed to Jesus. In fact, it complicates further what may have seemed like a simple disagreement of fact in regard to the question: Is Jesus the Messiah? Christians and Jews have to examine in detail the characteristics and titles attributed to Jesus. Christians are not going to give up what is fundamental to the existence of Christianity. However, they might reconsider the policy of assuming that the substitution of the term

Messiah for Christ is always a help to Jewish-Christian understanding.

Christians have to rethink their claims and realize that Jews may not be rejecting what Christians think they are rejecting. William Christian writes that when Christians say yes to "Jesus is Messiah" and Jews say no, this is not a contradiction.[35] The same author goes on to say that there are genuine disagreements which Christians and Jews can have over who Jesus was and what he accomplished. Paul Kirsch puts the difference well: "Christians are right in asserting that Jesus is the Christ; Jews are right in asserting that Jesus is not the Messiah."[36]

Can Christians live with the second part of Kirsch's statement that Jesus is not the Messiah? Suppose it were possible to bring in an outside negotiator who was neither Jewish nor Christian. What might he or she judge about the Messiah on the basis of public evidence? Christianity, it could be said, has a defensible case that Jesus fulfilled some elements of messianic hope. At the same time, Christians, in asserting that Jesus is the expected one of Israel, have always had to admit that the fulfillment was in a surprising way. That is, he was the expected one who was not expected to be as he was.

Thus, even in Christian terms, and obviously in any other discourse, the Jews have room to believe in a Messiah or a messianic age still to come. Jesus simply was not their Messiah, a statement that a twentieth-century Christian should be able to recognize as true, even though second-century Christians could not see their way to this acknowledgment. If Christians were to back off from their insistence that Jesus is the Messiah, it would give Jews a chance to express appreciation for their own Jesus, the rabbi from Nazareth.[37]

PRESENT AND FUTURE

There is a question implied in the above section not only about Messiah but about the tense of the verb to be used in reference to Christ, as well as Messiah. That leads us into the third distinction between the Christ that is and the Christ still to come.

Jews sometimes say that it is the newspaper that divides them from Christians. The Jew reads the daily paper and asks: Is this a redeemed world? For the Jew, the Christian position is clear — and incredible. The Christian believes that Christ means redemption; Christ has come; therefore, the world is redeemed. Arthur Cohen states the widespread Jewish belief: "Judaism asserts that history is not redeemed. Christianity maintains that it is. This is a fundamental and irreducible disagreement which divides Judaism and Christianity to the end of time."[38]

Cohen is probably right that there will always be disagreement here, but the difference is not a contradiction. Although Christians from the start have used phrases affirming that redemption has happened, there has always been another side to Christian language. And on the Jewish side, the denial that history has been redeemed does not necessarily mean that redemption can only be imagined as a "future event." For example, Abraham Heschel writes: "According to the Kabbalah, the redemption is not an event that will take place all at once at the end of days nor something that concerns the Jewish people alone. It is a continual process, taking place at every moment."[39]

Christians believe that a fundamental orientation (to use Rosenzweig's term) is revealed in Jesus. For a century or more at the beginning, the Christians believed that the era of peace and justice was at hand. They were wrong, or at least the intervening period has been far longer than they had anticipated. From the beginning of Christianity, however, there has always been the acknowledgment that if Christ means redemption, then Christ—the whole body of the Christ—has not yet been realized.

Christians came to speak of a "second coming," a rather clumsy admission that the world is still awaiting its complete redemption. A better image might have been that of Paul's saying that he fills up in his body the sufferings still lacking in Christ (Col. 1:24). When Paul speaks of being saved, he regularly uses present and future tenses.[40] Thus, in Christian usage, Jesus is related to Christ in both the present and the future tenses: Jesus *is* the Christ (there are no serious competitors for the title), and Jesus is *not yet* the Christ (no one can be the fullness of Christ until history reaches its culmination).[41] Redemption awaits human actions that will contribute to an era of justice. *Christ* is the name for an ideal embodied in a community whose emergence is still at issue.

I hope it is clear that this position is not a "postponing of the messianic claim for Jesus." A Jewish writer is understandably suspicious of what he sees as a "post factum rationalization" by some Christian writers today who defer the problem from present to future. "The messianic claim of Jesus vis-à-vis the Jewish people is cancelled for the present. If the first coming of Jesus makes a messianic claim on the world, the Jews are exempt; it is deferred to the future, the second coming."[42]

By distinguishing between Christ and Messiah, I have denied that a messianic claim was made on the (Gentile) world. Furthermore, this position does not assume that Jews will ever accept Jesus as Messiah (a position that is in accord with Paul's doctrine of salvation in Rom. 9-11).[43] Jesus' relation to the messianic hopes of Israel and the difference between Jewish and Christian understandings of "Messiah" are legitimate topics of discussion and debate that do not imply any missionary attitude on the part of Christians.

With these comments on the present and future Christ, we can draw up a summary of the uniqueness of Christ in relation to time. In *Meaning A*: "Christ is unique" means that God interrupted history, inserting into history such *things* as revelation, redemption, and salvation. At one moment, in one individual, there is something that is incomparable.[44] Redemption is there and nowhere else; God acted this one time and not again. The knowledge of this happening is transported from the past up to the present.

The most extreme case in this way of speaking is the phrase "Christ event."[45] It is a very modern phrase that is now so common that writers do not seem to notice how peculiar it is. One can make sense of Christ as a title given to a person, as an ideal of a coming community, or even as a metaphysical structure of the universe. But "Christ event" severs the connection between past and present, between Christians and non-Christians. Giving up the phrase is not an abandoning of traditional Christian belief; on the contrary, it would force Christian writers to think more clearly about who or what Christ is.

In *Meaning B,* "Christ is unique" is mainly about a hoped-for future, without excluding the present and past. Christ is the name of a personal and communal relation, rather than the name of event, person, or truth of the past. When Christians say that Christ is unique, that means (or can mean) they intend to work toward a greater inclusiveness, a more genuine community than the world has yet seen. The term Christ, without ceasing to be a title attributed to Jesus—indeed, precisely as a title attributed to that person in his community—foreshadows the concrete realization of a world of persons in peace with other human and nonhuman life. Is Christ now unique? Yes, to an extent. But the Christian task is to get on with the realization of a greater uniqueness of Christ.

CHRISTIAN INTENTION AND NON-CHRISTIAN UNDERSTANDING

The distinction between uniqueness now and uniqueness still to come has already led into the final distinction between what Christians may intend by *Christ* and what others, including Jews, can possibly understand by the term. In their best meaning of the Christ ideal, Christians intend an umbrella term for the meeting of all peoples; for Christian theology, Christ is *the* term under which the righteous of the earth are gathered. Karl Rahner is often criticized, sometimes ridiculed, for his phrase "anonymous Christian," but the idea is simply a liberalizing of Christian theology as far as it can go.[46] Rahner did not intend to say (though the words may indeed say) that non-Christians are, despite themselves, members of the Christian church. Rahner means that they are followers of that universal ideal which Christians call "Christ." A Christian theologian cannot pay anyone a higher compliment.

What is intended as compliment is not always received that way. Rahner's way of liberalizing Christian theology is probably better than other ways that proclaim themselves radical. For example, there is the position that Jesus is not the only Christ; Christians should recognize Christs in other religions. However well intended, the pushing of the term Christ into other religions can be taken as imperialistic.[47] If Christians are clear that Jesus is the Christ but not yet fully so, that the church is the community that embodies in flawed ways the Christ that is hoped for, then the uniqueness of Christ can be understood as an invitation to non-Christians to join in the greater realization of that unique ideal. Most people presumably will not accept the invitation, but none need be offended by it. Many people would cooperate with Christians under other formulations of a hoped-for world.

MEDIATION

In this context, the question that always comes up is: Why one? Isn't it preposterous to imagine that the salvation of the world is tied to a single person? I hope that the discussion of this and the previous chapter has situated the question in a better light. To a Hindu, the Christian claim seems unnecessarily narrow; perhaps Christianity will never be able to make its position very intelligible to eastern traditions. However, this is a question that Christians have to get straight with Jews before trying to talk incarnation with Hindus.

Jews do not accept most of the Christian claims about Jesus of Nazareth. However, the logic that Christians use should not seem preposterous, or even strange. There is a famous passage in the Jewish Mishnah that reads: "Why was only a single man created? To teach you that for him who destroys one man, it is regarded as if he had destroyed all men, and that for him who saves one man, it is regarded as though he had saved all men."[48]

Judaism, like Christianity, is interested in the salvation of the whole world; like Christianity, it sees the whole world present in a single person. The same Mishnah passage notes that when human kings stamp many coins, they are alike; whereas the Holy One "stamped every man in the mold of the first man, and yet not one of these resembles his fellow." Each human being represents all humanity; each human being is distinctly and uniquely himself or herself. There is no contradiction in saying that the redemption of the world is found in one person.

If Jesus were kept in the context of his time and his place, if he were centered in his Jewish community, then most of the Christian statements about salvation in one man would not be foreign to Jewish logic.[49] Not that salvation is present in this man as opposed to or instead of all others. Rather, Christians see a universal grace, revelation, and salvation represented in the personal life of Jesus. Because they have a focus of divine revelation and human acceptance in this one dramatic case, then their outlook can extend to every corner of the world.

The objection to redemption in the one Christ can involve a confusion of language. In Christian terms, two, two hundred, or two million Christs would not be enough. Christian hope is for nothing less than that all become Christ. Granted that Jesus' relation to Christ remains different, but once the breakthrough to personal uniqueness was made, it became unnecessary to repeat the breakthrough.[50] Jesus' uniqueness is the Christian guarantee that Christ's uniqueness does not slip into intolerance.

Much of the confusion surrounding the claim of one person being a unique source or agent of salvation is tied to the word *mediator*. Is Jesus the sole mediator between God and the human race? More basically, why should there be a mediator at all? One might state a general, if not universal, rule of religious reform: Reformers believe that their opponents have inserted a mediator between the Nameless One and the people. The reformers promise to restore immediacy of contact. Struggles between Catholic and Protestant, Shiite and Sunni, Mahayana and Hinayana, could be studied in light of this rule; so could conflicts between closely related religions, such as Buddhism and Hinduism, Christianity and Judaism. The amazing thing is that each side accuses the other of the same failure. Christians believe that they got rid of the intermediary of Jewish law and restored the immediacy of God's grace. Jews believe that Christianity is a religion lacking in warmth and intimacy because it inserted a mediator between God and the people.[51]

Stanley Rosenbaum, with no intention of attacking Christianity, writes:

> Here, I think, Judaism and Christianity are remarkably close in outlook. For most Christians, salvation is an act of grace, which is a free gift of God. For Jews, too, salvation is an act of God's *hesed* ... The major difference between us is that Christian grace is obtained through the intermediacy of Jesus, while our gimlet-eyed Jewish business mentality moves us to diminish the middle man and apply directly from the great wholesaler.[52]

It is understandable that a Jew could see Christianity in this way. It is, nonetheless, a terrible accusation to make against any religion that—at its best—it deals with a middleman. Many forms of Christian piety represent such a corruption, but Christian reformers have continually protested against such an interpretation. Rosenbaum is possibly unaware that anti-Jewish Christians believe that Jews are blocked from direct contact with God; and, indeed, Jewish reformers have also had to struggle with what is a form of idolatry. If Rosenbaum's last sentence were correct (or the corresponding description of Jews by some Christians), then the two religions would not at all be similar. The first part of Rosenbaum's statement is accurate. Both religions are concerned with God's grace as found in person, community, and the whole world.[53]

Are terms such as mediator, mediation, and intermediacy legitimate religious terms? As might be guessed by this point, there are two directions in which the idea of mediation can go. Mediators and mediation can be a case of Meaning A of uniqueness; they can also be developed under Meaning B.

MEANING A

The mediator can be a *thing* that excludes as many common notes as possible with any potential competitor. Nothing else except this unique thing can be the source of grace, revelation, salvation, redemption. This middleman can be constituted by legal prescriptions that have lost connection with their communal significance. In Christian history, sacraments that are no longer the action of the community but things that guarantee grace can be that kind of mediator. A vast, impersonal bureaucracy called "the church" can be set up as middleman. And even "Christ," as a thing or a doctrine, can be conceived that way. In this pattern, "Christ is unique" means that if you wish to have access to grace or redemption, see the agents who are in sole possession of that unique thing.

MEANING B

In the alternate meaning of unique mediator, there is no middleman (more exactly, no middle thing). The operation of this logic of uniqueness is missed by many reformers. As a result, they miss the secret of successful religious reform: The way to get rid of a single (exclusive) mediator is to make everything and everyone potential participants in mediation. Where is grace to be found? Everywhere. What is revelatory of God? Every gesture. How does God save? In even the smallest action.

Reformers often shoot down one middleman only to have another pop up in its place (sometimes the reformers themselves). Human life requires one form or another of mediation. Revelation, grace, or salvation need mediation in the sense of finding bodily representation.[54] In the grand sweep of both Christian and Jewish thinking, everything in the universe represents divine creativity and creaturely response. Living organisms particularly express this relation, and animals even more so. Human beings bring the relation to its (most nearly) unique expression, a conscious and free response to divine activity. Christians find this process summed up in Jesus, the one in whom divine love and human response are embodied.

The Christian church attributed various titles to Jesus to capture this understanding (Christ, Savior, Son of God). Sometimes these titles undermined the very relation of divine and human that they were intended to describe. When the term Christ obscures Jesus the Jew, then Christ is *neither* divine nor human; *it* is a system of exchange between God and the individual soul. But when Christ is a title indicating that Jesus is the revelation of God within a community, then Christ is *both* divine and human, signifying the presence of God in all creation and inviting a human response to God's grace on behalf of all creation.

CONCLUSION

At the center of Christian life is God; at the center of Christian life is Christ. They are not competing centers, something that is suggested by a confusing discussion about christocentric versus theocentric theologies.[55] The One beyond names has to be imagined and symbolized in relation to all creation. For Christians, the term Christ is a summary of the rich variety of relations between divine and created. Jesus is the person who reveals the meaning of personal uniqueness and keeps the Christ idea from turning into one more metaphysical abstraction. In Christian terms, Christ is the axis of the world, the relational reality that guarantees equal opportunity for all human beings, who are themselves representatives of nonhuman creation.

In summarizing a discussion in contemporary Christian theology, John Bowden writes: "Once Christ was put at the center, the gaze of Christians was predominantly backwards, to what *had* happened in him."[56] There is an obvious inconsistency of imagery here. If Christ is at the center, then the gaze of Christians is not *backwards* but to the *center*. Actually, the real problem has been that Christ (and Jesus' relation to Christ) is so seldom at the center of Christian theology.

The place where Christ is often to be found is not at the center but at the *top*, where a god is clothed in human appearance. Then the term Christ means a person who was not really a person, a Jew who is not recognizable as Jewish, and an impersonal instrument of divine truths given to authoritative agents. In short, "Christ" becomes the unique mediator who excludes bodily representation, even that of Jesus' representation of God. The alternative to that impersonal Christ at the top is a transpersonal Christ at the center. The symbolism of center is indispensable in testing out the Jewish and Christian logic of uniqueness. Such a testing is found in the ecological movement of today, a topic that we turn to in the next chapter.

6

The Unique Animal

Humans at the Center

One of the most important places to test the Jewish and Christian logic of uniqueness is in the ecological discussion of today. In contrast to the other areas discussed in the previous chapters, the word *uniqueness* does not frequently appear in this literature. My thesis here is that uniqueness is the very idea that is lacking in ecology. The relation of the human person to all other beings in the cosmos cannot be adequately imagined and stated without recourse to Meaning B of uniqueness.

I wish to note, right from the beginning of this chapter, that its concern is feminism as well as ecology. Within the logic of uniqueness, it becomes evident that feminism and ecology are ultimately a single issue; both have to be worked at, or else both will fail. Most feminist writing is aware of this connection; almost always there is some advertence to ecology. But much of ecological literature remains astonishingly unaware of this connection.

There has been some progress in the last decade. However, the existence of a subdivision of ecology called "eco-feminism" can unwittingly result in bracketing off feminist awareness from the rest of ecology. To a large extent, ecology remains a hotbed of sexist writing that is gamely trying to rethink where "man" belongs in nature.

The drive toward uniqueness has been evident in western history for at least two millennia. Human life, as I pointed out in chapter 1, is a confusing mixture of two kinds of uniqueness. The call to an ever increasing inclusiveness in Meaning B is genetically based, but its realization depends upon a psychological openness, a moral readiness, and a metaphysical courage. The willingness to live out Meaning B of uniqueness includes the acceptance of mortality, a theme I return to in the next chapter.

Meaning A of uniqueness, in contrast, depends on a simple physical displacement in space and time. My space is not your space; I know that I exist because I am not that, nor that, nor that. Existence depends on resistance to intrusion, on getting as far away as possible from competitors and their control. This kind of uniqueness is firmly possessed only if one has the power to dominate everyone and everything else. Death is the reminder that this kind of uniqueness is not a permanent possession, which is why death has to be banished from consciousness.

It could therefore be said that our ecological crisis is simply the historical triumph of Meaning A over Meaning B. In an ecologically sane world, Meaning B of uniqueness in human life contains Meaning A. For example, the territorial imperative to strike out at intruders to one's space is restrained by listening, understanding, tolerance, and compassion. Other animals have these restraints built in; the human breakthrough to Meaning B means that the capacity for receptiveness is greater and, alas, when something goes wrong in their development, the humans are the great killers. The humans are the only wild animals, those who can kill indiscriminately, even their own kind. The triumph of Meaning A of uniqueness over Meaning B subverts the best of human life and eventually turns human beings into a terror to the whole earth.

A recovery of Meaning B of uniqueness requires a careful rethinking of the relation of person to community, local community to universal community, human community to biotic system. This question cannot be stated in the crude abstractions of "man and nature." The language required is one of the relations between men and women and their discriminating relations to each level of being. Contemporary ecology is in danger of freezing itself in an orthodoxy that can block out elementary truths about human existence, men and women, and their responsibility to the nonhuman world.

THE ECOLOGICAL PROBLEM

As almost everyone knows by now, the ecological crisis can be simply put by saying that human beings are destroying the very environment that sustains them. But why are they doing that, and how can they be stopped? To ask this question using the pronoun *they* reveals the peculiar nature of the problem, because the they is, of course, we. We are not asking a question about another species ("How can we control the mosquito problem?") nor about a wayward individual ("How do we get Johnny to behave?"). But many of the solutions seem to miss this paradox. They are answers of the kind: "Let's send the human beings to their room without dinner," or more drastically, "Let's see if we can eliminate the human beings as far as possible."

The inappropriate logic used in such an approach relies heavily on size and measurement. The humans, it seems, have exaggerated their importance; they have to be cut down to size. Intimidating data are therefore brought forth from astronomy, physics, and geology, all designed to put the human race in its place. That place is as one species among others, a mere speck in physical space and a brief moment in geological time. If only people were more enlightened with the facts of modern science, they would acquire some humility and begin treating the environment with respect.

Human beings keep getting out of line and interfering with nature's wise ways. When that happens regularly, a logical if bizarre conclusion is drawn, namely, wouldn't it be better if human beings did not exist? Paul Taylor's *Respect for Nature* is one of the most elaborate studies of "environmental ethics." Without a hint of irony, Taylor can write: "Given the total, absolute and final disappearance of *Homo Sapiens*, then, not only would the Earth's Community of Life continue to exist but in all probability its well-being would be enhanced."[1]

Taylor is not alone in drawing this conclusion. He is merely being logical with the principle of equality accepted in much of ecology. Each thing has its place, and it does not take long to find out who refuses to stay equal with all the other animals: "man." But do not such writers perceive the absurdity of humanly advocating that life would be better without humans?

Writers on this subject are forced into absurdity because they are going in the opposite direction from where they should be going. The people who keep telling us that "man" is small and insignificant are the ones controlling all the data. The men who are speaking and their activity of control give the lie to professions of equality, of being merely one species among billions. Instead of trying to lessen human dignity, they should be trying to enhance it. Instead of trying to get the human being out of the center of the picture, that is exactly the place of the human. Instead of more scientific data to intimidate the impressionable, we need a context in which to situate science itself.

One of the reasons ecology cannot find the logic it needs is that this way of thinking is embedded in both Jewish and Christian histories, and some of the bitterest anti-Christian polemic to be found today is in the ecological movement.[2] Ecology is, as it were, the new religion of the world. From the standpoint of ecology's new religious fervor, Christianity is the religion that failed. The Christian religion takes the brunt of emotional attack, much as Judaism did from Christianity. And just as Christianity needs to recover its own logic within Judaism, so ecology has to examine the complex strands of Christian history that have helped to shape today's environment and today's environmentalists.

A modest essay by Lynn White, Jr., in 1967, "The Historical Roots of Our Ecological Crisis," set off controversy in this area and established the terms of the debate.[3] Numerous books and essays responded to White's essay; White himself wrote several subsequent essays, though none got the attention of the first.[4] White offered two theses: "The root of the ecological crisis is Christianity," and "The remedy must be essentially religious." There was widespread agreement with the first thesis, that Christianity is the culprit. There was less agreement with the second. But many people who did agree that something "religious" was needed looked either to the recovery of the pre-Christian religion in the West or to eastern religions.

Stephen Toulmin's *Return to Cosmology* is an example of the first approach; Fritjof Capra's *The Tao of Physics* exemplifies the second.[5]

Lynn White, Jr., tried to find an alternate strand of Christianity. He concentrated on Francis of Assisi, who has subsequently become the patron saint of ecology. Francis is undoubtedly worthy of study, but White's description is brief and misleading. He writes that Francis "tried to substitute the idea of equality of all creatures, including man, for the idea of man's limitless rule of creation."[6] The statement is wrong on both counts. Francis, like other medieval Christians, believed in a hierarchy of God's creating. He did not have a theory of equality; he was a preacher of compassion, love, and human responsibility. When he did use the word equality, it was in reference to our standing before God; that is, all creatures are equally nothing apart from grace.[7]

As for White's reference to "man's limitless rule of creation," no such doctrine existed. Christian doctrine could be rigid, but it was never that obtuse. Whatever was its fault in practice, the Christian church never lost sight of the reality of human finitude. To be a creature is to be finite, that is, not limitless.

The isolating of Francis does not explain where he came from or why he touched such a chord of Christian piety. Roderick Nash writes that "it is well to emphasize that within the Christian tradition Francis was unique in his point of view. He was the exception that proved the rule."[8] Francis was indeed unique, but in an opposite sense from what Nash assumes. His unique person was largely an imitation of Jesus of Nazareth. He was and is one of those distinctive personalities that is more unique (more nearly unique) than other people. As other giants of the Middle Ages, he lived from the portrait of Jesus in the New Testament, from devotion to his church (with which he disputed), and with a sensitivity to the entire chain of being.

Stories abound of Francis's relation to the animal world and other living forms. The danger has always been that his life is enveloped in a misty romanticism; the saint of the birdbath, without the rigorous discipline of life which he practiced.[9] Recent ecological literature, in attributing to him a love of nature, has not clarified the picture. Actually, Francis never used the term *natura* in his writings. This omission is explained in Chesterton's biography of the saint: "Francis was a man who did not want to see the wood for the trees. ... He did not call nature his mother; he called a particular donkey his brother or a particular sparrow his sister."[10]

This attitude is admirable and inspiring; it remains important today. However, one has to question whether this kind of outlook is adequate to our ecological problems. René Dubos, in one of the responses to White, suggested that Benedict of Nursia would be a better model for ecology. "The Benedictine rule ... seems inspired rather from the second chapter [of Genesis] in which the Good Lord places man in the Garden of Eden not as a master but rather in a spirit of stewardship."[11] Benedict's monks preserved the learning of the West while using the appropriate technology to till the earth and develop an understanding of agriculture.

Dubos's reference to the second chapter of the Book of Genesis is to God's command to the human pair to "dress it and keep it." (Gen. 2:15). Many writers intent on attacking the "Judeo-Christian tradition" do not seem to get past the first chapter of Genesis and the word *dominion* in verse twenty-eight. The human beings are told to master the earth and have dominion over it. There is some room for debate over the term *radah,* translated as dominion. The term is used elsewhere in the Bible for the relation of master to hired servant or a king to his people (Lev. 25:43; Ps.72).[12] The part of the same verse that reads "replenish the earth" should not be neglected in understanding the meaning of dominion. In any case, a single word in this mythical story of human origins did not determine the Jewish and Christian attitudes to the earth.

The frequent reference to the ecological attitude of the "Judeo-Christian tradition" is symptomatic of an abstract, blanket attack that neither locates the problem nor formulates an effective alternative. As I pointed out in chapter 1, "Judeo-Christian tradition" is largely an invention of nineteenth-century secular thought. The phrase was used for referring to the residue of the two religions that was still acceptable to modern thinkers. However, what the nineteenth century praised in the "Judeo-Christian tradition" is what the twentieth century is attacking: The supremacy of man over nature and the autonomy of the individual person.

"Judeo-Christian tradition" may be responsible for this problem, but Jewish and Christian religions are another story. That is, some people seem to confuse Christianity with the secular philosophy that largely replaced it. Our ecological problems do have roots in Hebrew, Greek, early Christian, and medieval Christian worlds. But the ecological crisis emerged as Christian influence began to wane. In the nineteenth century, Auguste Comte was certainly intent on "man's limitless rule of creation," but he correctly understood that Christian thought was a chief obstacle to his scheme. In Comte's vision, humanity is the "Great Being, achieved when man masters nature and gains direct control of his destiny."[13]

The language of "man over nature" had been developed by Comte's predecessors in the seventeenth and eighteenth centuries. Scientific discoveries and technological innovation held out the hope of turning the tables on nature. Nature had always been on top, controlling man; now it was man's turn. The sexual imagery Francis Bacon used was integral to the whole pattern of thought. Man was to establish a "chaste and lawful marriage between mind and nature." The new science provided a "nuptial couch for the mind and the universe."[14] Note that the marriage is between *mind* and universe. The man on top of nature is the disembodied mind of man, free to penetrate from the outside. The claim so frequently made today, that medieval Christianity placed man on top of nature, would have amused the early modern scientists and technologists. Only with the new knowledge and its resulting power did man finally have hope of being liberated from and triumphing over nature.

There seems to be agreement today on what the problem is: Man is outside nature and above nature. The solution would seem to be obvious: Man should come inside nature; man should not be above but equal. Much of ecological literature does in fact assume that such a reversal is the answer. Unfortunately, reversals of language are often not an escape; they perpetuate the very image embodied by the language. In this case, "man and nature" is hopelessly inadequate language to explore the relations of men and women, human and nonhuman animals, living beings and their environment.

HIERARCHY

The image that guided western thought up to a few centuries ago was a "chain of being(s)."[15] It was a hierarchy not of man and nature but of every kind of thing. Philosophers and theologians believed that once God had decided to create, he had to create every kind; there could be no missing links in the chain. Each kind had its place and its importance. No one could give an exact location to each species; however, the humans were somewhere near the middle of the chain. Even in its most literal sense, such a chain is more descriptive, more open to scientific and artistic detail, than either a hierarchy of "man and nature" or its proclaimed alternative: no hierarchy at all.

I bring up here one of the most frequently attacked words in ecological writing: *hierarchy*. To most writers, the only image of hierarchy seems to be a pyramid, with "man" occupying the pinnacle and all of "nature" trampled under his feet.[16] The alternative to hierarchy is assumed to be egalitarianism, not just equality among the humans but among all the species. Paul Taylor, for example, attacks the idea that humans are "thought of as carrying on a higher grade of existence when compared with the so called 'lower orders' of life. The biocentric outlook precludes a hierarchic view of nature."[17]

Neither Taylor's book nor other pronouncements on the evils of hierarchy convince me that the claim is intelligible and that the advocacy can be made without self-contradiction and absurdity. Why is "biocentrism" not a hierarchic preference? How does writing a book on anything escape "value gradients"? As a position to be advocated, a nonhierarchic world is senseless. But unfortunately as a description of the way things have been moving, the elimination of hierarchy may have some ring of truth. Wendell Berry writes of the present that "it is as though Noah's Ark has just landed and opened its doors. Every creature is hesitating, not knowing where to go or what to do."[18] The humans are the most free and therefore the most confused of all. "If all things were equal," continues Berry, "all places would be in dispute, to be contended for. The result would be a free-for-all, which in turn could only result either in a restoration of hierarchy or in total annihilation."[19]

Short of annihilation, our choice is between a hierarchy based on sheer power or a hierarchy based on the cycles of life. The first refers to a one-way exercise of power, from oppressor to oppressed. The second is based on several kinds of exchanges of power. In the exquisite texture of life on earth, the more complex organisms depend upon lesser forms of life. Ultimately, in a cyclical pattern, everything depends on everything else.

This interdependence is presumably the reason for the insistence on equality. Each kind plays a part; no kind should be disparaged or destroyed. But each creature has its own unique form, with some creatures being more unique (more nearly unique) than others. The excitement, the beauty, the wonder of life on earth is that no two humans, no two snowflakes, are the same. E-quality (not quality) is desirable in a few aspects of life (for example, when appearing in court), but it is not a practical or desirable characteristic in most of life.

A strange facet of much ecological writing is that while it concerns the *cycle* of life, its imagery is all straight lines. The third chapter of Roderick Nash's *The Rights of Nature* is entitled "Ecology Widens the Circle," but neither in that chapter nor in the whole book is there a hint of circular, cyclical, or spherical imagery.[20] Writers who object to "man standing above" want "man standing next to." The only imagined alternative to above seems to be below. The solution that is offered to "man outside nature" is "man inside nature."

I said that the premodern West was largely governed by the metaphor of a chain of being. One can imagine such a chain as a plumb line, a single undifferentiated line from top to bottom. But the image was more complex, both in quality and direction. The human beings, it must be repeated, were not at the top but in the middle. Furthermore, the humans did not progress to the top by climbing up the steps above them. Their vocation was to go out to the other earthly creatures and return to themselves. The whole of being was present right where they were; they were to stay in their place, which was the center.

In human experience the chain was more like a circular bracelet than a plumb line. Even in Plotinus, the philosopher best known for the chain of being, circular image predominates; being is a kind of chorus in which the One is found in the song as well as the singers. In Thomas Aquinas's grand metaphysical scheme, the movement of intellect is out-around-back to reach the plentitude of being. Such movement is found in the Creator and in his chief representative on earth.[21]

The main religious image of hierarchy is not a pyramid but concentric circles, "a wheel within a wheel" (Ezek. 1:16). I suggest that this is the image that contemporary ecology needs. The only effective alternative to "man on top" is "men and women at the center." The man on top is not a flesh-and-blood individual. The "man" in this case refers to the supposedly unique characteristic (in Meaning A) that separates man from beast: the rational, penetrating, coercive mind.

In contrast, at the center is not only "a man" but men and women. The relation between men and women is perhaps the ultimate symbol for Meaning B of uniqueness. Nearly all religions have sensed that the human being is a microcosm; the human is the "workshop of all creation."[22] Within the human, the relation between men and women symbolizes the relation of human and nonhuman. The men and women at the center recognize that everything surrounding them is a sister, a brother—is indeed themselves. The humans' existence is an incorporation or incarnation of all earthly life.

The logic in Jewish and Christian traditions could be helpful in ecology today. An anti-Christian bias may be blinding ecologists to what is in front of their eyes and surrounding them on all sides. I have argued in previous chapters that the Bible is a book of peculiar logic in which those who claim to have power are revealed as weak and those who are vulnerable reveal a surprising strength. At the center are the people Israel and Jesus of Nazareth. A universal truth is revealed in their sufferings: Only out of patient endurance is life reborn and justice restored.

Those who are chosen by God are not placed in a high position and given coercive power. On the contrary, the chosen are placed at the center, to represent all. Such representation occurs by being open to all and, in some sense, by including all. The chosen one is a microcosm, embodying in itself the whole world. Each thing is not equal to every other thing; some are chosen to bear greater responsibility. They have the power to listen, to discover the other, and to answer for all.

In the Bible, Israel and Jesus are chosen within humanity. But there is a larger pattern of chosenness to the story. Ultimately, the chosen people are people, the human beings. Jews are a stand-in for all humanity, and Christianity has the effect of heightening the centrality of person. A big claim, but not an arrogant claim, is made for humanity. The importance of the human race does not depend on size or the power to dominate. Scientific discoveries have not essentially changed the question. As Chesterton notes, "it is quite futile to argue that man is small compared to the cosmos; for man was always small compared to the nearest tree."[23] In their vulnerability, that is, their power to receive and respond, human beings are the place of meaning in the world.

The mathematical sciences of the sixteenth and seventeenth centuries began as a rejection of this logic. What was now to count were objectivity, neutrality, rationality, and, as far as is possible, the elimination of the human subject. Unfortunately, much of contemporary writing is strapped to this premise. When measuring the distance between planets, one can almost forget the human observer. But in asking many questions about the texture of life on earth (for example, the relation between animal and human worlds), the elimination of the humans—their distinctiveness, their (near) uniqueness—is self-defeating.[24]

ANTHROPOCENTRISM

One of the accusations that Lynn White, Jr., made in his 1967 essay was that "Christianity is the most anthropocentric religion the world has seen."[25] He may be right. Certainly, the centrality of the humans is the glory of Christianity (and Judaism). The message was that the humans—each unique person—embody the cosmos and are the centers of meaning. Modern humanism in the West liked that part of Christianity and tried to build a new religion on that one dogma. The problem is: Can you have man at the center of creation if there is no creator? More basically, is there any center? The insistence of humanistic thinkers that human life is all-important was up against a logic that went from displacing the earth from the center of the solar system to displacing the idea of center at all. Arthur Lovejoy notes the big change begun in the sixteenth century: "The change from a geocentric to a heliocentric system was less momentous than the change from a heliocentric to an accentric one."[26]

Like the term hierarchy, there are few words used so pejoratively in ecological writing as anthropocentrism. In fact, this latter word is used as a kind of summary of everything that is wrong with the "Judeo-Christian tradition." Where nineteenth-century humanists saw the one redeeming feature of Christianity, twentieth-century ecology sees the worst quality of "Judeo-Christian tradition."

I have no great enthusiasm for the clumsy term anthropocentrism. Unlike the term hierarchy (a sacred order) whose elimination would be a real loss, "anthropocentrism" is a recent invention that has become popular as accusation. My argument here is that if the word is going to be used, it should not be as a slogan that obstructs imaginative and practical examination of what the problem is and what can be done about it.

The worst disease anyone can have is one in which the name of the cure has been given to the disease. There is no way to begin looking for the cure if everyone is calling that the disease. Such a confusion is engendered by the term anthropocentrism, which is taken to mean that man is perched on a pinnacle at the top of nature. I agree that the problem is an image of man on top, but the solution is flesh-and-blood humans at the center, that is, an *anthropos*-centered world. Calling the image of man on top anthropocentrism makes no sense, because the disease is a lack of centeredness. The cure for this disease of isolation and illusion is to return the man to the center of his body, his person to the center of a community of women and men, and the human species to its place in the middle of the cosmos.

I cite an analogy, or what is perhaps a manifestation of the same problem. There are many attempts to "decentralize" bureaucratic organizations; the attempts are doomed to fail. You cannot decentralize a bureaucracy, because what it lacks is centeredness. You could "de-top" a bureaucracy, but that is a fundamentally different image. In fact, the way to de-top a bureaucracy is by centralizing power: each person having a center, each small community having a center. The ideal alternative to a pyramidic bureaucracy is a well-ordered series of concentric circles. Power flows in toward the center and outward from the center.

Attempts at decentralizing bureaucracies begin by the man (usually) at the top announcing that power belongs to the people. He hands down some of his power to his lieutenants, who are to hand down some of that to their underlings. If any power does eventually trickle to the bottom, no one is likely to be interested in that kind of power. The people at the bottom may have believed the announcement of reform and may have started organizing their own communal base of power. With that kind of movement there is inevitable confusion; so after a decent interval of this confusion, the man at the top announces that the reform has not worked; it has been proved that the people are not ready for power. For the good of everyone, there-fore, the power must be restored to the center (that is, the top).

The term anthropocentric can have two meanings. One is a simple fact, the other a debatable perception of how the world should be. The first meaning is an acknowledgment that at the center of human speech, human thought, every picturing of the world, is a human subject. The term envi-ronment suggests this fact of life. Humans are surrounded by a world; they perceive that world from the center of it. In this sense, each human indi-vidual is egocentric. Wherever I perceive the world, whatever I perceive the world to be, I am at the center of the perception.

Egocentric is a term that usually carries a negative note. The individual, who expects as an infant that the world should cater to his or her demands, is supposed to grow up and discover that other people are also important. By an extension of this idea, we use ethnocentric as a negative term. One group of people who think they are superior to everyone else can be dan-gerous. The use of the word anthropocentric seems to have developed from what purports to be a further extension of this logic. Actually, it misun-derstands the logic and leads to the absurdity of no moral position at all. The *anthropos* is the ethical center of thought and speech. Here is the link to the second meaning of anthropocentric.

The second meaning is in regard to how one imagines or conceives the world to be. The first meaning is the picturing; this second is the picture. What *place* do humans have in the picture? If they are to take the morally responsible place, it will be in the center of the picture. Any other place is a flight from responsibility. At its best, Christianity led from the factual kind of anthropocentrism to the second kind, the moral ideal of anthro-pocentrism. At its worst—and this is Christianity's ecological failure—it glorified the individual male instead of praising men, women, and their physical environment. Thus Christianity and, to a lesser extent, Judaism are culpable. They made it too easy for the early modern era to talk about the abstraction of "man" on top of another abstraction, "nature."[27]

The condemnation of anthropocentrism as an extension of egocentrism and ethnocentrism does not express a greater humility. On the contrary, the humans' proper humility comes from listening to their brothers and sisters all around them and then exercising care in all their dealings. Humans are the only morally responsible animals we know of; their responses can affect all life on earth. Pitting the biocentric against the anthropocentric is senseless. Central to earth is life, and central to life is human life. The question, for those who wish life on earth and not human life to be central, is why they assume that earth is central. If one is really going to be egalitarian, isn't everything on earth an insignificant speck? Is not talk of biocentrism a pre-Copernican anachronism?

The existence of the science of ecology presumes that meaning is better than meaninglessness. There would be no talk of equality of the species or biocentrism unless meaningful questions emerged in human speech. We do not know if there is some greater realm beyond the human, and we are still discovering to what degree nonhuman animals share our perceptions of meaning. A religious group that sees the human as expressive of the divine can hold to an anthropocentric world that is also theocentric. The nonreligious person does not have that flexibility. He or she is forced to hope that this is an anthropocentric world—that there is meaning to human life—despite much evidence to the contrary.

In practice, the Christian believer and the secular thinker share much of the same belief and much of the same doubt. The Christian doctrine of incarnation is difficult to make any sense of, if imagined as God stepping down from heaven to pretend being a man. But as thinkers from Paul of Tarsus to Teilhard de Chardin have speculated, perhaps there is some much greater drama at issue. The humans must cling to the center because they are the most unique beings brought forth on earth. However, they are not totally unique. Although tiny in stature even among tiny earth's creatures, the unique human being is the fragile center of all meaning so far available.

Uniqueness in Meaning B is another way of describing this geocentric/biocentric/anthropocentric experience. The increasing inclusiveness is toward the center of concentric circles or toward the center of a sphere. Successive levels of creatures incorporate previous levels of life. Finally, at the very center, is the glory and danger of the whole process. Other living things on earth have natures; they are born with well-formed dimensions, they mature, they die. Human nature is nature going beyond itself, the hole at the middle of nature where all natures meet. Humans are not inside nature as something is inside a box; humans are the inside of nature, in the sense of being the incorporation of all natures.

Is such a picture a claim to human superiority? In some sense it obviously is. If one values value, if one considers meaning more important than size, the humans have always made the claim, and no one else on earth has made a counterclaim. The problem is with the intoxication that comes with the obvious fact that humans can do more than amoebas, that humans can name (a kind of control) the other animals. One of the earliest extant paintings is found on the walls of Lascaux. A man has thrown a spear at an animal; now the human looks like he is just discovering that in that kind of conflict and in the attempt to dominate, the humans are not necessarily superior. What each human being has to discover (and what "modern man" has found particularly difficult) is an ultimate paradox of power: Coercive, dominating, violent imposition from the outside can be an impressive-looking power, but it is the human temptation to evil.

The humans' lasting power appears as weakness, a vulnerability, a suffering from other forces. The humans' superior form of strength is an openness, a receptivity to everyone and everything. In Christian mystical tradition, the human is called a "no-thing," an empty place at the center. For example, in the paintings of Hildegard of Bingen, the human egg is often at the center of the choirs of angels and the rest of creation. Sometimes, however, at the center of such paintings is simply an empty hole.[28]

The survival and sanity of the human race depend upon its moral responsibility, its ability to listen carefully and then to act compassionately. When it comes to responsibility, the humans are the greatest. When it comes to accepting this responsibility, the humans are easily tempted by the lure of liberation: escape from their place, flight from their bodies, and refusal to sympathize with other living creatures.

I am amazed that so many writers casually assume that anthropocentrism is equivalent to utilitarianism, that is, if the humans are the center then everything else becomes mere means to an end.[29] Actually, if man is at the *top*, then everything below is turned into a stepping stone on the way to the last point. The only way to avoid means-to-end exploitation is by placing humans at the center. Everything moves toward the center, everything moves from the center; there is no end in the sense of termination point. Is everything *for* the human? Not in the sense that things are reduced to something less than themselves. But everything is for the human in the sense of what is represented by the human and what is at least potentially under the care of the human.

Human life should not be reduced to a mentality of possession, use, and consumption. Generally speaking, if human beings make something, they have the right to possess it and use it. They have no such rights over living things (extending to topsoil, oceans, and mineral formations). They have these gifts on loan, to be used in such a way that the resources do not dry up. Only at the center do the humans have a 360-degree view of the world, of what they are responsible to and responsible for. Only at the center are the humans kept in place by their kin. Nicholas Johnson, of the Federal Communications Commission, used to say that the way to keep a government official upright is to lean on him from all sides. The humans have to be kept in sight from every side; their environment is not just to surround them but to provide mutual exchange. Otherwise, the humans are liable to start thinking that they own the world and can do anything they please.

OUR NEXT OF KIN

Some further words should be said about the closest circle to the human. What to call this relation is a question that reveals the problem. The words "human animals and nonhuman animals" suggest that the humans are simply one species of animal. That would be to evade human responsibility for the animal world. On the other hand, the more traditional language of "man and beast" does not accept the kinship: Humans really are found among the animals, representing the whole animal world. The reality cannot be grasped without the uniqueness of Meaning B. Human life is neither one of a kind nor a different kind of animal. Humans differ from (the other) animals neither by degree nor kind, but by an increasing inclusiveness of degree and kind. I will use the term "human-animal" to indicate this closest of kinship together with the recognition and acceptance of responsibility.[30]

The aspect of ecology that has received the most popular attention is the "animal rights movement." The positive thing to be said immediately is that if many people have become more sensitive to animal suffering, this development represents great progress. It would mean, at least, that many adults are rediscovering what most children know: Each deer, horse, wolf, or hamster has its own uniqueness and therefore suffers. To cause animals to suffer simply for the entertainment of humans (for example, in the making of movies) is evil. Where humans believe that some suffering is necessary (for purposes of food or medical experimentation), every effort should be made to keep the suffering to a minimum.

The drawback to the animal rights movement is that it is using a moral category that is severely limited and, as a result, the category does not extend all the way into the animal world, let alone the nonanimal world.[31] The animal rights movement, instead of being too radical, is not a big enough revolution. At the most, it might save some chimps, dolphins, whales, deer, and so forth, but the saving will be a pyrrhic victory unless an ecological movement alters the relation of human-animal to all animals and all life.

The idea of individual rights has roots in both Greek and Hebrew traditions, but rights language became our moral currency only in the era of western enlightenment. Not accidentally, it was the era when man got on top of nature; man has rights, things do not. Today's advocates of animal rights are correct in sensing that when there is a single line drawn between man and thing, then a dog or a dolphin is more like a man than like a thing. Thus the rights line had been drawn between "man" and things of "nature." Now some of the (other) animals are being brought up across the line.

This widening of the language of rights has much to commend it. Even though political and civil rights have not been gained by every human individual, we can be working at the extension of rights to elephants, whales, and the whole world of mammals. This extension is not an easy, logical movement, from men to women to ... white mice. Human rights, it has to be realized, were asserted against the "natural world" as much as against human dictators. *Rights* is "a legal term describing privileges of each contractor. It is a competitive, confrontational term (they have rights against one another), not a term which helps to arbitrate such clashes."[32] That the attempt to protect laboratory animals causes bitter controversy is not surprising; the assertion of one set of rights is pitted against another set of rights.

Where humans can recognize unique individuality, then the extension of rights is consistent. That could include more than animals.[33] In legal language, a tree could have "standing" as well as an animal. When someone deliberately poisoned an eight-hundred-year-old tree in Austin, Texas, the perpetrator was prosecuted. On the other hand, not every animal can or should be protected by law. Humans recognize that a housefly has no discernible individuality. If all the eggs of one fly were hatched and were to live, it would by the seventh generation have several trillion offspring.[34] Nature seems to have something else in mind with this vast profusion of life. No one seriously means that *every* animal (each individual of every species) has an equal right to protection of its life, because no one can even imagine what such a proposition means. The human vocation is to join with forces of nature in their patterns of restraint, balance, and interaction.

The claim that animal rights language gets us away from anthropocentrism is a peculiar assumption about where this language comes from and how it is applied. Peter Singer writes in complaint of a writer who says that "rights are uniquely human in origin and application."[35] Nothing greater could be said of rights than that they are uniquely human in origin; they emerged with the emergence of human uniqueness. Rights are also uniquely human in application, which is not to say that they are exclusively the possession of human individuals. Because human uniqueness is one of increasing inclusiveness and a representing of earth's creatures, then uniquely human rights extend—with no single, obvious cutoff point—to the nonhuman world.

What is obvious is that some animals who live with us, in our homes or in the field next door, should be extended the protection of moral rights. What may not be so obvious, but is morally imperative, is that no species be destroyed, even if it seems merely pesty to the humans (as in the dangerous word pesticide). The humans did not make any species; they have no right to destroy any of them. If a virus is a human killer, then humans have to find ways to restrain the species and keep it away from human contact.

Is it utilitarianism to maintain those conditions that make human life possible? If humans are to preserve and develop their life, then their rights will at times take precedence over other creatures. The issue then is negotiating with all creatures concerning particular advantages and disadvantages. Humans have to clear space for settlements; the individual rights of each insect in the ground do not come first. However, that is not equivalent to saying that because humans have greater rights than insects, they can bulldoze and spray their way through every tract of land. Humans are more important, but not every wish and fashion of theirs is more important. Restraint is a word that should never be far from human lips. I suspect that the conservationist was exaggerating when he said, "I would kill a man before a rattlesnake." On occasions when the choice is necessary, the man should come first. But many times the choice is between the life of a magnificent creature (for example, an elephant or a rattlesnake) and satisfaction of a human appetite for fancy food or decoration.

The human animal at the center will have to accept that there are many animals that he or she cannot see; living organisms overflow in abundant mystery. Furthermore, the elephants, giraffes, and bear in the front row block the view. Human thought and language tend to blur distinct beings into general categories. A "love for nature" or a "love of life" is an admirable feeling, but it needs concrete expression. The way to love life is to test out one's concern for animals by caring for this cat, this dog, this cow, this lizard. Such animals can be part of our community. I think it is a mangling of language to talk about "the monkey community." Nevertheless, it is entirely appropriate to talk of the human community that can extend to monkeys, dogs, or horses. To the extent that such animals are unique, they can share in human love and compassion. Furthermore, these animals become more unique as humans share love and compassion with them.[36]

While praising Jane Goodall's book on the Gombe chimp, Stephen Jay Gould is highly critical in one respect: "I was shaken by occasional statements in the worst tradition of the chain of being: 'It is evident that chimpanzees have made considerable progress along the road to humanlike love and compassion'." Gould thinks that such a way of looking at chimps is unscientific, and he asks: "What are we missing because we have made ourselves for reasons of blind vanity and hubris the measure of all things?"[37]

Although some of her phrases might be questionable, Jane Goodall understands chimps because she uses humanlike love and compassion as the measure. Her language is not one of "blind vanity and hubris." Chimps are rightly said to have a degree of love and compassion. But no one would use these words to describe chimps unless one knew of love and compassion in human beings. Indeed, the words love, compassion, and for that matter, any words of description, have to be born in human beings. Goodall is not forcing the chimps toward being humans; she is understanding them with *humanlike* qualities. The humans have a greater capacity than chimps for love and compassion; they also have a greater responsibility. After twenty-five years of living with chimps, Jane Goodall knows this, and I dare say the chimps do too.

In the logic of uniqueness, the choice is not between "man as the measure of all things" and scientific objectivity. Instead, the choice is between man at the top as exploiter and human beings at the center as nurturers of life ("replenishers of the earth"). Plato's objection to Protagoras was not that he had said "man is the measure of all things," but rather that *man the user* is the measure of all things.[38] If man thinks of wind only to move his boat, said Plato, he mistakes what the wind is. The measure of all things is the human being as poet, as nurturer, as contemplator, as lover, as painter, as athlete.

Jewish and Christian traditions are not incompatible with a reverence for the "sentient" animal, our next of kin. Starting with the first chapter of Genesis, it should have been clear that we sit at the same table with the (other) animals. Many prescriptions of the Hebrew Bible concern taking care of beasts of the field, and giving them proper rest. The covenant, as noted in chapter 4, includes all living flesh. One can hardly deny, however, that the record of Jewish and Christian religions has not been outstanding on this point. Other religions, for example, Buddhist or Native American, have a better record in practice.

In their haste to affirm the "uniqueness of man," Jewish and, more so, Christian religions jumped over some of the concentric circles on their way to the center. "The poets and storytellers in this tradition have tended to be interested in the extraordinary activities of 'great men' — actions unique in grandeur, such as may occur only once in the history of the world."[39] What is now evident is that the jump to the unique feats of great men may undermine the genuine uniqueness of ordinary men and women and non-human animals. When that happens, Christianity is left with the uniqueness of Meaning A — an aggressive and dangerous claim to superiority by great men that leaves the rest of human-animals and other animals gasping for breath. If every man and woman is to be unique, then one has to recognize the uniqueness of our closest kin.

THE GIFT OF FOOD

Although the extension of rights to some animals is one of the important moral projects of our time, an animal rights movement is only a small part of ecology/environmentalism. When the movement tries to seize all the moral currency, it can be a dangerous distraction from the need to reorient human-nonhuman relations. This concluding section will comment on these relations, especially as manifested in the nature of food.

The term *food chain* was coined in 1927, the word *ecosystem* in 1935.[40] Both terms are common today, and both are helpful reminders to the humans. Like the words animal and nature, ecosystem and food chain refer to realities that humans cannot remove themselves from. But neither is the human just one link in the system, similar to all the other links. Ecosystem and food chain as transfers of energy have to be kept in tension with community, person, and freedom. Ecosystem cannot substitute without remainder for these human qualities which constitute the hole at the center of the system.

An ecosystem is a relatively autonomous part of the world wherein a complete cycle of life, death, and rebirth occurs. A forest, for example, contains the necessary variety of living forms and the environment in which these forms interact. An ocean is obviously an ecosystem containing untold forms of plant and animal life. But a lake and even at times a mud puddle can be an ecosystem with a cycle of life and death transpiring within its borders.

An ecosystem has three indispensable elements: producers, consumers, and decomposers. The main producers are green plants, those forms of life that transfer the sun's light into carbohydrates. They do their work quietly; their modest appearance, starting with microscopic algae, belies their importance. The consumers are the animals; they take in products of plant life. The animal world transfers energy in an inefficient way, but that is just the cost of staying alive. The decomposers—bacteria and fungi—have the most thankless job; they return animal remains to a form in which the material can go into production again. Each of the three levels depends on the other two. While life takes varying forms of complexity, each level is equally important to the cycle of living beings.

The human beings make their appearance in the middle of the animal world. They can perform dazzling feats, but they are also the great consumers, the inefficient and unpredictable element in the biological cycle. The humans are "the center of all surprise in the world."[41] They are able to transform nature(s), an ability they could not abandon if they were to try. The danger is, because they cannot grasp either the concept or image of interconnection of all things, they can call something progress which is in fact the destruction of a larger ecosystem.

The most primitive form of agriculture is already the creation of an artificial ecosystem. The humans are animals of art and artifice. The question is always whether the artifice is in accord with the rhythms and cadences of nature. Not everything that can be done should be done by them. Religion throughout the centuries has been a restraint here. The last few centuries have seen an unprecedented break with those restraints. Exorbitant demands have been made upon the land, the forests, the rivers, and the oceans.

Everything has tended to become subordinate to the business deal, that is, contracts of investment, interest, selling price, and profit. This relation is an ancient one, practiced by most people. The Hebrew Bible had restricted this relation to the outsider; one should not treat a member of the community on these terms. The Christian ideal was to do away with the outsider and recognize all people as members of the same body. The ideal failed to be realized; in fact, the business relation of commodity exchange reasserted itself in western history to such an extent that it has threatened to obscure every other relation.

What traditionally complemented and restrained the business relation is the relation of gift giving. When anthropologists first started studying gift exchange in tribal religion, the logic of the relation seemed mysterious and primitive. The gift had symbolic and sacred meaning as it passed from one tribe member to another. In some North American tribes, the gift was called a *potlatch,* a term sometimes given to all such gifts.

What has begun to emerge recently is that the cycle of life has many of the characteristics of the potlatch or gift relation. Human life is possible because of the many gifts that are received each day. The most dramatic gift is food, something that human beings must be grateful for several times daily. Not by accident, the potlatch was often food. In this case, the gift is consumed and another gift of food is passed on.

Food cannot be stored as wealth; it has to die in order that life can continue. A plant is a gift of food for an animal; one animal is a gift for another. The gift should be received with a proper ritual of thanksgiving. "In the case of food, literally, and in the case of much else metaphorically, we die into one another's lives and live into one another's deaths."[42]

The religious practice of sacrifice acknowledges that the humans are in the cycle of birth, death, and rebirth. The cycle of Jewish and Christian holy days was integrated with the cycle of the seasons. Even if they live in an urban setting, humans should not forget that they live on the earth with creatures who are producers of food that others consume. In their turn, the consumers become food for other consumers, and the material for reproduction of new life forms.

One could view this process as a horrible spectacle of endless killing; nature's balance is achieved by ruthless means. However, one can also accept the part of creature and recognize that we are part of some great undertaking beyond our imaginations. "To live, we must daily break the body and shed the blood of Creation. When we do this knowingly, lovingly, skillfully, reverently, it is a sacrament. When we do it ignorantly, greedily, clumsily, destructively, it is a desecration."[43]

In E. M. Forster's *A Passage to India*, the Englishman says: "You cannot eat your cake and have it, even in the world of spirit." To which the Muslim replies: "If you are right, there is no point in any friendship." It is precisely the logic of gift relation that the only way to have your cake is to eat it, the only way to pass on the cake is to consume it. The fundamental structure of the life cycle is that we cannot possess goods by holding on to them, that to consume is to reproduce, that a gift has to keep moving until it returns to the giver.[44]

Gifts can be exchanged between two people, but the danger here is that gift giving slips toward commodity exchange. In our culture, days like Christmas become a balancing of price tags. Gift giving becomes an anguishing chore of guessing what he will give me or remembering how expensive was her gift last year.

One way out of this narrowed-down world is to give a gift that has no price tag. A child's gift that is worthless in money terms may be invaluable as a gift. Likewise, adult love and affection cannot be evaluated in money terms. Another way out, practiced in tribal religions, is to move the gift in a circle. The wider the circle, the less likely are the participants to act as salespersons or investors. The sacrifice to God is the acknowledgment of the widest possible circle, the complete cycle of creation that encompasses all of nature's gifts.

Some writers refer to the food chain as the traditional chain of being turned upside down. That misses the point: The food chain is circular. Ancient religions lacked the scientific description of producer, consumer, and decomposer, but they usually had a strong sense of circular imagery. Like Ezekiel's vision of life as a wheel within a wheel, images were complex constructions of increasing inclusiveness, with movement toward a center point that is never reached.

Around the still point of a turning world, life continues to rush forth in a "round river."[45] A theoretically convincing and practically effective ecology needs circular — or more exactly, the three-dimensional spherical image — to describe the emergence of the (very) unique human-animal. This creature can either perfect the flow of gifts through responsible interaction from the center, or assuredly, it will desecrate the gift of life from a spiritual isolation at the top.

7

Human Development

Uniqueness unto Death

The unique human being, as described in the previous chapter, has a "geography," that is, an ecological context. One aspect of that geography was not elaborated, namely, the *human* surroundings of the human individual. The human species is itself very unique, but the most unique accomplishment on earth is the human individual whose uniqueness depends on interaction with other human beings. This chapter begins, therefore, with a discussion of interhuman geography, that is, the relation between the human individual and the human community.

In addition to examining this most central circle of biotic geography, the present chapter looks at the history of the human individual. From interaction with the entire biotic system, including other human beings, the individual person changes over time. Like other animals, the humans are born, they grow, they decline, they die. Nothing is more obvious than this steady and inexorable march from birth to death. And yet, behind the surface, there is a mysterious depth in the way each individual encounters the interval between birth and death.

The human beings are born unique; as indicated earlier, the phrase unique person is practically a redundancy. Meaning B of uniqueness emerged with the idea of person. However, the assertion of uniqueness always implies more unique (or more nearly unique) than something else. If the human individual is considered on its own, the comparison of uniquenesses can be between temporal versions of the same individual. The successful development of a human individual means that the person becomes more (nearly) unique in the course of his or her lifetime. The culmination of such unique development is the act of dying, which is the most unique of the individual's experiences.

This chapter has three preliminary sections that converge upon the fourth. The first section is a reflection on the relation between person and community. This relation is the precondition and the context of the individual's history. The second section is a reflection on the nature of time, particularly the contrasting meanings of uniqueness in relation to the present. The third section concerns the term *development*, one of the distinguishing words of the modern era; once again there are two sharply contrasting meanings of development. All three of these sections feed into the concluding reflection on human dying. In this last consideration, I introduce the Jewish and Christian symbol of resurrection, which I interpret to be the final affirmation of Meaning B of uniqueness.

In the sections on community and development, I draw some broad pictures of what constitutes human possibilities. I do so without offering scientific data or embracing one of the theories of "human development." It is not my wish to reject the helpful information about human individuals that has been pieced together in this century. However, I do resist the contemporary assumption that "human development" is a subset of the field of psychology. While I take what I can from psychology about how people develop, I assume that numerous fields of study are necessary for the full study of human development.

To the social or psychological expert, I make the same statement of limits I did to the experts on the Holocaust, Christian theology, and ecology. I am not pretending to be an expert who can substitute my voice for the voices that speak with authority in each of these areas. My interest in this chapter, as it is throughout the book, is to raise a single question of language. How does the term *unique* get used, and how better might it be used to clarify controversies in this area? As in the previous chapters, the distinction between Meanings A and B of uniqueness illuminates the question of development unto death.

PERSON AND COMMUNITY

Describing the ecological crisis in chapter 6, I said that one could interpret it as the triumph of Meaning A of uniqueness over Meaning B. Human beings are a confusing combination of the two uniquenesses. Within Meaning A, humans can never leave behind a concern for the exclusive control of their space; every human being resists a knife put into his or her ribs. However, this unavoidable concern needs to be placed within an overall attitude toward life that emphasizes receptivity and an ever-increasing inclusiveness.

When the context has been prepared and the person gives consent, the individual's identity is not threatened by the presence of other people, even if the other person is spatially very close. Indeed, entrance into one of the body's orifices and acceptance of such entrance can be among the pleasures of human life. This fact might suggest that the relation of men and women is one of the links in understanding the relation of human and nonhuman within Meaning B of uniqueness.

Much of ecological discussion is trapped in the categories of "man and nature." This obscurantist phrase hides the fact that some men dominate other men, some men dominate women, and other oppressive relations operate within the abstraction of *man*.[1] There is an attitude inherent to the human condition, perhaps more prevalent among men than women, that says: My life needs preserving and protecting; the intruder must be repulsed and, if necessary, destroyed. When this attitude is let loose, it can overwhelm other considerations. The white European invaders, for example, had a more pronounced attitude of individualism, possessiveness, and aggression than did the North American natives; however, the latter group had their own share of death and destruction.

The language of "man and nature" provides no room for maneuvering and negotiating. Worse, it identifies the opponents as the human race on one side and all of (nonhuman) nature on the other. This picture implies that whatever warring there is within humanity is peripheral to the contest with nature, a distraction from the main war. In that case, the bears, elephants, and kangaroos should be worrying that the humans might settle their differences and stop their wars. Then a unified "man" could launch the final assault to control "nature."

The above reasoning is a possible interpretation of how intra-species and inter-species conflicts are related, but it seems to me all wrong. The attitude within "man" that leads to indiscriminate destruction works its havoc on human and nonhuman alike. Human wars are not kind to the ecological system; conversely, kindness and compassion between human beings is not especially dangerous to most animals. There are situations in which otherwise kind human beings are oblivious to the sufferings of many animals, but that is a problem of ignorance that can be corrected.

A human grasping for the wrong kind of uniqueness will lead an individual to strike out at feared competitors, whether the recipient of violence is man, woman, child, or cat. A human individual who does this is often described as acting like an animal or a wild beast. The accusation is unfair to the animals. The violent lunge after uniqueness is specifically human; it springs from a heightened rationality that is at war with its own biological basis. Rape, for example, as is now generally accepted, is not an overflow of animal eroticism; it is a highly rational act of violence to ward off a perceived threat from some stereotype of female control.

I would therefore posit that the relation of person and community is not the opposite of the relation of "man and beast." Indeed, there is much that can be learned about human relations by studying human–nonhuman and nonhuman–nonhuman relations. Humans have to learn that their most important uniqueness does not depend on their being bigger and tougher than the other animals. And each human individual has to learn a similar lesson as he or she grows up among humankind; pretentious claims to superiority are not the best policy. A man can say to his dog: "I'm unique and you're not." The man gets no argument, even though the statement is inaccurate. He perhaps feels comforted by thinking himself superior to his dog. But if he says to his brother-in-law, "I'm unique and you're not," he could get an earful in return. When this issue of a unique self surfaces in childhood, it is one of the greatest problems confronting the fragile person: How can I be myself if there are billions of people who are just like me?

I would think there would be numerous studies of this issue of uniqueness in individual development. The issue is implied in many social and psychological studies, but the theme of uniqueness and the paradox in the term uniqueness are seldom treated at length. One of the few full-length studies is *Uniqueness: The Human Pursuit of Difference.*[2] The authors, Snyder and Franklin, refer at the beginning of the book to an "apparent paradox," but the paradox is real, not apparent.[3] That is, people have a desperate need to be the same as other human beings (no one wishes to be inhuman) and at the same time different (to be a self). This real paradox (an apparent contradiction) cannot be resolved by human beings; they have to learn to live with the paradox. Meaning B of uniqueness is the best way to understand this paradox.

The problem that the book addresses has become more acute in recent centuries, perhaps especially in the last few decades. Both sides of the paradox have been continually heightened. The gospel of the individual is incessantly proclaimed. "I've gotta be me" is drilled into the individual from infancy. At the same time, much of the effect of modern industrialization and technology is toward homogenization. Sheer quantity alone becomes a problem if the individual is trying to find a mark, a characteristic, an expression of personal style that no one else has. The person might seem to be succeeding in being different within the family or the neighborhood, but can he or she really withstand comparison to five or six billion?

The pressure to maintain a difference can obstruct the individual from experiencing whatever self he or she does have. Philip Slater writes: "In a society that places a value on individualism, this inability to experience oneself leads paradoxically to a cry for *more* uniqueness, more eccentricity, more individuation, thus increasing the symptoms."[4] Slater equates uniqueness with eccentricity, a term that usually has a negative meaning. To the extent that Meaning A is assumed, then eccentricity is the most likely outcome. Striving to be different, to maintain some spark of originality in dress, hair color, earrings, size of house, make of car, length of weapon, and so forth, succeeds only in throwing a person off center (ec-centric) in human terms. In contrast, Meaning B of uniqueness situates the individual more and more toward the center of the whole human race.

The thesis of Snyder and Franklin is that people are characterized by "a striving to maintain a moderate sense of dissimilarity relative to other people."[5] This formulation does very little to unravel the complexity of the problem. The authors never seem to sense the paradox within the very idea of uniqueness. They continually refer to the *pursuit* of uniqueness. If one sticks to Meaning A of uniqueness, then pursue is what one does, even if one eventually discovers that the pursuit is illusory.[6] Meaning B of uniqueness comes into play only when we stop seeking.

The paradox of finding by not seeking is central to both Jewish and Christian traditions; terms such as grace or salvation point to this experience. Not just in the modern era, though perhaps especially here, individuals seek to rise above all others in accomplishments and to secure complete control of their lives. In religious terms, they seek salvation by ordering life according to a preestablished structure of rules of success.

The religious experience consists of a change of heart, a realization that we have been encountering the world with the wrong attitudes. The most intense moments of life — experiences of compassion, love, suffering, bereavement — shake us out of our illusory assumption that our lives are under the control of the human will. As the beauty of the world, the suffering of humanity, and the sense of our own mortality are received into the center of our personal beings, Meaning B of uniqueness emerges. How does one maintain a sense of difference? By forgetting about that problem and allowing all the similarities to flow into one's life. The interweaving of all these similarities is the way an individual becomes distinctive. The greater the immersion in the common qualities of humankind, the greater the unmistakable and unique identity of the person.

The relation of similarity and difference is not a zero-sum game. When compassion, love, power — indeed any genuine human characteristic — is shared, the result is increase rather than diminishment. The personal uniqueness of Meaning B does not depend on fending off competitors to human possessions. Instead, it depends on recognition that personal existence is a gift of the human community and that one's life is an embodying of all humanity. The first thing called for is gratitude.

Person and community, therefore, are reciprocal categories; they grow together and are diminished together. Persons make up a community, and communities are composed of persons. The more one becomes a person, the greater is the community. A community is that form of unity in which persons are differentiated by becoming united. Where there is no community, there are no persons; instead, there are individuals who do not recognize a universal humanity within themselves.

When community is weak or broken, one often hears the call for heroes, powerful individuals who can rise above the rest of us and show the way. I think one has to approach with skepticism the oft-heard question: Where have all the heroes gone? Perhaps what we really need are not a few super individuals (traditionally, male individuals), but thousands or millions of persons who, in becoming unique within their communities, offer moral guidance to their own people. Occasionally, such ordinary courage rooted in ordinary communities will inspire a wider response; ancient figures like Jesus or Gautama, contemporaries like King or Gandhi are ready examples.

The uniqueness of the person is not something to be followed, as if the solution to one's own life could be found by mechanically imitating a hero or leader. However, the uniqueness of a highly developed person offers endless instructive examples for those who are willing to listen and respond in their own way. This point is misunderstood by Theodore Roszak in saying: "Uniqueness provides no grounds for contest or comparison — only for self evaluation."[7] Meaning A suggests that there is nothing to compare: my self is not your self. But the uniqueness of Meaning B invites comparison with all unique people, from each of whom we could learn something.

The author of a book on mid-life crisis begins with the premise: "I have made a deliberate attempt in this book to avoid using examples and case studies. The reason for this is that people tend to follow examples, but you and your life are unique."[8] I think the fallacy in this statement is obvious. Precisely because one's life is unique, storytelling and examples are the closest that an author can get to providing directions for personal life. The only alternative is a lot of preaching and scientific generalities.

UNIQUE PRESENTS

This section is an excursion into the nature of time, a meditation that is needed before we can look at the question of lifelong development. Theories of human development always presuppose some image of time; in fact, theories about almost anything do. If one does not examine the image of time, then the culture's dominant image of time is likely to control the discussion. In the terms of this book, that image of time will be associated with Meaning A of uniqueness. Meaning B of uniqueness will not be denied; it simply will not get a hearing.

I have dealt with time in several of the previous chapters. In those places, I considered time within the large patterns of Jewish and Christian history. In this chapter, I am narrowing the focus to individual human development. To an extent, therefore, this chapter applies to the individual what has been said about the historical group.

There is also some application in the opposite direction, a movement that might throw light on confusion about the meaning of history. It is generally said that Judaism and Christianity are historical religions, with the usual implication that other religions are not. However, prominent Jewish, Christian, and other voices take issue with both the assertion and the contrast.[9] When one gets deeply into this debate, it becomes apparent that *history* and *historical* are very complex terms. Many different questions get mixed together under the aegis of history/historical.

I have no intention of taking on this whole debate. I view this chapter as a step back from history to a simpler issue that is part of the problem. My sole interest in this section is the individual's encounter with time. What does it mean for a person to experience the present? I argue that there are two main possibilities. Either the individual experiences the present as an isolated moment between a past that has disappeared and a future that has not arrived, or the present is experienced as gathering up and recapitulating the past, with the future experienced as the quickening possibilities of the present. The first image of time is Meaning A of uniqueness; the second is Meaning B. As is always true of uniqueness, both experiences are limit cases. No one experiences the present as a totally isolated moment, although a psychopath is a person who approaches that limit.[10] Likewise, no one totally gathers all experience into the present, although some people in the act of dying may approach that limit.

UNIQUE PRESENT: MEANING A

I will now sketch out with a few more details each meaning of uniqueness in relation to time, especially to the present. Because Meaning A envelops us in the modern western world, the problem is not one of describing this image but of convincing people that it *is* an image, and it is an image that much of the world does not assume. To this day there are people who resist this image, and there are voices in the late twentieth century warning us that we cannot continue indefinitely with this image. Nonetheless, our modern mechanized and technological world is practically unthinkable without this image of time.

The fundamental characteristic of this image is that of a two-dimensional line. Often it is assumed (especially in Christian theology) that the choice of image for time is between a circle and a straight line.[11] Actually, these two are slight variations on the same linear image found throughout western history. Circular imagery was popular during the Renaissance period; far from being a sign of pessimism, the circle represented a hope that the glories of the past were not lost.[12]

In the modern period, the circle became straightened out into a horizontal line. The line had need of an arrow to indicate the direction of the future. The idea of future, as a distinct segment of time, was thus invented, and with it the dream (or dogma) of progress.[13] The nineteenth century's mass production of timepieces confirmed the social reality of a time that consists of a present moment, a past that is disappearing at the rate of sixty seconds a minute, and a future which has not arrived. In the late twentieth century, the digital clock is finally eliminating the vestiges of a circular movement to time.

The word that goes with *present* in this image is *moment*, a disappearing point between past and future. In mathematical terms, the present is a one-dimensional point that does not exist on its own. But if the past is no more, the future is not yet, and the present never really is here to stay, where is a human being (or a nonhuman animal) to stand? The answer is that no one should stand still; everyone should run toward the future. "Gatsby believed in the green light, the orgiastic future that constantly recedes before us. But no matter, tomorrow we shall run faster, stretch out our arms farther . . . "[14]

This image of time can be viewed as an optimistic one, especially at the "macro" level. The nineteenth century was convinced that "the golden age of the human species is not behind us, it is before us."[15] Although generations of immigrants who came to the United States were disappointed at what they found, they were sustained by the fervent belief that "life will be better for our children." Usually, their hopes were not entirely misplaced; life did become better in terms of less labor, more pleasure, longer lives. But despite this seeming progress of society, the individual still confronts the inevitable cycle: birth, growth, decline, death.

If time is experienced as only a series of points, then the individual seems caught in a losing situation. Within the time of Meaning A, the individual speaks of time saved, spent, wasted, lost, made up, slowed down; eventually, however, time "runs out."[16] Society may be playing a winning game, but the individual always loses. From the first moment, the individual can sense that the cards are fixed. A character in a Samuel Beckett play says: "Two and a half billion seconds. Hard to believe so few."[17] The irony, of course, is that two and one-half billion is hardly "so few." But in the context of this image, another billion seconds would be no more satisfying. The real problem is that one can run until tired, and then all one can do is wait. "Do you believe in the life to come?" asks Clov in Beckett's *Endgame*. "Mine was always that," replies Hamm. "Moment by moment, pattering down, like the millet grains . . . and all life you wait for that to mount up to a life."[18]

Samuel Beckett's image of time as grains of sand or millets of wheat expresses nature's insistence that time cannot be reduced to one-dimensional points. "Time doesn't pass, don't pass from you, why it piles up all about you . . . it buries you grain by grain . . . buried under the sand, saying any old thing, your mouth full of sand."[19] While humans keep talking about leaving the past behind them, the past comes up to cover them. The characters in Beckett's plays and novels stubbornly wait, but they have no idea what or whom they are waiting for. In the image of time in which their lives are caught, waiting is all they can do.

UNIQUE PRESENT: MEANING B

Beckett's picture of the modern individual cannot be put aside; it is a powerful indictment of the contemporary scene. Philosopher William Barrett, late in life, wrote: "We might indicate the religious task of our time in the following way: How to let prayer re-enter the world of Samuel Beckett (which is where modernity leads us finally)."[20] I would interpret this task of "let prayer re-enter" to mean a change in the way people encounter the present, a change that includes an interiority of life, an acceptance of bodiliness, and a reestablishing of genuine interpersonal relations. All of these changes are indicated by the symbols of depth and centeredness.

In Meaning B of uniqueness, the present is best imagined as the center of a sphere. The image has to be three-dimensional so that the present is not a disappearing point along a line but rather the convergence of lines at the center of a sphere. The first meaning of present is not moment, but a relation, or a matrix of relations. To be present is to be in the presence of. To be present is to be oneself, but that requires the presence of others, both human and nonhuman. To live in the present is to resist the temptation to flee from one's body, one's people, one's place, and other dimensions of one's finitude.

Where in this image of time is the past imagined to be? It is deposited in one's body, and is the ground one stands on. An individual's past experiences have not disappeared "behind the back." For the time-full self, the past is still present.[21] The attempt to flee from what is painful in our past can only tie us more firmly to past failure. "All that we have felt, thought and willed from our earliest infancy is there, leaning over the present which is about to join it, pressing against the portals of consciousness that would fain leave it outside."[22]

The present of the individual person also contains the past of his or her people: family, tribe, nation, ultimately all humanity. From this vast, unimaginable storehouse, what comes into the light of consciousness is usually what has been gathered up, preserved, and ritualized by previous generations. The statement that Judaism or Christianity is a historical religion can easily mask the important truth that Judaism and Christianity are religions of the present, a present that includes the past. They are religions of tradition, of memory, of a living God who speaks in the present.

In this image of time, what happened ten centuries ago may be closer to the surface than what happened ten years ago. In tradition's view, the measure of what is important is not finally determined by "the small and arrogant oligarchy of those who happen to be walking about."[23] Of course, if the world of a thousand or three thousand years ago is to have its voice heard, then particular rituals must be observed by a community and by individuals who willingly participate in such exercises.

Jewish tradition is unexcelled in this awareness of the past that lives within the present. The Talmud advises: "In each and every generation, let each person regard himself as though *he* had emerged from Egypt."[24] Yosef Yerushalmi explains this Jewish attitude by saying: "The historical events of the biblical period remain unique and irreversible. Psychologically, however, those events are *experienced* cyclically, repetitively, and to that extent, at least, atemporally."[25] I would put the matter a little differently: The uniqueness of personal experience today is dependent on the unique biblical experiences whose meaning is still present. The image is best captured in the observance of Sabbath, a strange celebration of nonactivity, but one that centers the cleaving unto God throughout the work week.[26]

What of the future? There is less to say of it than of the past, but some kind of orientation toward the future is an indispensable dimension of the present. In Jewish and Christian terms, the future exists as promise, as that which is hoped for. The future as a segment of a time line, something to be planned for and speculated upon, can be a dangerous distraction. But this modern invention could be worthwhile if it does not diminish the present or obliterate the past. Now that the idea of a future has spread throughout most of the world, societies do need some hope that life can be improved.

For the individual, the future exists at the mysterious juncture of the deposit of the past and the imagination of novelty. The past controls the future, though not entirely; the individual can gently reshape what the past offers as a gift. The future also controls the past to the extent that the meaning of the past has not reached its conclusion. The death of Jesus or the destruction of the temple in Jerusalem are still to be determined in meaning; the same is true of the bombing of Hiroshima or the murder of Martin Luther King, Jr.

It can be plausibly argued that the central virtue of Christianity and Judaism is hope; faith is a kind of hoping. Twentieth-century thinkers from Heidegger to Beckett have emphasized waiting.[27] Waiting can imply a degree of hope, but the waiting needs a present experience of oneself, one's neighbors, and a sense of the All. If the present is rich enough in meaning, then the future becomes promise. Religions attempt to sustain hope in the face of evidence to the contrary. The issue of religion, wrote W. P. Montague, "is whether the things we care for most are at the mercy of the things we care for least."[28]

The individual's difficulty is that no matter what glossy pictures are painted of the world's long-range future, the individual's future is death within a few score years. When time is understood as a series of points, then the movement toward death is almost of necessity a march of despair. Erik Erikson describes despair as the feeling that one is running out of time.[29] But many people do not experience the approach of death this way. They have discovered from religion or somewhere else a meaning of time in which the present is constantly being enriched by the past; they are content with the day. "He who lives with a sense of the present," writes Abraham Heschel, "knows that to get older does not mean to lose time but rather to gain time."[30] One sinks into the middle of time, toward the still point at the center of the world. "And do not call it fixity, where past and future are gathered."[31]

UNIQUE DEVELOPMENTS

The term development is not only a modern word, it is one of the terms that defines modernity. Evolution and progress are its closest kin, but both of those words have remained restricted in application and open to debate. *Development*, in contrast, has continued to become more widely used from psychology to economics; and almost no voice can be heard in opposition to the idea of development.

The modern idea of development arose in rebellion against a closed world with a preordained end. In the age dominated by medieval Christianity, the emphasis was on a fair distribution of the world's goods and the salvation of the individual soul. There was a path of success leading to heaven, and there was the alternative of total failure: not finding the path at all.

Under the influence of numerous forces — especially the discovery of new lands, the rise of empirical science, and its attendant technology — the idea arose that life could be improved here and now. Christianity and Judaism had oriented history toward God. The project of modernity was to retain the arrow forward while liberating humanity from the endpoint of God and heaven. With a new way of looking at wealth as something that can be increased or developed, the modern world had an alternative to an endpoint, namely, the indefinite expansion of goods.

Psychologists arrived rather late on the scene of development. But starting in the late nineteenth century, development became individualized; each human person was now seen to undergo a process of "growth and development," the two words becoming almost synonymous. Jean Piaget and others showed how the development of mental capacities in the child paralleled physical growth. For a long time, and to some extent even today, development was applied only to children; "human development" became a subdivision of child psychology.

The restriction of development to the child was almost a self-contradiction. Development does not have an endpoint, even one called adulthood. The individual has to be freed from any preordained path that would limit his or her growth. Slowly but surely, the idea of development has spread to mid-life and finally to elderhood. Middle-aged men go through their crisis of mid-life development; middle-aged women demand liberation from a fixed track of dependency. And now the old wish to be liberated and to have the means to live free and independent lives.

As in the previous section on time, I will briefly describe the two meanings of uniqueness in relation to development. One can readily see the parallel between images of time and the understanding of development. Both meanings of time and development have their roots in Jewish and Christian history. Even at their narrowest, Jewish and Christian traditions had a sense of unique individuals who were called to greatness. Modern secular thinkers have tried to throw off the confinement of the religious tradition while retaining the sense of unique human individuals.

Modern developmental theory can, therefore, be the chief competitor to Judaism and Christianity. But as in the ecological question, a deeper strand of Jewish and Christian traditions may reveal that the religious and secular approaches need each other's help. As ecological imagery needs the humans at the center for a responsible ecological system, so development needs a cyclical or conversionary movement on the part of the individual.

At their best, Christianity and Judaism call the individual to a unique development, a circling about a center. This kind of movement is ultimately the only way to be liberated from the control of either an endpoint or an ecologically disastrous image of unlimited expansion. What counts is the richest, deepest sense of life in the present. Modern secular thinkers attack the idea that this life is merely a test for which one is rewarded at the end. What most secular thinkers seem unaware of is that prophets, saints, and mystics throughout the centuries have made the same protest.[32]

MEANING A

Development, within Meaning A of uniqueness, assumes that the individual is not yet differentiated from the mass at life's beginning. The task of development is an increasing differentiation that ultimately places the individual on one time line unlike anyone else's. Zvi Lamm describes this development:

> The realization of what is human in the individual is the realization of what is unique and different in him. To develop means to advance along the road leading to this differentiation. Uniqueness cannot be predicted or planned. Educating the individual toward self-actualization means educating him without any ready-made models that he must try to emulate.[33]

The absence of ready-made models is, from one perspective, liberating. But having no one to emulate also means an increasing isolation of the individual. The little boy is to become his own independent self, disregarding previous history and present society that tempt him with ready-made models. Every man is to be Robinson Crusoe.[34]

The little boy's problem is to detach himself from the mother and hold his ground against the father. If he repeats that process with every other power that seeks to control him, he will become an *autonomous man*. Meaning A of uniqueness implies separation, independence, and autonomy. Negatively considered, uniqueness can mean disconnectedness, isolation, and loneliness. One is distanced even from the moments of one's own life.

This negative side to autonomy has generated considerable criticism from women during the last two decades. They argue that theories of human development have been theories of male development.[35] Most powerfully in Freud, but even in a writer like Erikson, the little boy's search for separation and autonomy skews the issue of *human* development. Little girls, for better or worse, do not separate from the mother or confront the father the way boys do. Women argue that even for men there is a need to reconsider the emphasis upon independence and autonomy, the extraordinary claim that a man is whatever he makes himself to be. The following description of "man's development" is not untypical: "A human life is composed of performances, and each performance is a disclosure of a man's beliefs

about himself and the world and an exploit in self-enactment. He is what
he becomes; he has a history but no 'nature'. This history is not an evolutionary process or a teleological engagement."[36]

In this author's determination to fight the confinement of fixed nature
and the oppression of a teleological point of control, he is thrown into the
opposites, namely, performance, self-enactment, and a man's life being
what he becomes. Perhaps there are other choices besides dependence
versus independence, nature versus history, teleology versus self-enactment.
It is almost impossible to imagine a woman writing the above passage, not
just because of the male pronouns but because the imagery is so foreign to
women's experience.

If one is born male, healthy, white, and rich, development within Meaning A of uniqueness is certainly attractive. The only question is whether
one can exercise sufficient reason and will to become the independent self
that is so desirable. When one starts with all the advantages of gender,
race, education, health, and wealth, the development of an autonomous
self is not really so difficult. The man becomes more unique, an isolated
self with the power to control his wife, his children, his dog, his employees,
his time, his cash flow, his body. The arrow goes forward and upward; each
self-enacted moment seeks to be an increase over the previous ones.

Even for the most advantaged man, however, this theory of unique development eventually shows its limits. In fact, it is the successful man who is
often hardest hit by male mid-life crisis. The trigger may be the death of a
friend or the first heart attack; man is mortal. The occasion may be rebellion
by his wife or his teenage daughter; man is not in complete control. The
man senses in his own body that he is no longer on the ascent. Within the
confines of his imagery, the only way he can see himself moving is downward, away from a uniquely autonomous self to a dependent and blurred
selfhood.

Sometimes it is said that middle-aged men fear they are running out of
time; this description misses the point of the imagery. The man's real problem is that he sees years and decades stretching out before him—all of
them running downhill. He has believed since infancy that life is supposed
to keep going up to better and better things. But this construct of a lifetime
can be shattered in the course of an hour. Now the man needs a new
meaning for "unique self." The meaning can come from voices within his
own body, as well as the voices of his wife, his children, his elders, or anyone
else who has been pressed to discover another meaning of uniqueness.[37]

MEANING B

In Meaning B of unique development, a person is born with a unique
self. It is the gift of previous generations, of one's parents, of the cosmos,
of God. One is also called by these forces to become more unique, that is,
a more nearly unique self. A sixth-century Christian author wrote: "God is

really wonderful and extremely wise in having distinguished each of his creatures by a unique disposition lest unseemly confusion overwhelm them."[38] The Jewish and Christian doctrine of creation does not refer to an isolated fact at the beginning of things. It refers, instead, to the continuing support of this "unique disposition."

Where Christian and Jewish thought sometimes erred was in thinking that God provides a unique self and that the individual's task is simply to hold on to it. But the unique self is called to develop into a more (nearly) unique self. In the language of Irenaeus, each human being is born an *imago* of God and is called to become a *similitudo*.[39] The child is already related to the cosmos; its vocation is to transform those relations so that the world consciously and freely flows into his or her person. This process takes time; it includes the bad days as well as the good. If the process is successful, each stage of life recapitulates all of one's previous life.

Each stage of life has its own uniqueness; there is no need to press forward to the next step. A child ought to be allowed to be a child, neither a minor version of an adult nor a station on the way to adulthood. The teenage period, at least in the modern era, is most in tension with a uniqueness of continuous development. Emerging from childhood, one is tempted to try eliminating the past and inventing oneself anew. A great danger is that the uniqueness that teenage adolescents seek can turn into the model for a whole society when it fails to appreciate the unique stages of middle age and elderhood.

Adolescence has perhaps gotten a bad name by being totally identified with teenagers. *Adolescence* means becoming adult; if there is such a thing as lifelong development, then everyone is an adolescent. One can reach greater degrees of adulthood, but one can never reach a fixed state or final point called "adult." This theory of development and adulthood seems, in fact, to be working its way into the contemporary world. Middle-aged men are sometimes embarrassed to be having experiences similar to those of their children; they need not be. Even seventy-year-olds may be thinking of getting new work and finding a sexual partner. Such things were once associated with teenagers, who were allowed a period of changeableness before they were supposed to settle down in their twenties.

If everyone becomes an adolescent, would that not be a disaster? That depends on which set of adolescent characteristics predominates. On the positive side, adolescence can mean fluidity, spontaneity, and openness to the future; life has not been fixed into a final form. Unfortunately, however, adolescence can also mean instability, emotionalism, and a flight from one's past. Teenaged adolescents remain especially vulnerable to such chaos unless they have older adolescents to provide encouraging examples and advice.

Forty-year-old adolescents should have stability without rigidity, be affective without being irrational, and recognize that the future is the past reshaped. The forty-year-old adolescent should be able to look to seventy-year-old adolescents who have further developed into stable and unique selves. A forty- or a seventy-year-old who is still just experimenting with sexual partners may be a case of retarded development, but the rest of us adolescents should be slow to judge the success or failure of a person's life. In any case, by the time of elderhood, people should be more unique than teenagers or young adults. Even dependencies that resurface in old age can be a sign of the uniqueness that relates us to the whole universe.

Can the human race, or even a major part of it, succeed in doing away with a fixed point at the end while retaining meaningful direction and order? The answer is not yet clear. What is needed for success is the experiencing of *end* (direction, purpose, meaning) in everything we do. These ends are found in the interior of our selves, in the middle of communal activity, in our relation to the center of the cosmos. As for an ultimate end that orders everything, it can only be imagined as the mathematical center of a sphere. This center point orients movement, even though the point itself is never reached.

In religious terms, God is the fixed point of meaning at the center (not the termination point) of life. Meister Eckhart and other mystics have used at times shocking formulas to deny that God is a reward at the end of the line. A contemporary Catholic monk, after saying that God is no-thing, writes: "God is the direction in which we go in our quest for meaning."[40]

The lifelong quest is important, but God will not be found as an object. God is the direction which emerges as one practices justice and love. The practicing of such virtue is not done for the reward but because the activities are worth doing. From the time of the Pharisees onward, Jews and Christians have been told to do things "for the sake of the thing itself."[41] God is discovered or revealed in silence, in rituals of remembrance, in acts of compassion, in the refusal to accept evil as the final condition.

A MOST UNIQUE EXPERIENCE

The culminating test of the meanings of uniqueness is the experience of dying, or the sense of mortality that is implicit from the beginning and may blossom at any stage of life. How we deal with vulnerability in our lives and the lives of those we love prepares the context in which we have what is likely to be our most unique experience: dying. Thus, the attitude toward death that I describe in this section cannot have its development postponed until old age. The hour of our birth is the hour of our beginning to die. To each arriving infant, the sign is posted: "Welcome to earth; the death rate here is 100%. One out of one dies."[42]

John Hick notes that the presence of death in human life brings about a uniqueness, or rather a double uniqueness, in comparison to other animals: The individual knows that he or she is going to die, and, in an important sense, he or she doesn't believe it.[43] To the extent that Meaning A of uniqueness governs one's life, death must be banished from consciousness.

The individual believes that he or she is immortal, despite the overwhelming evidence to the contrary. Other animals cannot foresee their own deaths and are therefore saved from denying their mortality. Human beings are pressed to deny death because to go on with daily life seems unbearable if all the struggles are in vain, if the joy as well as the sorrow ultimately counts for nothing. Tolstoy wrote in his *Confession* that "the most basic question of life—the simplest kind of question, and one which is lying in the soul of every man, from the silliest child to the wisest old man is the question: 'Is there in my life a meaning which would not be destroyed by my inevitable, imminent death'?"[44]

In recent decades, an attempt has been made to bring the topic of death out into the open, to reverse a century or more of near silence on the issue. This new "speaking about death"—thanatology—is unavoidably in danger of chattering on about life's most mystery laden experience. Thanatology is sometimes accused of romanticizing death into something positive that can be lovingly embraced.[45] Dying would then be one more pleasant and interesting experience.

Paul Ramsey, understandably upset at some of the trivializing talk, wrote an essay entitled "The Indignity of 'Death and Dignity'."[46] In it, Ramsey argues: "To deny the indignity of death requires that the dignity of man be refused also. The more acceptable in itself death is, the less the worth or uniqueness ascribed to the dying life." Ramsey's reaction is distorted by his simple opposition between "accepting death" and "unique life." Accepting death need not mean praising it or eagerly seeking it. The acceptance of death can mean that one finally recognizes life and death are not opposites, and that life becomes unique precisely in the acceptance of death.

The connection between a unique human life and the acceptance of death is captured in the final paragraph of Elisabeth Kübler-Ross's classic, *On Death and Dying*:

> Watching a peaceful death of a human being reminds us of a falling star, one of the million lights in a vast sky that flares up for a brief moment only to disappear into the endless night forever. To be a therapist to a dying patient makes us aware of the uniqueness of each individual in this vast sea of humanity. It makes us aware of our finiteness, our limited lifespan. Few of us live beyond our three score and ten years and yet in that brief time most of us create and live a unique biography and weave ourselves into the fabric of human history.[47]

Kübler-Ross in this passage uses the word *unique* in two metaphorical contexts: a falling star and the weaving of a fabric. I think that her second metaphor for the individual's unique biography—"weave ourselves into the fabric of human history"—assumes Meaning B of uniqueness and is appropriate for her intentions. Kübler-Ross's first image of a falling star, flaring for a moment, tends toward Meaning A of uniqueness, thereby evacuating the meaning that she has been dealing with throughout the book. The controlling metaphor for the relation of life and death is crucial to the meaning of human uniqueness. Death becomes a ratification of the uniqueness that the individual has lived.

In Meaning A of uniqueness, life is understood to be a quest for autonomy, independence, and control. Within this meaning, the individual is separated from the body, the present is separated from the past, and life is separated from death. These separations are never completed, but each moment, event, occasion, performance, self-invention, can be a striving toward splendid and solitary isolation. This search for total independence must put death out of mind, but it does not succeed in eliminating death from life. This way of life can lead to a cruel "last moment" in which dying is experienced as the ultimate aloneness. In Meaning A, the most unique and most isolated moment is the act of dying.

Meaning B, in contrast, is movement toward communion throughout all of life. Love and care for particular beings during life prepare one for a greater communion that is beyond imagination, though not beyond hope. Dying is not the last moment but the central experience, the revelation of our interdependence with all creation. Most people do not embrace death as something desirable; they accept death because their experience has led them to the conclusion that living and dying are not separate processes. Dying is what each being does in small ways every day; living is what buds forth from death.

For the individual to sustain this second meaning of uniqueness, in which dying is entrance into deeper communion, the social context should reflect this meaning. People ought to be able to die among the living; they ought to be able to sink into the center of a human community and a cycle of nonhuman life. A problem today is that people die in hospitals surrounded by or hooked up to machines. Modern medicine can be a great benefit; there is nothing glorious about dying in excruciating pain. However, we are only starting to develop an ethic to deal with the mechanizing and indefinite prolongation of the act of dying. Both Jewish and Christian traditions support an ethic in which the dying are allowed to die. In Meaning B of uniqueness, biological death is not the worst of happenings; it is something to be accepted when most of the signs in the present point to its appropriateness.

Some of the most creative thinking on death in Christian theology has been done by Karl Rahner. He combined the traditional Christian belief that "Christ redeemed us by his death" with twentieth-century thinking, especially Heidegger's, that "man is a being unto death."[48] In Rahner's theology, death is not a last point on the line; it is the guiding presence in all of life and the final recapitulation of individual existence. One's life moves toward either greater isolation or deeper communion; the act of dying reveals what may have been unclear about the journey and gives us a final chance to ratify or reject the choice. Each of us can die alone, or we can die with humanity. In Christian theological terms, dying in communion with all means dying "in Christ." Jesus' life was summed up and ratified by his death; each person's death is the most nearly unique experience that recapitulates one's previous experience. One is freed from limited communion for greater communion; at death one becomes not a-cosmic but pancosmic.

Karl Rahner's work provides a theological interpretation of the meaning of death and resurrection. But if one tries to turn this interpretive idea into an empirical description of each person's conscious experience, then one goes beyond the evidence. Also, one may be adding an unnecessary burden on the individual who is approaching death. Although many people who have brushed with death say "my whole life flashed before me," there is no persuasive evidence that each person has to make one great decision about his or her life at the moment of dying. "Christianity must always remain realistic, even about death, and should refuse to increase its burden. Therefore, it will not demand a surcharge of fantasy at the very moment when that is least possible."[49]

The belief that "death is not god" is surely one of the most universal religious beliefs, if not the foundation of religion itself. All religions reject the notion that dying is simply the last of a series of points. Rather, death is summation and transition, a revelation of what life is for. Jews often criticize Christians for glorifying death and for teaching that this life is merely a trial for getting into heaven. Christianity and Judaism over the centuries have moved apart on this issue, but the differences are a matter of emphases within a commonality of belief.

Christianity, more than Judaism, has been tempted to deny the uniqueness of the *person*, that is, the temporal, bodily, communal, ecological unity of human existence. The temptation is to negate death by imagining that the human being is really not a person but a spirit held captive in a bodily prison. Death in this picture is liberation from the body. In this earthly life, one is not inclined to struggle for justice; all supposed progress is illusory.

The other way to cope with death is to see existence as a constant transformation of life into death, death into life. The individual's bodily death is a stage in this transformation. The Christian and Jewish term for the affirmation of life in spite of real death is resurrection. Instead of describing some other world, resurrection is a negative, or more precisely, a double negative term. It affirms life by negating the negation of life, especially those theories that the human being is not a bodily unit in the first place. Resurrection, according to Rahner, "only forbids in a *negative* sense the exclusion of particular elements of man from the outset as of no consequence for his final state."[50] Thus, the secular critics of the idea that "we change horses and ride on" are not necessarily opposed to the Jewish and Christian doctrine of resurrection.[51]

Like most things Christian, resurrection was a Jewish idea before it became central to Christian teaching about Jesus. In writing about Jesus in chapter 5, I barely adverted to this claim, even though it came first in the preaching of the Christian gospel. In our day, introducing the term resurrection without ample preparation is likely to turn the referent for this belief into a magical trick. The problem is not, as Bultmann claimed — that no one can believe in the resurrection after the invention of the electric light bulb — but that the *meaning* of resurrection has always demanded a communal and cosmic context that has seldom been available. The ground for such a meaning may be stronger today than in most of the previous 2200 years.

There is no doubt that the early Christians saw resurrection as central: "The unique claim of Jesus upon his followers is sealed by the fact that he was raised from the dead."[52] The Christians did not invent the term or the hope that it represents. Resurrection seems to have arisen in Judaism with the beginnings of Pharisaism several centuries before the common era. A God who lovingly cares for all creation and every human individual cannot allow death to be the final statement. In some sense, all of life must be "saved."

The announcement of Jesus' resurrection was to an audience already familiar with the term. Such a resurrection stood within Jewish tradition, but with one discrepancy: "If you had the faith of the Pharisees, his appearance would have startled you, but it would not have surprised you. You would have been stunned chiefly that he was *alone*."[53] The announcement "Christ is risen" was and is premature; what the first Christians believed was that Jesus had risen (or was raised) as the first fruits or downpayment for the resurrection of the whole Christ.

Many people, including some Jews, think that resurrection is a Christian term. Thus it is assumed that Christians believe in "life after death" but Jews do not. I have acknowledged a difference of emphasis in the two traditions, but the two need not be contradictory. Christians could learn from Jews to celebrate the only life and only world we know as the way to affirm resurrection. Jews could learn from Christians not to close the gate on a belief that is embedded in Jewish tradition, even though the belief has often been used to devalue the joys and struggles of this life.

What Jews and Christians should be able to agree upon is that the meaning of resurrection has to arise out of experience in the present. More particularly, resurrection has to derive its texture of meaning from: 1) the life cycle of the ecological system; 2) the integrity and joy of individual bodily life; 3) the communal fight against evil.

ECOLOGY

A reference to ecology may seem as though I am imposing a contemporary concern on an ancient doctrine. Actually, the Jewish and Christian doctrine probably has roots in a much older doctrine of death and resurrection as they are experienced in the seasons of the year. Resurrection is about the rebirth of the earth each year and all those whom the earth has gathered to itself. For example, in the excavations at New Grange in Ireland, there is clear evidence that this community of five thousand years ago had some belief in the rebirth of its dead, the belief connected to the rising of the sun and the change of seasons. The bones of the dead are gathered in a burial mound that is built with such geometric precision that light enters the interior only on the day of the winter solstice. The sun begins its annual ascent, and all that is buried in the earth stirs to life.

Even to urban dwellers today, this experience of a living earth and a life-giving sun remains central to the interpretation of human life.[54] It is the earth as a whole that is alive, and the humans share in that life. The ascent of the sun, the change of seasons, and the yield of new crops may seem to some Christians a long way from Jesus and resurrection. But as Archbishop William Temple put it: "Only if God is revealed in the rising of the sun in the sky can he be revealed in the rising of a son of man from the dead."[55]

INDIVIDUAL LIFE

Resurrection can only make sense to those who value and enjoy life.[56] If someone has cared for individual living things and has loved particular human beings, then he or she will affirm life even in the face of death. Resurrection stands in contrast to "saving one's soul," which is usually a defensive and egocentric movement. Resurrection is an outward movement that is primarily concerned with the death of a loved one. "The man who can see his beloved die, believing that it is forever, and say 'I don't care,' is a traitor to his beloved and to all that their love has brought them. He has no right not to care."[57] For those who have loved dearly, it is impossible to imagine that the loved person is simply no more. Reflecting on the death of his friend Charles Williams, C. S. Lewis wrote: "When my idea of death and the idea of Williams thus met in my mind, it was the idea of death that was changed."[58]

If we follow the developing uniqueness of a human being until death, we cannot imagine simply another segment of life after death. But we also cannot believe that the entire movement toward greater uniqueness was an illusion. Science has no real countervailing evidence; a lifetime of experiencing uniqueness is the best evidence we have on which to judge. Resurrection is the refusal to accept death as the final word. Not life after death is demanded, but life out of death, a life into which the loved person has been taken.

JUSTICE

A struggle for justice by a community is what makes its use of the term resurrection credible.[59] Various liberation movements in Christian theology have been rediscovering this theme, one that has been present in most of Judaism. In Jewish tradition, one does not speculate about an afterlife or even about God. The human task is to "heal the world," to do justly with the goods of creation. The effort to improve the world has to be rooted in one's own immediate community, but it should not exclude any human being. The stranger, the outcast, the one furthest away is the test of our protestations of human love.

A terrible part of medieval Christian theology was the belief that one of the joys of heaven is observing the pains of the damned. Most contemporary people — religious and secular — are repelled by the idea. We have not solved our problems of human division and enmity, but we do seem to have developed an ideal of human solidarity. As some Christian Fathers of the church realized, the harsh language of the New Testament need not mean that God tortures individuals for eternity. Religions do imply the possibility of radical failure. Perhaps some people do not become receptive enough (at least in one lifetime) to enjoy God's love, but that is not ours to pronounce.

In summary, the Jewish and Christian doctrine of resurrection can be understood as a realistic affirmation about life and its inevitable accompaniment, death. We are given life, which is a kind of miracle. Human uniqueness is the experience that life has possibilities beyond anyone's imagination. Most paradoxically, the greatness of this unique experience is based on weakness, vulnerability, and mortality. "If in this life we know that we are poor, that we are nothing and have nothing which we are not receiving from the unknown, then it will not seem uniquely strange that life should continue to be given beyond the boundaries of physical death."[60]

Whatever physical and psychological facts were the case in the experience of Jesus' disciples (an issue that the original documents can never resolve), the term resurrection indicates breakthrough to unique personhood. Resurrection is a reference to the cosmos before it is a puzzling fact about Jesus. It does not refer to another world on top of this one or after this one. Resurrection is about living and dying and living, about doing your work the best you can and loving those around you. In the beautiful words of Dietrich Bonhoeffer: "Wherever the world of death is illumined by the miracle of resurrection . . . one neither clings convulsively to life nor casts it frivolously away. One is content with the alloted span and one does not invest earthly things with the title of eternity; one allows to death the limited rights which it still possesses."[61]

Conclusion

The preceding chapters have traced the pattern of usage for the term *unique*. Two contrasting logics were found to be embodied in the use of this peculiar word. Both of these logics were traced to their emergence in Jewish and Christian traditions. Many of the main concepts in these traditions (for example, faith, revelation, chosen, covenant, mediator) were examined in relation to uniqueness. The final two chapters have extended the analysis to a wider sphere, what I called the geography and the history of the individual person.

The meaning of a term does not neatly divide into two parts. What I have called Meaning A and Meaning B of uniqueness are sharply opposed *directions* within the meaning of the term. They are movements in opposite directions away from the common note of "different from all others." In both cases, the absolutist claim that seems inherent to the term is never reached. The peculiar nature of the claim to uniqueness is that it is never the case.

Is *unique* perhaps similar to *absolutely*, a word that has inundated popular speech in the last fifteen years? People say absolutely when they simply but enthusiastically mean yes. There is nothing very absolute these days about "absolutely." Many uses of the word unique reflect a similar inflation of ordinary speech. People say unique when they wish to be emphatic about the importance of something. Often, the difference between an event and a unique event is merely that the speaker wishes to call attention to the latter. Thus, Meaning A of uniqueness is often an exclamation point whose removal from a statement would not essentially change the statement.

However, when a Jew says that "the Holocaust is unique" or a Christian says that "Christ is unique," a powerful and emotionally laden claim is at stake. Such claims are usually attacked not on the grounds of redundancy or vacuousness, but, on the contrary, because they are assumed to be arrogant and imperialistic.

Even if people have not thought out Meaning B of uniqueness, they often sense an alternate logic that can be conveyed through the term. This logic is an alternative to the "fact plus reasoning" logic that has dominated much of the modern era. In this modern framework, general laws are formulated by abstracting from individual cases. In contrast, Meaning B of uniqueness takes its approach to the universal not through abstracting from the particular but by going more deeply into it. The universal is encountered by finding what is more and more (nearly) unique.

Religion and art have been two of the places where this way of thinking has been preserved. The rise of modern science had seemed to be in conflict with Meaning B of uniqueness, but evolutionary and ecological modes of thinking have been breaking down the conflict. Indeed, Meaning B of uniqueness emerges as the link between aesthetic and evolutionary thinking. An ecological science requires persons who are unique living in relation to an environment constituted by varying degrees of uniqueness.

Meaning B of uniqueness points the mind in a direction; at the same time, it asserts a movement that does not have an endpoint. Thus, one of the supreme paradoxes of a "movement in the direction of increasing inclusiveness" is that the movement proceeds by exclusion—the exclusion of an endpoint that would abort continued movement. Judaism, Christianity, and other religions are familiar with this paradox, namely, the need to exclude idols in the name of the all-inclusive God. Not surprisingly, the passions unleashed by the need for de-idolization often obscure the process of increasing inclusiveness. When the paradox is lost, religions become almost the opposite of what they profess to be, religions of love that seem filled with hatred; religions that praise God's creation but are suspicious of listening to God's creatures.

As I pointed out in chapter 1, the parallel formulas of "the direction of increasing exclusiveness" and "the direction of increasing inclusiveness" can be deceiving. Exclusion can be directly intended; inclusion usually cannot. An organization can exclude Jews or women or blacks simply by making clear the intention to do so. But the same organization does not become inclusive by announcing its intention to be so. An organization that wishes to be more inclusive has to look carefully at itself to begin excluding what is excluding one group or another. The obstacles to inclusion are usually unstated, often unconscious. Even after such problems are detected and solved, a process of increasing inclusiveness takes time, more likely measured in years, rather than hours.

The logic of uniqueness needs to be carried into the arenas of racial, sexual, and political conflicts. The issue of pluralism or diversity is threatening to erode the social cohesion of neighborhood, nation, and world. We are going to need much patience and genuine dialogue if there are to evolve language, educational curricula, and political policies that are more inclusive of diverse groups.

In recent years, the phrase "inclusive language" has become the preserve of the feminist movement, as if "inclusive language" were equivalent to "gender-inclusive language." If we are to start with one problem of unfair exclusion, a good case can be made for choosing gender. But all language excludes and includes. The phrase inclusive language suggests that some group knows how to speak such a language. People who assume that they know how to speak inclusively usually speak in impersonal and vague abstractions. The bureaucratic language that dominates modern life is very inclusive; it subsumes personal differences in high-level abstractions. It is not an accident that many people today will say that inclusive language means using "gender-free" or "genderless" prose. What begins as a promise to include women ends by eliminating both women and men.

If one group is underrepresented in language or in an organization, the solution may seem to lie in a process of *addition*. Where there has been "he," let there be "he and she." This strategy seems to work well if the discussion is restricted to one group. However, if we try to get an increasing inclusiveness by going this route, the process will collapse under its own weight. Groups quickly begin to overlap other groups in complex ways (race, gender, age, sexual orientation, physical disabilities). A school curriculum can and should give attention to the two sexes of the human race that are present in the urban classroom. But what does one do with 37 or 57 ethnic/racial/national/cultural groups? Is anyone even sure whether there are 37, 57, or 157 groups? We seem to be reaching some point of terrible conflict resulting from the good but naive intention to be all-inclusive by addition.

The description of uniqueness in this book is not offered as a simplistic solution to these bitter disputes. But it might at least offer a warning when we are working with faulty logic. It might also suggest the line of development for the alternative logic. The uniqueness of life and death, person and community, history and tradition, provides the basis for patient dialogue. If the language we speak is deeply rooted in the concrete realities of personal and communal experience, then we might be able to hear what other uniquenesses have to offer. From there, the actuality of dialogue requires careful attention to every important category that shapes speech. With the exclusion of obstacles that hinder exchange, an increasing inclusiveness can proceed at its own pace. The task of uniqueness cannot be finished; neither should it be abandoned.

Notes

INTRODUCTION

1. Martin Buber, *I and Thou* (New York, Charles Scribner's Sons, 1937).

2. See Ludwig Wittgenstein, *Tractatus Logico-Philosophicus* (London, Routledge and Kegan Paul, 1971).

3. Ludwig Wittgenstein, *On Certainty* (New York, Harper Torch, 1969), p. 67.

4. G. K. Chesterton, *Orthodoxy* (Garden City, Image Books, 1957), p. 83.

5. Karl Rahner, *Foundations of Christian Faith* (New York, Seabury, 1978), pp. 178–321.

6. Nicholas Lash, *Easter in Ordinary: Reflections on Human Experience and the Knowledge of God* (Charlottesville, University of Virginia, 1988), pp. 208–10.

7. John Hick and Paul Knitter, eds., *The Myth of Christian Uniqueness* (Maryknoll, Orbis Books, 1987).

8. Gavin D'Costa, ed., *Christian Uniqueness Reconsidered* (Maryknoll, Orbis Books, 1990).

9. S. Mark Heim, "Crisscrossing the Rubicon: Reconsidering Religious Pluralism," *Christian Century*, July 10–13, 1991, 688–90.

10. Joseph Campbell, *Myths to Live By* (New York, Viking, 1972), p. 254.

11. Jonathan Z. Smith, *Drudgery Divine* (Chicago, University of Chicago, 1990), p. 36.

12. Ibid., p. 39.

13. Arthur Cohen, *The Myth of the Judeo-Christian Tradition* (New York, Harper and Row, 1972), p. xviii; see also Martin Marty, "A Judeo-Christian looks at the Judeo-Christian Tradition," *Christian Century*, Oct. 8, 1986, 58–66; for a criticism of Cohen's argument, see Mark Silk, "Notes on the Judeo-Christian Tradition in America," *American Quarterly*, 36 (Spring, 1984), 65–85.

14. Arthur Cohen, *The Myth of the Judeo-Christian Tradition*, p. xviii.

15. Krister Stendahl, *Paul among the Jews and Gentiles* (Philadelphia, Fortress, 1976), p. 37.

1. A VERY UNIQUE WORD

1. Jean Baker Miller, *Toward a New Psychology of Women* (Boston, Beacon, 1976).

2. I have no inclination here to glorify suffering in the lives of Jews or anyone else; certainly, powerlessness is never desirable. I agree with Irving Greenberg that "the redemptive nature of suffering must be held in absolute tension with the dialectical reality that it must be fought, cut down, eliminated." See "Cloud of Smoke, Pillar of Fire," *Auschwitz: A New Beginning?* ed. Eva Fleischner (New York,

KTAV, 1977), 7–56; see also the helpful insights on suffering in Leszck Kolakowski, *The Presence of Myth* (Chicago, University of Chicago, 1989), pp. 88–94.

3. Nels Ferre, *The Universal Word* (Philadelphia, Westminster, 1969), p. 142.

4. Frithjof Schuon, *The Transcendent Unity of Religions* (New York, Harper Torch, 1975), p. 18.

5. A. J. Toynbee, *A Study of History* (London, Oxford University, 1961), XII, p. 11.

6. Martin Buber, *Hasidism and Modern Man* (New York, Harper Torch, 1966), p. 110.

7. Michael Marrus, *The Holocaust in History* (New York, Meridian, 1988), p. 18.

8. Maurice Wiles, *What Is Theology?* (New York, Oxford University, 1976), p. 185.

9. Yehuda Bauer, *The Holocaust as Historical Experience* (New York, Holmes and Meier, 1981), p. 37.

10. Lawrence Kohlberg and Rochelle Mayer, "Development as the Aim of Education," *Curriculum: An Introduction to the Field*, eds. James Gress and David Purpel (Berkeley, McCutchan, 1978), p. 69.

11. René Dubos, *A God Within* (New York, Charles Scribner's Sons, 1972), p. 71.

12. Margaret Furse, *Mysticism: Windows on a World View* (New York, Abingdon, 1977), p. 74.

13. Lawrence Blum, *Friendship, Altruism and Morality* (Boston, Routledge and Kegan Paul, 1980), pp. 94–95.

14. Herbert Marcuse, *The Aesthetic Dimension* (Boston, Beacon, 1977), p. 41.

15. Ben Shahn, *The Shape of Content* (New York, Vintage, 1957), p. 54.

16. Michael McGarry, *Christology after Auschwitz* (New York, Paulist, 1977), p. 70.

17. In *Christian Faith in a Religiously Plural World*, eds. Donald Dawe and John Carman (Maryknoll, Orbis Books, 1978), p. 106.

18. Lewis Thomas, *The Medusa and the Snail* (New York, Viking, 1979), pp. 2, 7.

19. Ibid., p. 2.

20. See Carol Gould, *Women and Philosophy* (New York, Capricorn, 1976), p. 26 for her distinction between "essentialist" and "concrete" universality.

21. John Kenneth Galbraith, "Dan, You're No Strunk and White," *Harper's*, June, 1989, p. 26. Galbraith was incorrect in referring to adjectives; he meant adverbs.

22. Richard Nixon, *In the Arena* (New York, Simon and Schuster, 1990).

23. James Charlesworth, *Jews and Christians* (New York, Crossroad, 1990), p. 14.

24. Quoted in H. E. W. Turner, *Jesus the Christ* (London, Mowbrays, 1976), p. 18.

25. Lewis Thomas, *The Medusa and the Snail*, p. 2.

26. Hannah Arendt, *The Human Condition* (Chicago, University of Chicago, 1958), p. 176.

27. See Lewis Thomas, *Lives of a Cell* (New York, Viking, 1974); Wendell Berry, *Standing by Words* (San Francisco, North Point, 1983) and *The Unsettling of America* (San Francisco, Sierra Club, 1973); Loren Eiseley, *All the Strange Hours* (New York,

Charles Scribner's Sons, 1975) and *The Unexpected Universe* (New York, Harcourt, Brace and World, 1969).

28. William Clebsch, *Christianity in European History* (New York, Oxford University, 1979), p. 245.

29. Theodosius Dobzhansky, "The Pattern of Human Evolution," *The Uniqueness of Man*, ed. John Roslansky (Amsterdam, North Holland, 1969), pp. 43–44.

30. Peter Medawar, "The Uniqueness of the Individual," *The Uniqueness of the Individual* (London, Methuen, 1957).

31. Ibid., pp. 154–55.

32. Ibid., p. 185.

33. Maurice Friedman, *Touchstones of Reality* (New York, Dutton, 1972), p. 154.

34. Eugene Borowitz has written that he is the only Jew he knows of who is a student of christology; see *Contemporary Christologies: A Jewish Response* (New York, Paulist, 1980), Introduction.

35. CBS News, July 16, 1980.

2. IS THE HOLOCAUST UNIQUE?

1. See Irving Howe, "Writing and the Holocaust," *Writing on the Holocaust,* ed. Berel Lang (New York, Holmes and Meier, 1988), p. 179.

2. Vera Laska, *Nazism, Resistance and Holocaust in World War II: A Bibliography* (Metuchen, Scarecrow Press, 1985).

3. See Elie Wiesel, "Does the Holocaust Lie Beyond the Reach of Art?" *New York Times,* April 17, 1983; and "Trivializing the Holocaust: Semi-Fact and Semi-Fiction," *New York Times,* April 16, 1978.

4. Irving Howe, "Writing and the Holocaust," p. 190.

5. *New York Times,* April 15, 1985.

6. Franz Mussner, *Tractate on the Jews: The Significance of the Jews for the Christian Faith* (Philadelphia, Fortress Press, 1985), p. 44.

7. For example, see the exchange between Timothy Garton Ash and Israel Shahak over whether the Holocaust is unique, *New York Review of Books,* Jan. 28, 1987, 49.

8. Quoted in Anne Roiphe, *A Season for Healing: Reflections on the Holocaust* (New York, Summit, 1988), p. 217.

9. See Saul Friedlander, "On the Possibility of the Holocaust," *The Holocaust as Historical Experience,* ed. Yehuda Bauer and Nathan Rotenstreich (New York, Holmes and Meier, 1981), p. 6.

10. For example, James Charlesworth, *Jesus within Judaism* (Garden City, Doubleday, 1989), p. 5: "Only a historian can clarify to what extent 'uniqueness' is conceivable and point out that a historical person cannot be totally unique."

11. Richard Rubenstein, *The Cunning of History* (New York, Harper, 1975).

12. Nathan Rotenstreich, "Postscript," *The Holocaust as Historical Experience,* p. 276.

13. Arthur Cohen, *The Tremendum* (New York, Crossroad, 1988), p. 36.

14. Ibid, p. 41.

15. Michael Marrus, *The Holocaust in History*, p. 29. The italics are mine.

16. See Elisabeth Schüssler Fiorenza and David Tracy, eds., *The Holocaust as Interruption* (Edinburgh, T & T Clark, 1984).

17. *New York Times*, April 29, 1985.

18. I think that this is the main point that Philipp Jenninger tried to make in his much misunderstood speech marking the fiftieth anniversary of *Kristallnacht*. Ironically, the speech was attacked as anti-Jewish: "Whatever happens in the future or whatever else may be forgotten, Auschwitz will be remembered to the end of time as a part of our German history. That is why the call to 'finally put an end' to our past is senseless. Our past will not be quiet, it will not go away, independently of the fact that the young cannot be held guilty." *New York Times*, Nov. 12, 1988.

19. Leo Kuper, *Genocide* (London, Harmondsworth, 1981), p. 22.

20. See Paul Mendes-Flor and Yehuda Reinharz, *The Jew in the Modern World: A Documentary History* (New York, Oxford University, 1980).

21. For Jewish objection to the use of *Holocaust*, see Walter Laquer, *The Terrible Secret* (Boston, Little, Brown, 1981), p. 7.

22. Lucy Dawidowicz, *The Holocaust and the Historians* (Cambridge, Harvard University, 1981), p. 15.

23. Ibid., p. 16; as another example, consider this statement from a fund-raising letter of the National Council of Synagogue Youth: "In the 1940's Jews faced annihilation. In the 1980's we face it again. This time, however, we face a much more insidious enemy. This time you and I face the scourge of assimilation. Dare I call it a second holocaust in the making?" Quoted in Leonard Fein, *Where Are We: The Inner Life of the Jews* (San Francisco, Harper and Row, 1988), p. 146.

24. Lawrence Kramer, *Report from the Holocaust* (New York, St. Martin's Press, 1988).

25. Emil Fackenheim, *To Mend the World: Foundations for Future Jewish Thought* (New York, Schocken, 1982), p. 280.

26. Ibid., pp. 12–13.

27. The same holds true for Dawidowicz saying that "listing in one breath Auschwitz, Hiroshima, and Vietnam is seditious *poshlost* (bogus profundity)." *The Holocaust and the Historians*, p. 17. I would suggest that anyone listing in one breath all kinds of horrors is not carrying out a careful comparison. A writer who said most strongly that no comparisons are allowed is Cynthia Ozick. She lays down three rules about the Holocaust: 1) It is improper to draw any analogy from it; 2) It is not a metaphor; 3) It is not to be "used." On the next page of the essay, however, Ozick writes: "Indeed, it may be that for Jews like us, who come immediately after the Nazi period, there *are* no 'unrelated issues'." See *On Being a Jewish Feminist*, ed. S. Heschel (New York, Schocken Books, 1983), pp. 134–35. On the value of comparisons, see Michael Berenbaum, "The Uniqueness and Universality of the Holocaust," *Holocaust: Religious and Philosophical Implications*, ed. John Roth and Michael Berenbaum (New York, Paragon House, 1989), p. 96: "Such comparisons do not innately obscure the uniqueness of the Holocaust; they clarify it. Inclusion of the Armenian experience, for example, in commemorating the Holocaust does not detract from the uniqueness of the Holocaust but deepens our moral sensitivity while sharpening our perception."

28. In a review of Jon Butler's *Awash in a Sea of Faith*, Jan Lewis writes: "Mr. Butler invokes the term 'holocaust' to underscore the horror of slavery. But the comparison of slavery and the Nazi death camps is inflammatory. What can be gained by likening two unique forms of evil?" *New York Times Book Review*, April 1, 1990. It might be debatable whether slavery is an appropriate experience for comparison to the (Jewish) Holocaust. But in answer to the more general question

raised, the answer would seem to be clear that much is to be gained by comparing unique forms of evil.

29. Arno Mayer, *Why Did the Heavens Not Darken?* (New York, Harper, 1975).

30. See Primo Levi, *The Drowned and the Saved* (New York, Summit Books, 1986); Richard Rubenstein, *The Cunning of History*.

31. See Richard Rubenstein and John Roth, *Approaches to the Holocaust and Its Legacy* (Richmond, John Knox Press, 1987).

32. Zigmunt Bauman, *Modernity and the Holocaust* (Ithaca, Cornell University, 1979), pp. 83–116.

33. Isaac Deutscher, *The Non-Jewish Jew and Other Essays* (New York, Oxford University, 1968), p. 163.

34. Raul Hilbert, "Discussion," *The Holocaust as Historical Experience*, pp. 255–56.

35. Yosef Yerushalmi, "Response to Rosemary Ruether," *Auschwitz: A New Beginning?* ed. Eva Fleischner (New York, KTAV, 1977), pp. 97–107.

36. Arthur Cohen, *The Tremendum*, p. 58.

37. Hannah Arendt, *Eichmann in Jerusalem: A Report on the Banality of Evil* (New York, Penguin Books, 1964).

38. Isaiah Trunk, *Judenrat: The Jewish Councils in Eastern Europe under Nazi Occupation* (New York, Macmillan, 1972); Eliezer Berkovits, *With God in Hell* (New York, Sanhedrin, 1979).

39. Emil Fackenheim, "Jewish Values in the Post-Holocaust Future: A Symposium," *Judaism*, 16 (Summer, 1967).

40. Martin Buber, *Eclipse of God* (New York, Harper, 1957), p. 45.

41. Quoted in Richard Rubenstein and John Roth, *Approaches to the Holocaust and Its Legacy*, p. 285.

42. Emil Fackenheim, *To Mend the World*, p. 291.

43. Conor Cruise O'Brien, "A Lost Chance to Save the Jews," *New York Review of Books*, April 27, 1989, 27–35.

44. Paul Friedlander, "On the Possiblility of the Holocaust: An Approach to an Historical Synthesis," *The Holocaust as Historical Experience*, p. 11.

45. Johann-Baptist Metz, "Facing the Jews: Christian Theology after Auschwitz," in Elisabeth Schüssler Fiorenza and David Tracy, *The Holocaust as Interruption*, p. 31.

3. UNIQUE REVELATION

1. Philip Lopate, "Resistance to the Holocaust," *Tikkun*, 4 (May/June, 1989), 64; similarly, Ismar Schorsch, "The Holocaust and Jewish Survival," *Midstream*, 27 (Jan., 1981), pp. 38–42: Arguing for the uniqueness of the Holocaust is a "throwback to an age of religious polemics, a secular version of chosenness."

2. "Dogmatic Constitution on Divine Revelation," *The Documents of Vatican II*, ed. Walter Abbot (New York, America Press, 1966).

3. I mean, for example, that a council that included both men and women would more nearly embody a revelation of the divine.

4. The United States Catholic bishops tried several times to address the question of revelation in an educational context. In response to a document passed at the November 1978 meeting, the Vatican's Congregation of the Clergy required among other changes: "It would seem to be less opened to misunderstanding if the

word 'revelation', standing alone, without modifiers, quotation marks or italics, were to signify public, divine revelation in the strict sense, and that other expressions be chosen to indicate the modes by which God manifests Himself to man." The irony of this statement is that it says the right thing—revelation without qualifiers should mean public, divine revelation—but the Vatican's meaning of "public, divine revelation" is what is specified and controlled by the church, or, more exactly, by officials of the Roman Catholic church.

5. Gordon Kaufman, *God the Problem* (Cambridge, Harvard University, 1972), p. 4.

6. See Emil Fackenheim, *To Mend the World;* Richard Rubenstein and John Roth, *Approaches to the Holocaust and Its Legacy.*

7. Emil Fackenheim, *What is Judaism?* (New York, Collier, 1987), p. 24.

8. See Joseph Blau, *Judaism in America* (Chicago, University of Chicago), p. 44; Leon Jick, *The Americanization of the Synagogue* (Hanover, University Press of New England, 1976), p. 193.

9. John Locke, *The Reasonableness of Christianity* (Stanford, Stanford University, 1958).

10. Quoted in Rosemary Haughton, *The Catholic Thing* (Springfield, Templegate, 1979), p. 25.

11. See Moses Mendelssohn, "Judaism as Revealed Legislation," *The Jew in the Modern World*, ed. Paul Mendes-Flor and Jehuda Reinharz (New York, Oxford University, 1980), pp. 87–88; of Mendelssohn's approach to revelation, Norbert Samuelson writes, in *Modern Jewish Philosophy* (Albany, State University of New York, 1989), p. 144: "Judaism only teaches specific obligations for Jews that are consistent with the universal, rational teachings of natural religion."

12. See Charles Taylor, *Hegel* (Cambridge, Cambridge University, 1975), p. 211; see also Langdon Gilkey, *Religion and the Scientific Future* (New York, Harper and Row, 1976), p. 10: "As the eighteenth-century debates about the use or uselessness of revelation show, for not a few the knowledge of God through nature had become the only relevant source of our knowledge of his power, and even of his benevolence."

13. Norbert Samuelson, *Modern Jewish Philosophy*, p. 148; see also H. Richard Niebuhr, *Christ and Culture* (New York, Harper Torch, 1951), p. 119: "Revelation, then, is either fabulous clothing in which intelligible truth presents itself to people who have a low IQ; or it is the religious name for that process which is 'essentially the growth of reason in history'."

14. Northrop Frye, *The Great Code* (New York, Harcourt, Brace and Jovanovich, 1982), p. 67.

15. Ibid., p. 29.

16. Martin Buber, *Eclipse of God*, p. 46; see also Emil Fackenheim, "Martin Buber's Concept of Revelation," *The Philosophy of Martin Buber*, ed. P. A. Schilpp and M. Friedman (Lasalle, Open Court, 1967), p. 279: "Hence both the I and the Thou of every genuine dialogue are irreplaceable. Every dialogue is unique."

17. In a 1917 letter, Rosenzweig called this insight ("Revelation is orientation") "the archimedian point of my thinking." He apparently got the idea from his friend Rosenstock. See Eugen Rosenstock-Huessy and Franz Rosenzweig, *Judaism Despite Christianity* (Birmingham, University of Alabama, 1969), pp. 119–20.

18. Franz Rosenzweig, *Star of Redemption* (New York, Holt, Rinehart and Winston, 1970), pp. 182–86; see also Michael Oppenheim, *What Does Revelation*

Mean for the Modern Jew? (Lewiston, Edward Mellen, 1985), p. 41.

19. Paul Ricoeur, "Toward a Hermeneutic of the Idea of Revelation," *Essays in Biblical Interpretation*, ed. L. S. Mudge (Philadelphia, Fortress, 1980), pp. 73–118.

20. Martin Buber, *Israel and the World* (New York, Schocken, 1948), pp. 89–102.

21. Martin Buber, *I and Thou*, p. 106.

22. Martin Buber, *Eclipse of God*, p. 36: "The meaning is found through the engagement of one's own person; it only reveals itself as one takes part in the revelation"; see also Nicholas Berdyaev, *Truth and Revelation* (New York, Collier, 1963), p. 52: "Man has always been active in the reception and interpretation of revelation and this activity of his has always been both good and bad. Revelation cannot be something which is finished, static, and which requires a merely passive attitude for its reception."

23. Emil Fackenheim, *What is Judaism?* p. 28.

24. Gershom Scholem, *Major Trends in Jewish Mysticism*, 3rd ed. (New York, Schocken, 1961), p. 9.

25. Ibid., p. 6.

26. National Conference of Catholic Bishops, *The Challenge of Peace: God's Promise and Our Response* (Washington, U.S. Catholic Conference, 1983); see also Philip Berryman, *Our Unfinished Business: The U.S. Catholic Bishops' Letters on Peace and the Economy* (New York, Pantheon, 1989).

27. Carl Becker, *The Heavenly City of the Eighteenth-Century Philosophers* (New Haven, Yale University, 1932), pp. 50–51.

28. Jon Roberts, *Darwinism and the Divine* (New York, Oxford University, 1988), p. 162.

29. Ibid., p. 159: The quotation is from William Newton Clarke.

4. UNIQUE PEOPLE OF THE COVENANT

1. Martin Buber, *I and Thou*, p. 106.

2. See W. Cantwell Smith, *Faith and Belief* (Princeton, Princeton University, 1979); my own position here maintains a closer relation between the two words than does Smith.

3. See Mordecai Kaplan, *Judaism as a Civilization* (New York, Thomas Joseloff, 1957); similarly, Judith Plaskow, *Standing Again at Sinai* (San Francisco, Harper and Row, 1990), pp. 96–107 rejects the idea of chosenness; she suggests that "distinctness" is the proper term: "It points to the greater unity to which different groups belong, making it possible to acknowledge the uniqueness of each group as part of a wider association of self differentiated communities" (p. 105). As Plaskow's use of "uniqueness" indicates, her intention is very similar to mine in this chapter.

4. Martin Buber, *Israel and the World* (New York, Schocken, 1948), p. 170.

5. Erik Erikson, *Young Man Luther* (New York, Norton, 1958), p. 132.

6. See Mekilta Bahodesh 5; Lam. R. 3:1; Shab. 88b; Exod. R. 5.

7. David Hartman, *A Living Covenant* (New York, Free Press, 1985), p. 3.

8. *Gates of Prayer: The New Union Prayer Book* (New York, Central Conference of American Rabbis, 1977).

9. Meg. 10b; see *A New Rabbinic Anthology*, ed. Claude Montefiore and Raphael Loewe (New York, Schocken, 1974), p. 52.

10. See Elie Wiesel, *Souls on Fire* (New York, Simon and Schuster, 1972), p. 133.

11. See George Mendenhall, "Covenant," *Interpreter's Dictionary of the Bible* (New York, Abingdon, 1962), pp. 714–23; John Bright, *Covenant and Promise* (Philadelphia, Westminster, 1976); Howard Greenstein, *Judaism: An Eternal Covenant* (Philadelphia, Fortress, 1983).

12. See, for example, the catechetical document published by the Vatican in 1985; its subject matter is how to present Judaism. The first footnote of the document defends the use of the term "Old Testament." This is not so disconcerting as its statement that "in any case, it is the permanent value of the Old Testament as a source of Christian revelation that is emphasized here." So long as it is assumed that "Christian revelation" is not problematic, then the Old Testament will be reduced to being "a source." "Notes on the Correct Way to Present Judaism," can be found in Roger Brooks, ed., *Unanswered Questions: Theological Views of Jewish-Catholic Relations.* (Notre Dame, University of Notre Dame, 1988), pp. 31–47.

13. See Dennis McCarthy, *Old Testament Covenant: A Survey of Current Opinion* (Richmond, John Knox, 1972), p. 1.

14. J. Coert Rylaarsdam, "The Two Covenants and the Dilemma of Christianity," *Journal of Ecumenical Studies*, 9 (Spring, 1972), 249–70; Paul Borchsenius, *Two Ways to God* (London, Valentine Mitchell, 1968).

15. Franz Rosenzweig, *Star of Redemption*, pp. 336–79.

16. For Rosenzweig, see Nahum Glatzer, *Franz Rosenzweig* (New York, Schocken, 1961); for the quotation from Judah Halevi, see Robert Gordis, *Judaic Ethics for A Lawless World* (New York, KTAV, 1987), p. 144.

17. David Novak, *Jewish-Christian Dialogue: A Jewish Justification* (New York, Oxford University, 1989), p. 108.

18. Franz Rosenzweig, *Star of Redemption*, pp. 122–24; 171–73; 225–27.

19. See Maurice Bowler, "Rosenzweig on Judaism and Christianity: The Two Covenant Theory," *Judaism*, 22 (1973), 475–81; Jacob Taubes, "The Issue between Judaism and Christianity," *Arguments and Doctrines*, ed. Arthur Cohen (New York, Harper and Row, 1970), pp. 408–12.

20. See George Mendenhall, *Law and Covenant in Israel and the Ancient Near East* (Pittsburgh, The Biblical Collegium, 1955); Delbert Hillers, *Covenant: The History of a Biblical Idea* (Baltimore, Johns Hopkins University, 1969); Dennis McCarthy, *Treaty and Covenant* (Rome, Pontifical Biblical Institute, 1963).

21. *The Encyclopedia of Judaism*, ed. Geoffrey Wigoder (New York, Macmillan, 1989); *The Encyclopedia Judaica* does have an entry on "covenant"; most of it refers to the Christian discussion referred to here; see *Encyclopedia Judaica* (Jerusalem, Keter Publishing House, 1971), V., pp. 1011–1021.

22. Arnold Eisen, "Covenant," *Contemporary Jewish Religious Thought*, ed. Arthur Cohen and Paul Mendes-Flor (New York, Charles Scribner's Sons, 1987), pp. 107–12.

23. Gershom Scholem, *On the Kabbalah and its Symbolism* (New York, Charles Scribner's Sons, 1965), pp. 37–65.

24. Lionel Blue, *To Heaven with Scribes and Pharisees* (New York, Oxford University, 1976), p. 86.

25. Michael Walzer, *Exodus and Revolution* (New York, Basic Books, 1984), p. 88.

26. Eliezer Berkovits, *With God in Hell*, p. 127.

27. The Books of Exodus and Joshua.

28. The Second Book of Samuel and Psalm 89.

29. Genesis 15 and Genesis 17.

30. Ronald Clements, *Abraham and David* (Naperville, Allenson, 1967).

31. See Delbert Hillers, *Covenant*; Dennis McCarthy, *Old Testament Covenant*, p. 46.

32. Krister Stendahl, *Paul among Jews and Gentiles* (Philadelphia, Fortress, 1976); E. P. Sanders, *Paul, the Law and the Jewish People* (Philadelphia, Fortress, 1983); John Gager, *The Origin of Anti-Semitism* (New York, Oxford University, 1983).

33. See Jacob Neusner, *The Bible and Us* (New York, Warner, 1990), p. 215.

34. See Donald Hagner, *The Jewish Reclamation of Jesus* (Grand Rapids, Zondervan, 1984).

35. Hayim Perelmuter, *Siblings: Rabbinic Judaism and Early Christianity* (New York, Paulist Press, 1990).

5. JESUS: A VERY UNIQUE PERSON

1. Arthur Cohen, *Myth of Judeo-Christian Tradition*, p. 68.

2. See Pinchas Lapide, *Israelis, Jews and Jesus* (Garden City, Doubleday, 1979).

3. Pinchas Lapide and Jürgen Moltmann, *Jewish Monotheism and the Christian Trinitarian Doctrine* (Philadelphia, Fortress, 1981), p. 73.

4. John Hick, "The Non-absoluteness of Christianity," *The Myth of Christian Uniqueness*, p. 16.

5. Arnold Toynbee, "What Should Be the Christian Approach to the Contemporary Non-Christian Faiths?" *Attitudes toward Other Religions*, ed. Owen Thomas (London, SCM Press, 1969), pp. 160–61.

6. John Cobb, "Beyond Pluralism," *Christian Uniqueness Reconsidered*, p. 94.

7. Jonathan Z. Smith, *Drudgery Divine*, pp. 39–40.

8. Ibid., p. 39.

9. For example, James Smart, *The Cultural Subversion of the Biblical Faith* (Philadelphia, Westminster, 1977), p. 53: "In this collection of widely different writings we have the absolutely unique once-and-for-all witness to what God has done, is doing, and yet means to do." This kind of claim is likely to contribute to the subversion of the Bible that the author is fighting.

10. For a summary, see John Bowden, *Jesus: The Unanswered Questions* (New York, Abingdon Press, 1989), p. 8.

11. Jaroslav Pelikan, *Jesus throughout the Centuries* (New Haven, Yale University, 1985), p. 85.

12. Jaroslav Pelikan, *The Spirit of Eastern Christendom* (Chicago, University of Chicago, 1974), p. 96.

13. Ibid., p. 90.

14. Nathan Söderblom, *The Living God* (Boston, Beacon, 1962), p. 352.

15. Aloysius Pieris, "The Buddha and the Christ," *The Myth of Christian Uniqueness*, p. 171.

16. Pinchas Lapide and Hans Küng, "Is Jesus a Bond or a Barrier?" *Journal of Ecumenical Studies*, 14 (Summer, 1977), 472.

17. See Emilio Castro, "Mission in a Pluralistic Age," *International Review of Mission*, 70 (July, 1986), 200.

18. James Charlesworth, *Jesus within Judaism*, p. 45; see also Bernard Lee, *The Galilean Jewishness of Jesus* (New York, Paulist Press, 1988), p. 126.

19. James Charlesworth, *Jesus within Judaism*, p. 5.

20. Franz Mussner, *Tractate on the Jews*, p. 113: "Jesus will be seen by Christians no longer as the one who divides them from Israel, but rather much more precisely as the one who in a unique way binds them with Israel."

21. Loren Eiseley, *The Night Country* (New York, Charles Scribner's Sons, 1971), p. 131.

22. Joseph Klausner, *Jesus of Nazareth* (New York, Macmillan, 1927), p. 397; see also Martin Buber, *Two Types of Faith* (London, Routledge and Kegan Paul, 1951), p. 75.

23. Pinchas Lapide, *The Sermon on the Mount* (Maryknoll, Orbis Books, 1982).

24. David Flusser, *Jesus* (New York, Herder and Herder, 1969), p. 46.

25. Geza Vermes, *Jesus the Jew* (Philadelphia, Fortress, 1971), p. 225.

26. John Howard Yoder, *The Politics of Jesus* (Grand Rapids, Eerdmans, 1972); for a reading of Mark's Gospel with a similar interpretation, see Ched Myers, *Binding the Strong Man: A Political Reading of Mark's Story of Jesus* (Maryknoll, Orbis Books, 1989).

27. Haddon Willmer, "Comments," *The Origin of Christology*, by C. F. D. Moule (Cambridge, Cambridge University, 1977), p. 160.

28. George Lindbeck, *The Nature of Religious Doctrine* (Philadelphia, Westminster, 1984), p. 68; see also Paul Griffiths, "The Uniqueness of Christian Doctrine Defended," *The Myth of Christian Uniqueness*, pp. 162–68.

29. For example, Gerald O'Collins, *Foundations of Theology* (Chicago, Loyola University, 1971), p. 44: "Outside Christ there is no revelation. Outside official Christianity there can be revelation, but it is always a divine disclosure which comes from and leads to Christ . . . Whether explicitly recognized or not, Christ constitutes the only true light which enlightens every man." This statement is more a definition of terms than it is a description of fact. A non-Christian who reads the words as a factual statement would no doubt find the statement arrogant and offensive.

30. J. Christian Beker, "The New Testament View of Judaism," *Jews and Christians*, ed. James Charlesworth (New York, Crossroad, 1990), p. 62.

31. N. A. Dahl, "The Messiahship of Jesus in Paul," *The Crucified Messiah and Other Essays* (Minneapolis, Augsburg, 1974), p. 40.

32. Ibid.

33. Ibid., p. 43.

34. Lloyd Gaston, *Paul and Torah* (Vancouver, University of British Columbia, 1987).

35. William Christian, *Meaning in Truth and Religion* (Princeton, Princeton University, 1964), pp. 15–16.

36. Paul Kirsch, *We Christians and Jews* (Philadelphia, Fortress, 1975), pp. 36–37; see also Andrew Greeley, *The Bible and Us* (New York, Warner, 1990), p. 281: "The only reasonable resolution of the Messiah argument is the conclusion that in some Catholic sense of the word Jesus was (the) Messiah but in no Jewish sense of the word. Beyond that it is perhaps time to declare a moratorium on the issue."

37. Pinchas Lapide, "Is Jesus a Bond or Barrier?" 482: "If the messiah comes and turns out to be Jesus of Nazareth, I would say that I do not know any Jew in the world who would have anything against it"; see also David Flusser, "To What Extent is Jesus a Question for Jews?" *Concilium*, 5 (1974), 596: "It seems to me very few Jews would raise an objection if the Messiah, when he comes again, were the Jew Jesus."

38. Arthur Cohen, *Myth of the Judeo-Christian Tradition*, p. 159; see also the same author's "Redemption," *Contemporary Jewish Religious Thought*, ed. Arthur Cohen and Paul Mendes-Flor (New York, Charles Scribner's Sons, 1987), pp. 761–65.

39. Abraham Heschel, *The Earth is the Lord's and the Sabbath* (New York, Harper Torch, 1962), p. 72; Martin Buber, who speaks of redemption as "pure prospect" can nevertheless write: "But suddenly we feel a touch as of a hand. It reaches down to us, it wishes to be grasped—and yet what incredible courage is needed to take the hand, to let it draw us up out of darkness! This is redemption." See *Israel and the World*, pp. 101–02.

40. John Ziegler, *Pauline Christianity* (New York, Oxford University, 1983), p. 71; for example: I Cor. 3:15; Rom. 5:9, 10:9.

41. Norbert Lohfink, *The Christian Meaning of the Old Testament* (Milwaukee, Bruce, 1968), p. 136: "The statements, 'In Christ God acted finally in history' and 'In Christ God will act finally in history', must be combined to form the Christian understanding of history."

42. Manfred Vogel, "The Problem of Dialogue between Judaism and Christianity," *Journal of Ecumenical Studies*, 4 (1967), 689.

43. John Koenig, *Jews and Christians in Dialogue* (Philadelphia, Westminster, 1989), p. 43.

44. For example, Paula Fredriksen, *From Jesus to Christ* (New Haven, Yale University, 1989), pp. 214–15. The author's careful ecumenical reading of the New Testament is undercut on these last two pages, in which she assumes that Jesus is the "unique occasion of divine revelation," language that is tied to an image of vertical intrusion into time.

45. John Pawlikowski, *Christ in the Light of Christian-Jewish Dialogue* (New York, Paulist Press, 1982).

46. Karl Rahner, "Christianity and Non-Christian Religions," *Theological Investigations*, vol. V (Baltimore, Helicon, 1966), pp. 115–34.

47. For a criticism of this tendency in Christian writers, see Leonard Swidler, *Yeshua: A Model for Moderns* (Kansas City, Sheed and Ward, 1988), pp. 112–28.

48. Mishnah Sanhedrin, IV, 5; see Ellis Rivkin, *The Shaping of Jewish History* (New York, Charles Scribner's Sons, 1971), pp. 80–81.

49. Jacob Neusner, *The Bible and Us*, p. 50: "Does that mean that God can become incarnate? It does. Does it mean that I should regard Jesus Christ as God incarnate? Yes, but. But not uniquely so . . . When you enter the claim of 'uniqueness', we have to part company. For, we see in the oral Torah, to me incarnation means all of us can be, some of us may be, but none of us *alone* is 'like God' " (my italics). I would say that the word *alone* in the last sentence is a restriction that Christians should also place on Jesus' incarnation of God. Jesus is the incarnation of God insofar as he is related to others, both human and nonhuman.

50. Karl Rahner, *Foundations of Christian Faith*, p. 254: "Jesus experienced a relationship to God which he experienced as new and unique in comparison with other men, but which he nevertheless considered exemplary for other men in their relation to God."

51. Franz Rosenzweig, *Judaism Despite Christianity*, with Eugen Rosenstock-Huessy (Birmingham, University of Alabama, 1969), p. 113: "Any and every Jew feels in the depth of his soul that the Christian relation to God, and so in a sense their religion, is particularly and extremely pitiful . . . As a Christian one has to learn from someone else, whoever he may be, to call God 'our Father'.

To the Jew that God is our Father is the first and most self-evident fact."

52. Stanley Rosenbaum, "On Jewish Worldliness," *Christian Century*, Dec. 18, 1982, 1253.

53. David Novak, *Jewish-Christian Dialogue*, p. 53: "For each community to recognize that what *appears* to mediate the relationship with God for the other community is *not* an idol is the most that can be done without surrendering to relativism."

54. Martin Buber, *Hasidism and Modern Man*, p. 20: "(The Zaddiks) mediated between God and man, but at the same time they insisted on the importance of the immediate relationship to God, which cannot be replaced by any mediator."

55. For example, Jean Milet, *God or Christ? The Excesses of Christocentricity* (New York, Crossroad, 1981).

56. John Bowden, *Jesus*, p. 173.

6. THE UNIQUE ANIMAL

1. Paul Taylor, *Respect for Nature* (Princeton, Princeton University, 1986), p. 188.

2. For example, see James Serpell, *In the Company of Animals* (New York, Basil Blackwell, 1986); Ian McHarg, "Values, Process and Form," *The Fitness of Man's Environment* (Washington, Smithsonian Institution, 1986); David Ehrenfeld, *The Arrogance of Humanism* (New York, Oxford University, 1978).

3. Lynn White, Jr., "The Historical Roots of Our Ecological Crisis," *Science*, March 10, 1967, 1203–07.

4. See Lynn White, Jr., "The Future of Compassion," *Ecumenical Review*, 30 (April, 1978), 106–08.

5. Stephen Toulmin, *The Return to Cosmology;* Fritjof Capra, *The Tao of Physics* (New York, Bantam, 1977).

6. Lynn White, Jr., "The Historical Roots of Our Ecological Crisis," 1206.

7. Roger Sorrell, *St. Francis and Nature* (New York, Oxford University Press, 1989), p. 8: "(The Bible) asserts the belief in a divine creation, organized according to a plan that is hierarchical and unchanging with all parts having their established positions and dependent on will and action. This was the most fundamental basis for Francis's conception of the natural world."

8. Roderick Nash, *The Rights of Nature* (Madison, University of Wisconsin, 1989), p. 94.

9. Paul Wiegrand, "Escape from the Birdbath," *Cry of the Environment*, ed. Philip Joranson and Ken Butigan (Santa Fe, Bear and Co., 1984), pp. 148–59.

10. G. K. Chesterton, *St. Francis of Assisi* (Garden City, Image Books, 1957), p. 87.

11. René Dubos, *A God Within*, p. 169.

12. See Ted Peters, "Creation, Consummation and the Ethical Imagination," *Cry of the Environment*, pp. 415–16.

13. See Samuel Preus, *Explaining Religion: Criticism and Theory from Bodin to Freud* (New Haven, Yale University, 1987), p. 125.

14. See Genevieve Lloyd, *The Man of Reason: Male and Female in Western Philosophy* (Minneapolis, University of Minnesota, 1984), pp. 11–15; Carolyn Merchant, *The Death of Nature: Women, Ecology and the Scientific Revolution* (San Francisco, Harper and Row, 1980), p. 168.

15. Arthur Lovejoy, *The Great Chain of Being* (Cambridge, Harvard University, 1961).

16. For a defense of vertical hierarchy (civilization/primitivism, learning/ignorance, men/women), see George Steiner, *In Bluebeard's Castle* (New Haven, Yale University, 1971), pp. 81–82.

17. Paul Taylor, *Respect for Nature*, p. 45.

18. Wendell Berry, *Standing by Words*, p. 170.

19. Ibid., p. 166.

20. Roderick Nash, *The Rights of Nature*, pp. 55–86.

21. Plotinus, *The Enneads* (London, Faber and Faber, 1969); for specific citations on circular imagery, see Gabriel Moran, *No Ladder to the Sky* (San Francisco, Harper and Row, 1989), pp. 55–56; on Thomas Aquinas, see Josef Pieper, *Guide to Thomas Aquinas* (New York, Pantheon, 1962); M. D. Chenu, "Body and Body Politic in the Creation Spirituality of Thomas Aquinas," *Western Spirituality* (Notre Dame, Fides, 1979), 193–214.

22. Eriugena, as quoted in John Macquarrie, *In Search of Deity* (New York, Crossroad, 1985), p. 95; for the same idea in Judaism, see Gershom Scholem, *Major Trends in Jewish Mysticism*, p. 269.

23. G. K. Chesterton, *St. Francis of Assisi*, p. 61.

24. It may be that a "postmodern" science with a different scale of size will return the human to the center: "Measured in terms of space and time, human kind is indeed, as scientists traditionally remind us, a tiny speck in the vastness of the cosmos. Measured in a more fundamental way, by density and complexity of information, we are already the largest objects in the universe." Frederick Turner, "Escape from Modernism," *Sacred Interconnections*, ed. David Ray Griffin (Albany, State University of New York, 1990), p. 147.

25. Lynn White, Jr., "The Historical Roots of Our Ecological Crisis," 1207.

26. Arthur Lovejoy, *The Great Chain of Being*, p. 109.

27. Wendell Berry, "Preserving Wilderness," *Wilderness*, Spring, 1987, 52.

28. Hildegard of Bingen, *Illuminations* (Santa Fe, Bear and Co., 1985).

29. For example, Bill McKibben, *The End of Nature* (New York, Random House, 1989), p. 151: "This ideology argues that man is at the center of creation and it is therefore right for him to do whatever he pleases."

30. See Willard Gaylin, *Adam and Eve and Pinocchio* (New York, Viking, 1990). This book is based on characteristics that define *homo sapiens* as unique. The author uses the word five times in the first five pages. His position is the same as those Christians who assert that Darwinism undermined the uniqueness of the human being, citing, for example, the animal rights movement as opposed to human uniqueness.

31. For criticism of the animal rights approach, see John Rodman, "The Liberation of Nature," *Inquiry*, 20 (1977), 83–131.

32. Mary Midgley, "Review of 'Rights of Nature' by Roderick Nash," *Commonweal*, June 16, 1989, 376.

33. Christoper Stone, *Should Trees Have Standing?* (New York, Avon, 1975); and with some modification of his position, *Earth and Other Ethics* (San Francisco, Harper and Row, 1987).

34. Paul Lutz, "Interrelatedness: Ecological Patterns of the Creation," *Cry of the Environment*, p. 268.

35. Peter Singer, "Letter to the Editor," *New York Review of Books*, April 13,

1989, 52; for an interesting essay on the extension of rights to animals, but differing sharply from Singer's argument, see Vicki Hearne, "What's Wrong with Animal Rights?" *Harper's*, Sept., 1991, 59–64.

36. Animals cannot be strictly said to have personalities, but they clearly do have degrees of uniqueness that can be quite powerful in relation to human uniqueness; for example, see Martin Buber's description of his cat in *I and Thou*, p. 146; or Roger Caras, *A Cat is Watching* (New York, Simon and Schuster, 1989).

37. Stephen Jay Gould, "Animals and Us," *New York Review of Books*, June 25, 1987, 24–25.

38. Hannah Arendt, *The Human Condition* (Chicago, University of Chicago, 1958), pp. 157–58.

39. Wendell Berry, *The Gift of Good Land* (San Francisco, North Point, 1981), p. 276.

40. Charles Elton, *Animal Ecology* (New York, 1927); Arthur Tansley, "The Use and Abuse of Vegetational Concepts and Terms," *Ecology*, 16 (July, 1935), 284–307.

41. Nicholas Lash, *Easter in Ordinary*, p. 193 for the summary of Buber.

42. Lewis Hyde, *The Gift* (New York, Random House, 1983).

43. Wendell Berry, *The Gift of Good Land*, p. 281.

44. Lewis Hyde, *The Gift*, p. 21.

45. The phrase is from Aldo Leopold, *Sand County Almanac* (New York, Oxford University, 1966).

7. HUMAN DEVELOPMENT

1. William Leiss, *Domination of Nature* (New York, Braziller, 1972), pp. 145–65.

2. C. R. Snyder and Howard Franklin, *Uniqueness: The Human Pursuit of Difference* (New York, Plenum, 1980).

3. Ibid., p. 16.

4. Philip Slater, *Footholds* (New York, Dutton, 1977), p. 38; see also Leszck Kolakowski, *The Presence of Myth*, p. 93: "The fragility of fashion is the outcome of a self-contradictory desire which underlies the effort to be fashionable: to be perfectly unique within perfect conformity."

5. C. R. Snyder and Howard Franklin, *Uniqueness*, p. 75.

6. Ibid., p. 216.

7. Theodore Roszak, *Person/Planet* (Garden City, Anchor Books, 1978), p. 106.

8. Homer Figler, *Overcoming Executive Mid-Life Crisis* (New York, Wiley, 1978), p. 111.

9. Yosef Yerushalmi, *Zakhor: Jewish History and Jewish Memory* (Seattle, University of Washington, 1982).

10. W. McCord and J. McCord, *The Psychopath* (New York, Van Nostrand, 1964), p. 16.

11. Oscar Cullmann, *Christ and Time* (Philadelphia, Westminster, 1950).

12. Frank Manuel, *Shapes of Philosophical History* (Stanford, Stanford University, 1965), p. 65; Ernest Tuveson, *Millenium and Utopia* (Berkeley, University of California, 1949), p. 65.

13. Johann Huizinga, *The Waning of the Middle Ages* (Garden City, Anchor Books, 1954), p. 38.

14. F. Scott Fitzgerald, *The Great Gatsby* (New York, Charles Scribner's Sons, 1925), p. 182.

15. Henri de St. Simon, quoted in Frank Manuel, *Shapes of Philosophical History* (Stanford, Stanford University, 1965), p. 102.

16. Edward Hall, *Beyond Culture* (Garden City, Doubleday, 1976), p. 16.

17. Samuel Beckett, *A Piece of Monologue* (New York, Grove Press, 1976).

18. Samuel Beckett, *Endgame* (New York, Grove Press, 1958), pp. 49, 70.

19. Samuel Beckett, *The Unnameable* (New York, Grove Press, 1958), pp. 143–44.

20. William Barrett, *The Illusion of Technique* (Garden City, Anchor Books, 1978), p. 280.

21. H. Richard Niebuhr, *The Responsible Self* (San Francisco, Harper and Row, 1963), p. 93.

22. Henri Bergson, *Creative Evolution* (New York, Henry Holt, 1911), p. 5.

23. G. K. Chesterton, *Orthodoxy*, p. 48.

24. Yosef Yerushalmi, *Zakhor*, p. 45.

25. Ibid., p. 42.

26. Perle Epstein, *Kabbalah* (Garden City, Doubleday, 1978), p. 108; Abraham Heschel, *The Earth is the Lord's and The Sabbath* (New York, Harper Torch, 1962).

27. Samuel Beckett, *Waiting for Godot* (New York, Grove Press, 1954); Martin Heidegger, *Discourse on Thinking* (New York, Harper and Row, 1966), pp. 62–79.

28. As quoted in John Baillie, *And the Life Everlasting* (New York, Charles Scribner's Sons, 1933), p. 193.

29. Erik Erikson, *Childhood and Society* (New York, Norton, 1963), p. 269.

30. As quoted in Eugene Bianchi, *Aging as a Spiritual Journey* (New York, Crossroad, 1982), p. 164.

31. T. S. Eliot, *Four Quartets* (New York, Harcourt, Bracc and World, 1971), p. 15.

32. Meister Eckhart in Matthew Fox, *Breakthrough* (Garden City, Doubleday, 1980), p. 215: "Now we say that God insofar as he is 'God' is not the perfect goal for creatures ... Therefore we pray God to rid us of 'God' so that we may grasp and eternally enjoy the truth where the highest angel and the fly and the soul are equal."

33. Zvi Lamm, *Conflicting Theories of Instruction* (Berkeley, McCutchan, 1976), p. 27.

34. The figure of Robinson Crusoe lurks behind most reform writing in education from the eighteenth century to the present. Rousseau's *Emile* is the founding document of this tradition in which the young boy must eventually rebel against his teacher for the sake of his own autonomy. The young girl is educated to provide companionship for the man.

35. Carol Gilligan, *In a Different Voice* (Cambridge, Harvard University, 1982); Jean Baker Miller, *Toward a New Psychology of Women*.

36. Michael Oakeshott, *The Voice of Liberal Learning*, ed. Timothy Fuller (New Haven, Yale University, 1989), p. 64.

37. Gabriel Moran, "Religious Education for Middle-Aged Men," *Interplay* (Winona, St. Mary's Press, 1981), pp. 131–42.

38. Cassiodorus, quoted in Philip Wheelwright, *The Burning Fountain* (Bloomington, University of Indiana, 1968), p. 35.

39. John Hick, *Death and Eternal Life* (London, Collins, 1976), p. 209.

40. David Stendl-Rast, *Speaking of Silence*, p. 135.

41. Martin Buber, *Two Types of Faith*, p. 92.

42. Charles Meyer, *Surviving Death* (W. Mystic, Twenty-Third Publications, 1988), p. 30.

43. John Hick, *Death and Eternal Life*, p. 55.

44. Leo Tolstoy, *My Confession* (Boston, Dana Estes, 1904), p. 26.

45. Paul Santmire, "Nothing More Beautiful than Death?" *Christian Century*, Dec. 14, 1983, 1154–58; Robert Herhold, "Kübler-Ross and Life after Death," *Christian Century*, April 14, 1976, 363–64.

46. Paul Ramsey, "The Indignity of 'Death and Dignity'," *Death and Society*, ed. James Carse (New York, Harcourt, Brace and Jovanovich, 1977), p. 136.

47. Elisabeth Kübler-Ross, *On Death and Dying* (New York, Macmillan, 1969), p. 276; the use of "unique" in this final passage of the book complements what the author had written in the Preface: "They [who work with the dying] will learn much about the functioning of the human mind, the unique aspects of our existence, and will emerge from the experience enriched and with perhaps fewer anxieties about their own finality."

48. Karl Rahner, *Theology of Death* (New York, Herder and Herder, 1961); Ladislaus Boros, *The Mystery of Death* (New York, Herder and Herder, 1965).

49. William Lynch, *Images of Hope* (Baltimore, Helicon, 1965), p. 108; John Hick, *Death and Eternal Life*, p. 240.

50. Karl Rahner, *Foundations of Christian Faith*, p. 269.

51. Ibid., p. 436.

52. Peter Selby, *Look for the Living* (Philadelphia, Fortress, 1976), p. 1.

53. Gerard Sloyan, *Jesus in Focus* (W. Mystic, Twenty-Third Publications, 1983), p. 146.

54. James Lovelock, *The Ages of Gaia: A Biography of Our Living Earth* (New York, Norton, 1988).

55. William Temple, *Nature, Man and God* (London, Macmillan, 1935).

56. Maurice Lamm, *The Jewish Way in Death and Mourning* (New York, Jonathan David, 1969), p. 23.

57. John Baillie, *And the Life Everlasting*, p. 62.

58. C. S. Lewis, *Essays Presented to Charles Williams* (Grand Rapids, W. B. Eerdmans, 1947), Preface.

59. Peter Selby, *Look for the Living*, p. 179.

60. Rowan Williams, *Resurrection* (New York, Pilgrim Press, 1985), p. 177.

61. Dietrich Bonhoeffer, *Ethics* (New York, Macmillan, 1965), p. 79.

Index

Abraham, 67-68
Adam, 68; second, 68
Adolescence, 125; middle-aged, 126
Adorno, Theodore, 25
Adult, 125-126
AIDS, 33
Akiba, Rabbi, 80
Anderson, Gerald, 14
Animals: human, 105-108; relation to humans, 16; rights of, 105-106, 149; uniqueness of, 107, 150
Anonymous Christian, 88
Anthropocentrism, 101-104
Anti-Semites, 35, 60
Arendt, Hannah, 15, 37, 141, 150
Armenians, 32-33
Art, 13, 16; human, 109; uniqueness of, 46-47
Ash, Timothy Garton, 139
Auschwitz, 25, 28, 32, 33, 39, 140
Autonomy, 36
Bacon, Francis, 97
Baillie, John, 151
Bal Shem Tov, 63
Barrett, William, 119
Barth, Karl, 43
Bauer, Yehuda, 12, 138, 139
Bauman, Zigmunt, 141
Becker, Carl, 55, 143
Beckett, Samuel, 119, 121, 151
Beker, J. Christian, 146
Benedict, Saint, 96; rule of, 96
Berdyaev, Nicholas, 143
Berenbaum, Michael, 140
Bergson, Henri, 151
Berkovits, Eliezer, 141
Berry, Wendell, 16, 98, 138, 149, 150
Berryman, Philip, 143
Bianchi, Eugene, 151

Bible, 1, 3, 51, 55, 57, 59, 64, 66, 81; animals and, 108; ecology and, 97; hierarchy in, 148; outsiders, 109; witness to revelation, 145
Bishops, U. S. Catholic, 54, 141, 143
Bitburg, 31
Blau, Joseph, 142
Blue, Lionel, 144
Blum, Lawrence, 13, 138
Bonhoeffer, Dietrich, 132, 152
Book of Deuteronomy, 67, 69
Book of Genesis, 97, 144; evolution in, 17
Borchsenius, Paul, 144
Boros, Ladislaus, 152
Borowitz, Eugene, 139
Bowden, John, 145, 148
Bowler, Maurice, 144
Bright, John, 144
Buber, Martin, 2, 12, 43, 57, 137, 138, 141, 142, 143, 146, 148, 149, 152; on revelation, 51-52; on vocation of Israel, 61
Buddhism: animals in, 108; Mahayana and Hinayana, 90
Buddhists, 46, 79
Bultmann, Rudolf, 130
Bureaucracy, 101-102; church as, 91; language of, 134-135; Holocaust and, 35
Butler, Jon, 141
Campbell, Joseph, 4, 5, 137
Capote, Truman, 1
Capra, Fritjof, 96
Caras, Roger, 150
Cassiodorus, 151
Castro, Emilio, 145
Catholic church, 38, 42; Bishops of, 54; Second Vatican Council, 43

Catholics, 49, 72, 90

Cats, 107, 114, 150

Center: Christ at, 92; of food chain, 109; of human race, 115; symbolism of, 92, 95, 101-102, 104, 119, 121, 126

Chain of being, 98, 107

Charlesworth, James, 14, 80, 138, 139, 145

Chenu, M.D., 149

Chesterton, G.K., 2, 100, 137, 149, 150

Children: development of, 122, 125; gifts and, 110-111; uniqueness of, 16

Chosenness: human, 62-63, 100; Jewish, 60-63, 100, 141

Chosen People, 60-63

Christ, 82-92; community and, 88; event, 70, 71, 88; future and, 86-88; meaning of, 85; mediation, 85; messiah and, 84-85; non-Christians and, 88-89; relation to Jesus, 77-78; resurrection, 89-91; uniqueness of, 5, 82-89; word and idea, 83-84

Christian, William, 86, 146

Christian Education: on the Holocaust, 39-40; revelation in, 141-142

Christology, 73, 139

Church leaders, 38, 43, 54

Circle: gift relation and, 111; of time, 118; symbol of, 92, 95

Clarke, William Newton, 143

Clebsch, William, 17, 139

Clements, Ronald, 145

Clocks, 118

Cobb, John, 75, 145

Cohen, Arthur, 6, 28, 37, 40, 74, 86, 137, 139, 141, 145, 147

Community: Christ and, 88; death and, 128; diversity in, 134-135; human, 107; insiders and outsiders, 109-110; interpretive, 68; Jewish, 60-63; person and, 113-117; revelation and, 51

Comte, Auguste, 97

Cousins, Norman, 81

Covenant, 57-70; Davidic, 68-69; dialogue on, 64; forms of, 66-69; metaphor of, 63; Mosaic, 68-69; reform of, 67; two covenant theories, 64-70

Creation, 52, 54, 57, 58, 91, 96, 110; doctrine of, 125; hierarchy of, 148

Creature, 96

Cullmann, Oscar, 150

Cyclical movement, 120, 122

Dahl, N.A., 85, 146

Dawidowicz, Lucy, 32, 140

D'Costa, Gavin, 137

Dead Sea Scrolls, 49

Death, 94, 112, 126-132; acceptance of, 127; communion and, 128-129; of Jesus, 121, 129; movement toward, 121; resurrection and, 129-132; study of, 127; time and, 124; uniqueness of, 152

Decentralization, 101-102

Descartes, René, 2

Deutscher, Isaac, 36, 141

Development, 121-126; Christian and Jewish roots of, 122; endlessness of, 126; feminist criticism of, 123; line of, 70-71; middle-aged, 124; of Christian doctrine, 80, 83-85; of revelation, 55

Dewey, John, 2

Dialogue: basis of, 135; Catholic-Protestant, 72; Christian-Jewish, 7-8, 25, 57; in covenant, 64; with East, 56

Distinctness: Jewish, 143; uniqueness and, 16-17

Dobzhansky, Theodore, 17, 139

Doctrine, Christian, 48, 59; Christ in, 77; incarnation, 103; on Jews, 36

Dominion, 97

Dresden, 34

Dubos, René, 13, 96-97, 138, 148

Eastern church, 78

Eastern religions, 56, 95

Eccentricity, 115

Eckhart, Meister, 126, 151

Ecology: animal rights, 105-106; anthropocentrism in, 104; as new religion, 95; death and, 130-131; feminism and, 93; food in, 108-111; hierarchy in, 98-101; paradox in, 94; resurrection, 130-131

Ecosystem, 108-109

Education: development and, 123; on the Holocaust, 39-40

Ehrenfeld, David, 148
Eiseley, Loren, 16, 17, 138-139, 146
Eisen, Arnold, 144
Eliot, T.S., 5, 151
Elton, Charles, 150
Enlightenment, 14, 26, 36, 55-56;
    human rights and, 105
Epstein, Pearl, 151
Equality: human, 21, 115; of species,
    99, 106
Erikson, Erik, 61, 121, 123, 151
Eriugena, 149
Ethics, 102; Christ and, 85; environ-
    mental, 95; Jesus' ideal, 81; of
    dying, 128
Event, 30, 50; Christ, 70, 71, 88; histor-
    ical, 30-31; revelation as, 48
Evil: historical, 46; human temptation
    to, 104; possibility of, 34; resistance
    to, 126
Evolution, 17, 79, 121
Exclusivity, 19; of language, 21, 134;
    mediation and, 90
Exodus, 67, 144
Ezekiel, 111
Fackenheim, Emil, 33, 37, 38, 140, 142,
    143
Faith, 58-60, 63; and beliefs, 59; test
    of, 35
Fein, Leonard, 140
Feminism, 10; criticism of develop-
    ment, 123-124; ecology, 93; inclu-
    sive language, 134-135; on power,
    11; sexist language, 9, 93
Ferre, Nels, 12, 14-15, 138
Figler, Homer, 150
Fitzgerald, F. Scott, 151
Fleischner, Eva, 137
Food: chain, 108; gift of, 108-111
Ford, Gerald, 23
Forster, E.M., 110
Francis of Assisi, 96
Franklin, Howard, 115, 150
Fredriksen, Paula, 147
Freud, Sigmund, 123
Friedlander, Saul, 139, 141
Friedman, Maurice, 18, 139
Frye, Northrop, 51, 142
Furse, Margaret, 13, 138

Future: as promise, 121; hope of, 119;
    idea of, 121; invention of, 118
Gager, John, 145
Galbraith, John Kenneth, 14, 138
Gandhi, 116
Gaston, Lloyd, 146
Gautama, 79, 116
Gaylin, Willard, 149
Genocide, 32
Geography, human, 112-117
Gift relation, 110-111, 116, 124
Gilkey, Langdon, 142
Gilligan, Carol, 151
Glatzer, Nahum, 144
Golden Rule, 49
Golgotha, 48
Goodall, Jane, 107
Gordis, Robert, 144
Gospel: Christ and, 76; of Luke, 82; of
    Mark, 146; resurrection and, 130;
    synoptics, 85
Gould, Carol, 138
Gould, Stephen Jay, 107, 150
Grace, 58, 72; act of, 90; law and, 68;
    reception of, 116; universal, 89
Greeley, Andrew, 146
Greenberg, Irving, 137
Greenspan, Howard, 144
Griffiths, Paul, 146
Hagner, David, 145
Halevi, Judah, 65, 144
Hall, Edward, 151
Hartman, David, 62, 143
Haughton, Rosemary, 142
Hearne, Vicki, 150
Heidegger, Martin, 2, 121, 150; Rahner
    and, 128
Heim, S. Mark, 3, 137
Herhold, Robert, 152
Heroes, 38, 116-117
Heschel, Abraham, 87, 121, 147
Hick, John, 75, 126, 137, 145, 152
Hierarchy, 96, 98-100; image of 99-
    100; in Bible, 148
Hilbert, Raul, 36, 141
Hildegard of Bingen, 104
Hillel, Rabbi, 80
Hillers, Delbert, 144
Hinduism, 47, 76, 90

Hindus, 21, 47, 59, 89
Hiroshima, 33, 34; meaning of, 121
Historians, 29-31, 72, 80
History: as redeemed, 86-87; Christ
doctrine in, 78; Christ in, 78; Holo-
caust in, 31, 140; Jesus of, 78; Jew-
ish, 41, 70-72, 80; of covenant, 67-
68; of Old Testament, 68; time and,
117; unique in, 12-13, 79
Hitler, Adolph, 34, 35, 37
Hittites, 69
Holocaust, 6, 11, 25-40
Hope: in future, 119, 121; resurrection,
130
Howe, Irving, 26, 139
Hughes, Howard, 20
Huizinga, Johann, 150
Humans: at the center, 101-102; place
of, 94-95, 98, 102; relation to nonhumans, 17, 105-108; superiority of,
103-104; violence and, 114
Hyde, Lewis, 150
Iconoclasts, 78-79
Idols, 78, 134, 148
Imagery: circular, 99; of development,
124; of growth, 124; of time, 119-
120
Incarnation, 59, 89; Jewish doctrine of,
147; meaning of, 103
Inclusivity, 20; Christ and, 88; Christi-
anity and, 76; christology and, 73;
human, 103; levels of, 20; mediation
and, 91; of covenant, 69-70; of language, 21-22, 134-135; of revelation, 53
Intervention, divine, 30, 35, 54, 68, 87,
147
Intolerance: Christian, 4, 76; religious,
47
Irenaeus, 125
Islam, 8, 46, 48, 65
Israel: covenant in, 63, 67; expected
one, 86; God of, 35; state of, 37, 61;
tradition of, 81; vocation of, 61, 100
Israelis, 33; children, 34
Jenniger, Philipp, 140
Jesus, 3, 42, 49; and Christ, 77-79; as
chosen, 100; as unique, 14, 79-82;
ethics of, 80-81; parables of, 82;

relation to Pharisees, 82; resurrec-
tion of, 130; St. Francis and, 96
Jick, Leon, 142
Johnson, Nicholas, 104
Jubilee, 82
Judaizers, 70
Judeo-Christian tradition: ecology and,
97, 101; origin of, 6-7
Justice, 68; practice of, 126; resurrec-
tion and, 131-132
Kabbalah, 87
Kaplan, Mordecai, 60, 143
Kaufman, Gordon, 43, 142
Kennedy, John, 10
King, Martin Luther, Jr., 116, 121
Kirsch, Paul, 86, 146
Klausner, Joseph, 81, 146
Knitter, Paul, 137
Koenig, John, 147
Kohlberg, Lawrence, 13, 138
Kolakowski, Leszck, 138, 150
Kramer, Lawrence, 140
Kübler Ross, Elizabeth, 127-128, 152
Küng, Hans, 145
Kuper, Leo, 140
Lamm, Maurice, 152
Lamm, Zvi, 123, 151
Language, 9-12, 107; definition and
meaning, 10; inclusive, 134-135;
metaphors, 63; of Bible, 57-58; of
rights, 105-106; of theology, 26;
religion, 84; sexist, 9, 93; technical,
83
Lapide, Pinchas, 74, 81, 145, 146
Laquer, Walter, 140
Lascaux, 104
Lash, Nicholas, 3, 137, 150
Laska, Vera, 139
Law, 68; rules of, 116
Lee, Bernard, 145
Leiss, William, 150
Leopold, Aldo, 150
Levi, Primo, 141
Lewis, C.S., 131, 152
Lewis, Jan, 140
Liberal Christianity, 6, 42, 55, 56, 70,
71
Liberation movements, 131-132
Lichtenberg, Bernhard, 38

Lindbeck, George, 84, 146
Lloyd, Genevieve, 148
Locke, John, 44
Logic: of inclusivity, 135; of unique-
  ness, 4, 41, 100, 133
Lohfink, Norbert, 147
Lopate, Philip, 141
Lovejoy, Arthur, 101, 149
Lovelock, James, 152
Lutz, Paul, 149
Lynch, William, 152
Ma'alot, 33
McCarthy, Dennis, 144
McGarry, Michael, 13, 138
McHarg, Ian, 148
McKibben, Bill, 149
McLuhan, Marshall, 2
Macquarrie, John, 149
Manuel, Frank, 150
Marcel, Gabriel, 2
Marcuse, Herbert, 13, 138
Marrus, Michael, 12, 29, 138, 139
Marty, Martin, 137
Mayer, Arno, 141
Meaning: center of, 101; of develop-
  ment, 124; of revelation, 43; of
  words, 10; source of, 103; universal,
  13-14, 27
Medawar, Peter, 17, 18, 139
Mediation, 89-91; forms of, 90-91, 148
Mendel, Gregor, 17
Mendelssohn, Moses, 142
Mendenhall, George, 144
Mendes-Flor, Paul, 140
Merchant, Carol, 148
Messiah, 69, 81; Christ and, 84-86;
  Jewish hope for, 85, 146; meaning
  of, 84
Messianism, 69, 81
Metaphors, 63
Method: historical, 28; of science, 2,
  55, 95, 100
Metz, J.B., 39, 141
Meyer, Charles, 152
Middle Ages, 48, 96
Midgley, Mary, 149
Mid-life: crisis of, 124
Midrash, 53, 61
Milet, Jean, 148

Miller, Jean Baker, 137, 151
Miracle, 30, 35; life as, 132
Mishnah, 89
Modernity: founders of, 55; project of,
  122; test of, 36; time and, 118-119
Moltmann, Jürgen, 145
Montague, W. P., 121
Mortality: sense of, 116, 124, 127, 132
Moses, 44, 48, 67
Muslims, 8, 43, 46, 53, 56, 65; Shiite
  and Sunni, 90
Mussner, Franz, 139, 146
Myers, Ched, 146
Mystics, 151; ecology and, 104; protest,
  123; tradition and, 53-54
Nash, Roderick, 96, 99, 148
Native Americans, 108, 110, 114
Nature, 96-98; human, 34, 103; human
  place in, 102; love of, 107; man and,
  94, 98, 105, 114; medieval attitude
  toward, 97-98; nonhuman, 98; St.
  Francis and, 96; transformations of,
  109
Nazis, 28, 31, 34, 35, 36, 40, 74
Nazism, 29, 36, 39
Neusner, Jacob, 145
New Age, 45
New Grange, 131
New Testament, 36, 45; Christ in, 77-
  79; damnation in, 132; gospel of
  Luke, 82; gospel of Mark, 146; the
  term, 64, 71, 74, 75
Niebuhr, H. Richard, 142
Nixon, Richard, 14
Noah, 47, 67, 98; commandments to,
  47
Novak, David, 144, 148
Oakeshott, Michael, 151
O'Brien, Conor Cruise, 141
O'Collins, Gerald, 146
O'Connor, Cardinal John, 26
Old Age: development and, 125; time
  and, 121
Old Testament, 6, 50; covenant in, 68-
  69; relation to New Testament, 64;
  use of the term, 64, 144
Oppenheim, Michael, 142
Orientation, 55; Rosenzweig on, 52,
  142; to the future, 120

Ozick, Cynthia, 140
Parables of Jesus, 82
Paradox: ecological, 94; of religion, 134; power, 104; uniqueness, 5, 115
Particularity, 50, 133; Jewish, 62; of religions, 50
Paul, Saint, 66, 83, 103; Judaizers, 70-71; messiah, 85-87
Pawlikowski, John, 147
Pelikan, Jaroslav, 78-79, 145
Perelmuter, Hayim, 145
Peters, Ted, 148
Pharisees, 126; Jesus' relation to, 82; resurrection, 130
Philosophers: Christian, 49; Jewish, 44; modern, 2
Philosophy: categories of, 80; Christian, 44, 97; Jewish, 44; modern, 2
Piaget, Jean, 122
Pieris, Aloysius, 145
Pittenger, Norman, 15
Place, 60; human, 15, 98, 102
Plaskow, Judith, 143
Plato, 9, 108
Plotinus, 99
Pluralism, religious, 4, 45, 47
Pope Pius XI, 38
Post-Darwin, 5, 17, 149
Potlatch, 110
Power: meaning of, 11; paradox of, 104
Prayer: Book of, 62; Christian, 77; covenant renewal, 67; modernity and, 119; of two hands, 38
Present, 117-121; and future, 118-119; experience of, 117-118
Preus, Samuel, 148
Progress, 121-122; challenge to, 36; idea of, 118
Prophecy: and revelation, 52
Prophets, 71; protest of, 123
Protestantism, 5, 42, 43, 76; neo-orthodoxy, 43
Protestants, 49, 72, 79, 90
Psalms, 69
Quayle, J. Danforth, 14
Qur'an, 1, 59
Rahner, Karl, 5, 137, 147, 152; anonymous Christian, 99; theology of

death, 128-129; use of uniqueness, 3
Ramsey, Paul, 127, 152
Rape, 114
Reagan, Ronald, 23, 24, 31
Reason, 18; distinguishing mark of humans, 99-100; natural revelation and, 49; revelation and, 44
Reconstructionist movement, 60
Redemption, 50, 54, 57, 58; Christians and Jews on, 74-75, 86; and the future, 52, 87, 197; Paul on, 87
Reformers, 90; Protestant, 79
Reform Judaism: platform of, 44, 62; prayer book of, 62
Reinharz, Yehuda, 140
Renaissance, 118
Representation, 100; bodily, 91
Response, 18, 57, 91; human, 100; to covenant, 66; to Holocaust, 35, 37-40
Responsibility, human, 100, 104, 107
Resurrection: and justice, 132; ecology, 130-131; of Jesus, 131-132; origin of, 130-131
Revelation, 41-56; as event, 48; as orientation, 52, 142; Christ and, 146; community as bearer, 51; creation, 52-53; interpersonal character, 48; liberal views, 42, 55-56; natural, 49-50, 142; prophecy and, 52; Second Vatican Council, 43
Ricoeur, Paul, 52
Rights: animal, 105-106; language of, 105; legal, 106
Ritual: covenant renewal, 67; nonhuman, 114; of remembrance, 120, 126; of restraint, 94; revelation, 52, 53
Rivkin, Ellis, 147
Roberts, Jon, 143
Robinson Crusoe, 123, 151
Rodman, John, 149
Roiphe, Anne, 139
Rosenbaum, Stanley, 90, 148
Rosenstock-Huessy, Eugen, 142, 147
Rosenzweig, Franz, 38, 43, 87, 142, 143, 147; on revelation, 52, 57; two covenants, 65-66

Roszak, Theodore, 117, 150
Rotenstreich, Nathan, 28, 139
Roth, John, 140
Rousseau, Jean Jacques, 151
Rubenstein, Richard, 139, 141
Rylaarsdam, J. Coert, 144
Sabbath, 120; Jesus and, 82
Sacrament: and salvation, 47; media-
    tion and, 91; of food, 110
Samuelson, Norbert, 142
Sanders, E. P., 145
Santmire, Paul, 152
Scholem, Gershom, 53
Schorsch, Ismar, 141
Schuon, Frithjof, 138
Schüssler Fiorenza, Elisabeth, 139
Science, 21, 100; death and, 131;
    method of, 2, 133; postmodern, 149
Seder, 63
Selby, Peter, 152
Sermon on the Mount, 81
Serpell, James, 148
Shahak, Israel, 139
Shahn, Ben, 13, 138
Shoah, 32
Silk, Mark, 137
Sinai, 48, 61, 67
Singer, Peter, 106, 149
Slater, Philip, 115
Sloyan, Gerard, 152
Smart, James, 145
Smith, Jonathan Z., 5, 6, 76, 137, 145
Smith, W. Cantwell, 143
Snyder, C. R., 115, 150
Söderblom, Nathan, 79, 145
Sorrell, Roger, 148
South Africa, 40
Species: destruction of, 106; equality
    of, 99, 106
Sphere, symbol of, 120, 126
Steiner, George, 149
Stendahl, Krister, 7, 137, 145
Stendl-Rast, David, 152
Stone, Christopher, 149
Storytelling, 30, 108, 117; Jewish, 37,
    52, 61-62
St. Simon, Henri, 151
Suffering, 137; animal, 105; chosen
    people, 61; comparison of, 38, 40;

Holocaust, 34-38; human, 62; rela-
    tion to power, 11; struggle against,
    137
Superiority: Christian, 70; claims to,
    114-115; human, 103-104
Swidler, Leonard, 147
Talmud, 67, 120
Tansley, Arthur, 150
Taubes, Jacob, 144
Taylor, Charles, 142
Taylor, Paul, 95, 98, 148, 149
Teilhard de Chardin, Pierre, 103
Temple, William, 131, 152
Temple of Jerusalem, 121
Testament, 64
Thanatology, 127
Theology: Christ in, 73, 92; christocen-
    tric vs. theocentric, 91; crisis in, 39;
    language of, 26; liberalizing of, 88;
    of death, 128-129; philosophy and,
    44; response to Holocaust, 37-38;
    the term, 73; time and, 118
Thomas, Lewis, 14, 15, 16, 17, 138
Thomas Aquinas, 99
Time, nature of, 117-119
Tolstoy, Leo, 127
Torah, 53; acceptance of, 61
Toulmin, Stephen, 96, 148
Toynbee, A.J., 12, 75, 145
Tracy, David, 139
Tradition, 100; human, 17; Jesus in, 82;
    Judeo-Christian, 6, 7, 97, 101; Mus-
    lim, 8; mystics and, 54; of Israel, 81;
    reforming of, 4
Trinity, doctrine of, 85
Truman, Harry, 34
Trunk, Isaiah, 37, 141
Turner, Frederick, 149
Turner, H. E. W., 138
Tuveson, Ernest, 150
Unamuno, Miguel de, 13
United States, 7-8, 34; citizens of, 33;
    empiricism of, 62; government of,
    33-34, 54; immigrants to, 119
Universality, 133; chosenness and, 63;
    Holocaust, 140; of promise, 68; par-
    ticularity and, 60; uniqueness and,
    13-14
Utilitarianism, 104, 106, 149

Vatican, 142, 144
Vatican Council, Second, 42, 43
Vermes, Geza, 82, 146
Violence, 114
Vocation, 61; human, 21, 99; of child,
    125; of Israel, 61
Vogel, Manfred, 147
Von Hügel, Friedrich, 45
Walzer, Michael, 144
War, 54, 114
Watergate, 32
Wheelwright, Philip, 151

White, Lynn, Jr., 95, 96, 101, 148
Wiegrand, Paul, 148
Wiesel, Elie, 26, 27, 38, 139, 143
Wiles, Maurice, 12
Williams, Rowan, 152
Willmer, Haddon, 82, 146
Wittgenstein, Ludwig, 2, 137
World War II, 29, 32, 34, 35, 37, 41
Yad Vashem, 26
Yerushalmi, Yosef, 120, 141, 150
Yoder, John Howard, 82, 146
Ziegler, John, 147

Other Titles in the Faith Meets Faith Series

Toward a Universal Theology of Religion, Leonard Swidler, Editor

The Myth of Christian Uniqueness, John Hick and Paul F. Knitter, Editors

An Asian Theology of Liberation, Aloysius Pieris, S.J.

The Dialogical Imperative, David Lochhead

Love Meets Wisdom, Aloysius Pieris, S.J.

Many Paths, Eugene Hillman, C.S.Sp.

The Silence of God, Raimundo Panikkar

The Challenge of the Scriptures, Groupe de Recherches
   Islamo-Chrétien

The Meaning of Christ, John P. Keenan

Hindu-Christian Dialogue, Harold Coward, Editor

The Emptying God, John B. Cobb, Jr. and Christopher Ives, Editors

Christianity through Non-Christian Eyes, Paul J. Griffiths, Editor

Christian Uniqueness Reconsidered, Gavin D'Costa, Editor

Women Speaking, Women Listening, Maura O'Neill

Bursting the Bonds?, Leonard Swidler, Lewis John Eron, Lester Dean, and
   Gerard Sloyan

One Christ—Many Religions, Stanley J. Samartha

The New Universalism, David J. Krieger

Jesus Christ at the Encounter of World Religions, Jacques Dupuis, S.J.

After Patriarchy, Paula M. Cooey, William R. Eakin, and Jay B. McDaniels,
   Editors

An Apology for Apologetics, Paul J. Griffiths

World Religions and Human Liberation, Dan Cohn-Sherbok, Editor

Leave the Temple, Felix Wilfred, Editor